I ⊕
→ 1. continual PRAYER
→ 2. much THANKSgiving
→ 3. fervent EVANGELISM

"He has paid for my sins and given me His own righteousness! Praise be to God!"

"I was first introduced to Nick Harrison through his book, *Magnificent Prayer*. It has richly blessed my prayer life as I have continued to read it from year to year. I look forward to reading this latest book, knowing he shares my heart's cry for revival. I'm confident Nick Harrison's insights will help me pray for a fresh spiritual awakening in such a way that heaven is moved."

Anne Graham Lotz, author and international Bible teacher

"The greatest need today is not a change in government but a change in the spiritual condition of Christian churches. Nick Harrison is on target and has provided fresh inspiration for those who understand the times we live in. These daily readings will hopefully provoke a heart cry for revival."

Jim Cymbala, senior pastor, The Brooklyn Tabernacle

"Prayer precedes revival. Whose prayers? Mine and yours! As our hearts long for an outpouring of God's presence and power, let's be faithful and passionate in our prayers to the only one who can truly bring about an awakening in our land and renewal of the church. This inspiring devotional is a timely guide to lead us in praying consistently and boldly for God's supernatural intervention. What could be more important than that?"

Lee Strobel, evangelist, author, and apologist

"The current cultural and moral situation in America, and around the world, requires an unusual and powerful work of God. Nick Harrison's devotional will stir your heart, increase your faith, and help you believe that what God has done in the past can happen yet again. I highly recommend it."

Chip Ingram, founder/CEO Living on the Edge
and author of *I Choose Peace*

"One of the hymns we used to sing when I was growing up was 'Revive Us Again.' I didn't think much about it then, but today it is the cry of my heart. I doubt there's ever been a greater need for spiritual awakening in our world, or for renewal in the church, than there is right now. But it must start with us. This powerful devotional by Nick Harrison, *Our Cry for Revival*, is an excellent tool for rekindling our hearts and passion for a fresh touch from the Lord. Pick it up. Read it each day. And join us in asking God to revive us again—quickly!"

Mark Mittelberg, author of *Contagious Faith* and *The Questions Christians Hope No One Will Ask (With Answers)*

"As the country we love is being shaken to its core, with increasingly unsolvable calamity and dire corruption within—there is one real hope, one real and dependable lifeline for any future at all. It is THE GOD LINE, the direct connection with our Maker who loves us, wants to hear from us, and who alone can help us recover who we once were, one nation under God. Thank you, Nick Harrison."

Pat Boone, legendary recording star, actor, and author

"Nick Harrison is a gifted writer with a deep knowledge of Scripture, and he has written a powerful devotional book that burns with the desire of seeing true revival break out in our world. I hope that as you read these daily devotions you will find yourself praying what I did, 'Lord, let the revival start with me!'"

Matthew West, Dove award-winning recording artist, songwriter, and author

"For those whose souls long for revival and renewal, *Our Cry for Revival* by Nick Harrison will deeply challenge, change, and encourage your prayer life. Full of Scripture, narrative, and quotes from faithful Christians through the ages, this easy-to-read devotional would be a great addition to your morning routine."

Mary DeMuth, author of *Jesus Every Day*

"Our world, and today's Church, is in desperate need of revival! Nick Harrison prepares hearts and minds for a true touch from God with compelling stories from history and today's movements of the Lord, then includes beautifully crafted, Spirit-led prayers for an entire year to prepare our souls for revival. This is a must read for all Christians and we anticipate entire churches will read and walk out the powerful prayers and principles to ignite revival worldwide."

Pastor Bill and Pam Farrel, bestselling authors of sixty books including *Men Are Like Waffles, Women Are Like Spaghetti*

"In *Our Cry for Revival*, Nick Harrison masterfully guides us through the depths of longing and prayer for a divine awakening. This book is not just a call to daily prayer; it's a summons to wholehearted surrender and expectancy. Whether you're a seasoned intercessor or a newcomer to the journey of revival, *Our Cry for Revival* will inspire and equip you to press into God's presence with renewed fervor."

Shane Pruitt, author of *Revival Generation: Awakening to a Movement of God*

NICK HARRISON

OUR
CRY FOR
REVIVAL

**365 DEVOTIONS
AND PRAYERS
FOR AN OUTPOURING
OF GOD'S SPIRIT**

Copyright © 2024 by Nick Harrison
All rights reserved.
Printed in China

978-1-4300-9586-6

Published by B&H Publishing Group
Brentwood, Tennessee

Dewey Decimal Classification: 242.2
Subject Heading: DEVOTIONAL LITERATURE
/ MEDITATIONS / PRAYERS

Unless otherwise noted, all Scripture quotations are taking from The Holy Bible, English Standard Version. ESV® Text Edition: 2016. Copyright © 2001 by Crossway Bibles, a publishing ministry of Good News Publishers.

Scripture quotations marked NKJV are taken from the New King James Version®. Copyright © 1982 by Thomas Nelson. Used by permission. All rights reserved.

Scripture quotations marked NRSVUE are taken from the New Revised Standard Version, Updated Edition. Copyright © 2021 National Council of Churches of Christ in the United States of America. Used by permission. All rights reserved worldwide.

Scripture quotations marked KJV are from the King James Version, which is public domain.

Cover design by Micah Kandros Design. Cover images by Muzi pear studio/Shutterstock and azarnov/Shutterstock. Author photo by Rebecca Gores.

1 2 3 4 5 6 • 27 26 25 24

For all who pray for revival . . .

O God, have mercy upon thy poor church, and visit her, and revive her. She has but a little strength; she has desired to keep thy word; oh, refresh her; restore to her thy power, and give her yet to be great in this land.
CHARLES SPURGEON

Will you not revive us again, that your people may rejoice in you? Show us your steadfast love, O LORD, and grant us your salvation.
PSALM 85:6–7

There is no subject which is of greater importance to the Christian church at the present time than that of revival. It should be the theme of our constant meditation, preaching, and prayers.
MARTYN LLOYD-JONES

Lord, bring revival. And let it begin with me.
PRISCILLA SHIRER

Introduction

If you've picked up this book, I'm going to assume you're one of the tens of thousands of Christians praying for local, national, or even global revival (or you want to be, and you're looking for a guide to help you). If so, thank God he has enlisted you in this life-changing and world-changing endeavor.

I say that because revival comes *only* through prayer. We pray, God answers. No prayer, no revival. But *how* do we pray for revival? And why doesn't God quickly answer our pleas for revival?

First, we must realize that God wants to bring revival to his people even more than we want to experience it. In fact, God begins the revival timeline by laying prayer for revival on the hearts of his intercessors. We may think our hunger for revival is something we choose. But in reality, God has created that hunger so that he might fill it.

Before we begin, we should consider what revival is. In these devotions I've quoted from many Christian men and women who witnessed revival or were instrumental in the revivals of their day—as well as a few contemporary men and women known for their desire to see revival. Here's how some of those I quote in *Our Cry for Revival* define revival:

> [Revival] is a visitation in which God is making man conscious of himself without any human agency.
> G. Campbell Morgan

> Revival is a time when God visits his people, and, by the power of his Spirit imparts new life to them, and through them imparts life to sinners dead in trespasses and sins.
> R. A. Torrey

> A revival is nothing else than a new
> beginning of obedience to God.
> CHARLES FINNEY

> Revival, in its essence, is the outflow of the
> Spirit of God through the human spirit.
> JESSIE PENN-LEWIS

Best-selling author, Dr. Tony Evans writes:

> Revival is the return of God's manifest presence to his people for the purpose of them renewing their relationship with him, with each other and for the good of the broader society.

Author and pastor John Piper writes:

> In the history of the church, the term revival in its most biblical sense has meant a sovereign work of God in which the whole region of many churches, many Christians has been lifted out of spiritual indifference and worldliness into conviction of sin, earnest desires for more of Christ and his word, boldness in witness, purity of life, lots of conversions, joyful worship, renewed commitment to missions. You feel God has moved here.

Pastor Jim Cymbala is right when he says,

> If you study any of the great revivals of the past, you will always find men and women who longed to see the status quo changed—in themselves and in their churches. They called on God with insistence, and prayer begets revival, which begets more prayer.

Author Robert Coleman, who chronicled the Asbury Revival of 1970 in Wilmore, Kentucky, in his book *One Divine Moment*, wrote, "Revival is that sovereign work of God in which He visits His own people, restoring and releasing them into the fullness of His blessing." Some readers will recall that Asbury University experienced another glorious revival in February 2023.

Perhaps my favorite description of revival comes from the late pastor Jack Hayford. Referring to Isaiah 64:3 (NIV), he wrote: "Awesome things for which we did not look, is a perfect description of genuine revival, because the unpredictable and unusual are the characteristics of great spiritual awakenings."

We must also note the words of Dr. Michael Brown as to what revival is not.

> Revival is not a series of special meetings at church. Revival is not what a church does a few times a year to simply draw in new converts (although we celebrate true conversions when they take place). Revival is not about the unusual, physical manifestations that tend to happen when people are "touched by the Holy Spirit."

Another caution comes from author Arthur Wallis:

> Revival is more than a big meeting. It is more than religious excitement. It is more than the quickening of the saints or their being filled with the Holy Spirit. It is more than a great ingathering of souls. One may have any of these without revival—and yet revival includes them all.

Wallis is right about mistaking revival as simply a big meeting. It's a common mistake to assume all revivals are large and well-known among Christians. The Great Awakening, The Welsh Revival of 1904, Azusa Street, even the Jesus Movement are fairly well-known among believers. But how many of us are familiar with the Kilsyth revival of 1839; the 1860 revival in Tinevelly, South India; or the Moravian revival of 1727? There are dozens of (mostly regional) revivals that we never hear about. Some even count the day of Pentecost as an example of revival. Though Christians may disagree on the theological significance and limitations of Pentecost, we can all admire the fervency of the great evangelist Dwight Moody in one of his last sermons in Boston (his spiritual birthplace) who said, "See how he came on the day of Pentecost! It is not carnal to pray that he may come again and that the place be shaken. I believe Pentecost was but a specimen day. I think the church has made this woeful mistake that Pentecost was a miracle never to be repeated. I have thought too that Pentecost was a miracle not be repeated. I believe now if we looked on Pentecost as a specimen day and began to pray, we should have the old Pentecostal fire here in Boston."

We could also ask about the sequence of revival, even as we admit God brings revival in his own, often unexpected, way. But generally, the sequence of revival goes something like this:

- God creates the hunger for revival in his people.
- We pray for the desired revival (often for years).
- God brings revival, which is characterized by a deep sense of his presence, which in turn brings conviction of sin.
- Earnest confession and repentance follow conviction.
- Forgiveness of confessed sins leads into profound worship and true appreciation for God's amazing grace.
- Though this part of revival is for God's people—his church—the usual result is that many previously unsaved people are also convicted of sin and are born again, entering the family of God.

This sequence of events is a short explanation—and subject to change as revival is unpredictable and often catches us off guard, even when it's been the focus of our prayers.

The big question is: Will the God, who has answered the pleas of his people in the past for revival, bring yet another revival before Christ's return?

Most intercessors are certain the answer is yes. Why else would he call so many to pray for revival unless he intends to answer those prayers? Why would he allow us to experience our own paltry efforts at living righteously in an unrighteous world? Why would he show us how empty the amusements of this present age are when compared to the joys of his kingdom?

So, if God is the one who initiates revival, what's *our* part to play? There is only one thing we can do—pray boldly and persistently. We dare not do anything else. True revival has only God's fingerprints on it. When we try to manufacture revival, we only thwart God's ability to usher in true revival. We must simply pray and trust God for revival. Our own hands cannot touch the working of God.

Even though we may not create revival, we can prepare for it as we pray for it. Which is exactly what this book is for. For the next year, we'll spend time both praying for revival and preparing for revival. You'll find many of the devotions on the following pages focus on prayer for revival. It's not possible to overpray for a fresh move of God.

And remember, when revival comes, it may not be what we expected. How God answers our prayers is up to him. The kind of revival we witness is rarely what we expect.

The devotions on the following pages are offered as an encouragement for us to engage in bold prayer and belief in God for true revival.

Each devotion contains a **Scripture to ponder** along with a **brief word of encouragement** from those who can speak of revival from personal experience. You'll encounter many familiar names among the contributors—Charles Spurgeon, Oswald Chambers, A. W. Tozer, Jonathan Edwards, Charles Finney, and many others. You'll also be introduced to men and women of faith who you may not know. For instance, Octavius Winslow, J. C. Philpot, J. C. Ryle, Jonathan Goforth, Hannah Whitall Smith, Anne Dutton, Thomas Watson, and other great heroes of the faith.

Consider, for instance, James Smith. Pretty much unknown by Christians today, Smith preceded Charles Spurgeon as pastor at New Park Street Chapel in London. It is said that his early sermons rivaled Spurgeon's in popularity.

Reading these seasoned voices in the faith will bless you, I promise. I've also included a few more recent Christian leaders. The increased frequency of messages on revival is just one more indication that revival is on the prayer lists of tens of thousands of believers.

Finally, each day's reading concludes with a **prayer prompt** to help us focus on that day's specific devotion. My hope is that these concluding prayer prompts will act as a jump start to your further prayers for the day's topic.

So now please join me and thousands of others as we pray for the revival we so desperately need.

JANUARY 1

New Beginnings

*He who was seated on the throne said,
"Behold, I am making all things new."*
REVELATION 21:5

Experiencing revival is getting a fresh start, similar to the beginning of a new year. From the moment revival touches us, all things, in a sense, become new. We see with new eyes. We feel with a fresh intensity. Our hope in God is renewed. But these blessings are not to be hoarded; they are to be shared. One sure sign of revival is a new boldness in sharing new life in Christ with others.

Consider the many people worldwide, and even in our own communities, who are still unreached for Christ. Consider how, if we do not see revival in our day, these souls will be lost. Then imagine what can happen if these same people are reached through revival. Praying for revival is not only prayer for personal change, but also praying for a fresh wave of evangelism, sparked by hearts renewed for Christ.

> Revivals begin with God's own people; the Holy Spirit touches their heart anew, and gives them new fervor and compassion, and zeal, new light and life, and when he has thus come to you, he next goes forth to the valley of dry bones. . . . Oh, what responsibility this lays on the Church of God! If you grieve him away from yourselves, or hinder his visit, then the poor perishing world suffers sorely!
>
> ANDREW BONAR

PRAYER PROMPT: *Father, you know the need for a fresh wave of your Spirit in our land. Bring the kind of revival that spurs us to evangelism. May revival result in the salvation of many.*

JANUARY 2

Power from on High

"Behold, I am sending the promise of my Father upon you. But stay in the city until you are clothed with power from on high."
Luke 24:49

The disciples were told to wait in the city until the promise of the Father, power from on high, was given them. Without this power they were men without a mission . . . yet. But when they were clothed with the Spirit, a new era began.

Likewise today, we can be entering new seasons of usefulness to God with each fresh revival. But unlike the disciples, we don't have to wait in the city for power from on high. That power has been made available to every believer. While it was the disciples who waited, now it is the Holy Spirit who waits.

Will we keep him waiting longer?

> Verily the day of revivals is not past. The Holy Spirit is still waiting to fill believers with power from on high.
>
> John Greenfield

PRAYER PROMPT: *Lord, thank you for the filling of your Holy Spirit. Today may I walk confident of the power within me to affect change.*

JANUARY 3

The Creative Christian

He has filled him with the Spirit of God, with skill, with intelligence, with knowledge, and with all craftsmanship, to devise artistic designs, to work in gold and silver and bronze.
Exodus 35:31–32

For many, a surprising fruit of revival is a surge of creativity among believers. Often new hymns are composed, poetry written, books authored, and an all-around rebirth in the church of artistic expression reflecting our Lord's own creativity.

Some may not see the importance of such endeavors, but we must remember that the Spirit of God gifts his people with skill, craftsmanship, and the intense desire to showcase the beauty that can be had when God's people, created in his image, use their talents to praise him.

It is a part of Christianity to convert every natural talent to a holy use.
Hannah More

PRAYER PROMPT: *Lord, thank you for the natural talents you give your people. Bring forth even greater creations as a result of revived artistic ability. Give fresh talents to those who ask for it. Allow your glory to be glimpsed through the gifts of your people.*

JANUARY 4

The Power of Personal Obedience

*"Has the LORD as great delight in burnt offerings and
sacrifices, as in obeying the voice of the LORD? Behold, to obey
is better than sacrifice, and to listen than the fat of rams."*
1 SAMUEL 15:22

Though revival comes only through prayer, we must also personally prepare for God's outpouring. Obedience is key. God shows us what to do, but we're sometimes reluctant to obey.

What has God called you to do? Will you do it? If you don't know how to proceed, ask God. He will not only show you what to do, but he will also do it through you. In the Christian life and especially in revival, we are vessels, as God pours his Spirit into us.

Ask, obey, and see the fruit of your labors.

> Does it make sense to pray for guidance about the future if we are not obeying in the thing that lies before us today? How many momentous events in Scripture depended on one person's seemingly small act of obedience!
> Rest assured: Do what God tells you to do now, and, depend upon it, you will be shown what to do next.
>
> ELISABETH ELLIOT

PRAYER PROMPT: *Lord, you require no burnt offerings from me. You ask for no unreasonable sacrifice. You only ask for my obedience. Show me what you would have me do. Empower me with your Spirit. Breathe into my being the personal revival that seeks your will. I ask this for all of us praying for revival. May our obedience bring forth lasting fruit—revival fruit.*

JANUARY 5

Saying Goodbye to the World

Do not love the world or the things in the world. If anyone loves the world, the love of the Father is not in him. For all that is in the world—the desires of the flesh and the desires of the eyes and pride of life—is not from the Father but is from the world. And the world is passing away along with its desires, but whoever does the will of God abides forever.
1 John 2:15–17

This present world is filled with lures. We can all identify the attractions that weaken us spiritually. Worldliness to a Christian is like Kryptonite to Superman. Our benefit from revival will be shown in what we do when we encounter those Satanic lures of the world. Are we hungry enough for God to cut ourselves loose from the desires of the flesh, the desires of the eyes, and the pride of life? From all that glitters in this present world?

A true revival means nothing less than a revolution, casting out the spirit of worldliness and selfishness, and making God and his love triumph in the heart and life.
Andrew Murray

PRAYER PROMPT: *Father, this world holds many attractions for me. But I know that by faith the greater joys come from your kingdom. To experience revival, I pray for an increased desire for the things of God and a decrease in the false glitter I see around me. Lord, call your people out of this ungodly culture. Help us stand strong for your kingdom. Equip us to reach others for Christ. May true revival blossom on earth as an invitation to the lost to enter your kingdom of light.*

Am I hungry enough for God?

JANUARY 6

Conviction of Sin

"I tell you the truth: it is to your advantage that I go away, for if I do not go away, the Helper will not come to you. But if I go, I will send him to you. And when he comes, he will convict the world concerning sin and righteousness and judgment: concerning sin, because they do not believe in me."

JOHN 16:7–9

A hallmark of all true revival is the conviction of sin. One role of the Holy Spirit is just that—to reveal our sin to us. If we claim to have no sin or feel no conviction, we need only to ask God to show us our sin. That's a prayer God always answers through Holy Spirit conviction.

In the light of God's presence during revival, there will be a newfound grief as sin is uncovered—even sin we were previously unaware of. A revival-believing Christian keeps short accounts with God—confessing sin as soon as it's revealed.

Allow your sin to be revealed and then experience a breakthrough as you confess and repent. He will be there to forgive.

When Holy God draws near in true revival, people come under terrible conviction of sin. The outstanding feature of spiritual awakening has been the profound consciousness of the Presence and holiness of God.

HENRY BLACKABY

PRAYER PROMPT: *O God, holy One; Lord of all creation and Lord of my life, reveal to me hidden sin so that I may confess, repent, and enjoy the glow of forgiveness. Help me keep short accounts with you. I desire a holy and fruitful life, indwelt by your Holy Spirit.*

JANUARY 7

Complete in Christ

In Him dwells all the fullness of the Godhead bodily; and you are complete in Him, who is the head of all principality and power.
Colossians 2:9–10 (NKJV)

God's goal is that we be complete in him. That we live as completed individuals. Thus, he has made provision for our completeness. Too often, we try to complete ourselves through appeals to the flesh, but they can never deliver the right and permanent connection to us. His indwelling us *is* a permanent and complete connection. To live this out, we must forsake the flesh and all that appeals to the flesh. God will not share us with the flesh or with Satan.

Yes, believers are complete—they have a fullness in Christ which nothing can exhaust; a love which passes knowledge, a strength which is omnipotent, and a faithfulness which cannot be questioned. And the more they dwell upon it, the deeper becomes the conviction of their own weakness and Christ's sufficiency, their own emptiness and his fullness, their own ignorance and his wisdom, their own utter inability to keep the path of duty, and their daily, hourly need of Christ to animate, sustain, and guide them.

John MacDuff

PRAYER PROMPT: *Lord, so often I feel like I still lack completeness, but your Word assures me I am complete in Christ, so I take that truth by faith. Thank you that, because of Christ, I am complete, totally who you desire me to be. Nothing lacking.*

JANUARY 8

The Suddenness of God

> *"Behold, I am coming like a thief! Blessed is the one who stays awake, keeping his garments on, that he may not go about naked and be seen exposed!"*
> REVELATION 16:15

When will Christ return? Will there be worldwide revival first? Will there be judgment here on earth? These are questions Christians ask, but God withholds the specifics, asking us to trust him and stay awake awaiting Christ's return.

Some Christians foresee a final revival, perhaps in the aftermath of some catastrophic event. Is that how revival will come? Again, we don't know. We must, however, not be shaken by world events that disrupt our comfort. Such an event may indeed lead to a large last-days revival. Be prepared. Stay awake!

> Times of suffering and crisis are a prompt for God's people to, again, link arms across oceans and denominations in visible, united, extraordinary prayer. What might God be pleased to do if we asked him for global revival, for the expansion of the glorious gospel of his beloved Son?
> RYAN GRIFFITH

PRAYER PROMPT: *Father, I pray for Christians around the world, particularly in countries where believers are already experiencing tragic events—political upheaval, life-threatening diseases, earthquakes, wars, and rumors of war. Lord, may they be awakened, praying for us even as we pray for them. So desperate is the world for revival, we will willingly suffer tragedy if revival comes with it.*

JANUARY 9
Radical Reformation
Revival

> *Draw near to God, and he will draw near to you. Cleanse your hands, you sinners, and purify your hearts, you double-minded.*
> — JAMES 4:8

For most of our problems, we deal with the symptoms more than the causes. Like a painful toothache, we can try painkillers, or we can have the tooth removed. Revival, as it comes to us, may be just the beginning of what God wants to do next. Are we ready for what A. W. Tozer calls a "radical reformation"?

> I believe that the imperative need of the day is not simply revival, but a radical reformation that will go to the root of our moral and spiritual maladies and deal with causes rather than with consequences, with the disease rather than with symptoms.
>
> A. W. TOZER

PRAYER PROMPT: *Father, may our motto be "whatever it takes" for a cure for our worldwide problems. May our churches rise to the occasion and root out causes, not merely consequences. Go deep with us, Lord. Go deep with me.*

Radical Revival
→ Draw near to God

JANUARY 10

Stress and Revival

Cast your burden on the LORD, and he will sustain you; he will never permit the righteous to be moved.
PSALM 55:22

We live in a stressful world. Each day seems to bring yet another stressful situation. Handled wrongly, stress affects our physical, mental, and spiritual health. In revival, stress can cause us to miss out on the changes God wants to make in us or the blessings God wants to give us.

But stress, rightly handled, can work for our good. Stress teaches us how to handle the hard things that come into every life. To be alive is to know times of stress.

While we grow through rightly handled stress—casting our burden on the Lord—we can rely on him to give us the strength and wisdom to make it through.

> God does not promise to save us from struggle and hardship, for in no other school could he make spiritual men of us. Nor does he promise to make the hard way easier for us, for that would be to lower the standard of attainment, and of character which he has set for us. But he has promised, when the stress is growing too sore, to give us strength, that we fail not.
>
> J. R. MILLER

PRAYER PROMPT: *Lord, you know the triggers for my stress. I pray those might become triggers to cast my burden on you. For you will surely sustain me. You will never permit me to be moved.*

JANUARY 11

A Clean Heart

> *Create in me a clean heart, O God, and*
> *renew a right spirit within me.*
> Psalm 51:10

We know that God, not man or woman, brings revival to a community or nation. So it is also true of personal revival—it's God's work, not ours. We can pray, read the Word, even lead others to Christ, but it counts for little unless God is empowering (and glorified in) the work being done in us and through us.

Asking God to create a new heart in us is a prayer for personal revival, and it's a prayer he desires to answer.

God is the author of revival. We Christians can prepare
the atmosphere through our earnest prayer, exemplary
living, and being contrite and humble. But only God
can revive the spirit and revive the heart of a person.

Billy Graham

PRAYER PROMPT: *Father, like David, I ask you to create in me a clean heart and renew a right spirit within me. May the inside job you do in me be seen by those who know me best, and may you be glorified by your wonderful work in me.*

JANUARY 12

Self-Control

> *God gave us a spirit not of fear but of power and love and self-control.*
> 2 Timothy 1:7

What some may term an unfortunate side effect of revival is the tendency to have certain strange manifestations appear among the congregation. Many who experience these manifestations may count it as a blessing, but others see it as a distraction—one that can soon bring an end to revival.

The truest manifestation of revival is the intense awareness of God's presence and the worship generated by his Spirit. A Christian never needs to lose control of his or her actions. Even during revival, we are still accountable. The Spirit we have from God is one of power, love, and self-control.

> The weakness of human nature has always appeared
> in times of great revivals of religion, by a disposition
> to run into extremes, especially in these three things:
> enthusiasm, superstition, and intemperate zeal.
>
> Jonathan Edwards

PRAYER PROMPT: *God, my nature is weak. Guide me always as I, through the power of the Holy Spirit, learn self-control and discipline. Keep me from being a distraction to others through my own intemperance. Let all be done decently and in order.*

JANUARY 13

Ready the Horse

*The horse is made ready for the day of battle,
but the victory belongs to the LORD.*
PROVERBS 21:31

All of us, in one way or another, have prepared ourselves for battle, but revival, like victory, belongs to the Lord. Yes, many fine churches hold "revivals," often with the results of seeing more people saved. But such efforts are simply preparing for battle; the victory belongs to the Lord.

When it comes to true revival, human effort short-circuits what God wants to do. Ready the horse, but then give God the reins and get out of the way.

> If we persist in describing human efforts and continue
> to think in terms of "annual revival meetings," believing
> that the good work we are doing for God is revival,
> then we must content ourselves with far less than God
> is willing and able to give. If, on the other hand, we
> can realize that revival is truly God at work in a most
> unusual fashion, then our entire being can be stirred
> with longings and supplications to see just such an
> outpouring of God's mighty power in our own day.
>
> RICHARD OWEN ROBERTS

PRAYER PROMPT: *God, victory belongs to you, even when we prepare for battle. Revival, too, is yours. Bring it forth apart from our clumsy efforts at doing what only you can do. Forgive us our presumption that any "revival" of our making compares with what you want to do in our midst.*

JANUARY 14

Sustaining Prayer

Praying at all times in the Spirit, with all prayer and supplication.
EPHESIANS 6:18

We know that prayer begets revival, but we must remember that prayer also *sustains* revival. When we stop praying, revival dries up like a wet sponge in the desert. Likewise, when we allow worship and prayer to wane, we might as well call it a day. That revival is, sadly, winding down.

Bold persistent prayer brings *and* sustains revival. Pray before, during, and after revival.

> From the Day of Pentecost, there has not been one great spiritual awakening in any land which has not begun in a union of prayer, though only among two or three; no such outward, upward movement has continued after such prayer meetings have declined.
>
> A. T. PIERSON

PRAYER PROMPT: *God, you have placed it on our hearts to pray for revival—not just for revival but for ongoing revival. Keep the burden upon us, Lord. Don't let us up from our knees. May our worship continue through the days and nights. May the glorifying of you not come to an end until your purposes have been accomplished.*

JANUARY 15

A New Thing = Revival

"Behold, I am doing a new thing; now it springs forth, do you not perceive it? I will make a way in the wilderness and rivers in the desert."
Isaiah 43:19

The mistake many Christians make is expecting revival to look like it's looked in the past. Rest assured, it won't. When revival is from God, it's because he's doing a new thing.

We would not expect there to be rivers in the desert, but that's God's vision. God wants to bring a mighty river of revival into our desert experience today. Will we welcome it if it doesn't match our expectations of what revival should look like?

Past awakenings brought fundamental changes to music and methods, for instance. Both John Wesley and [George] Whitefield struggled mightily with the idea of preaching in the fields. They were proper Oxford men, after all! But their use of such a "profane" method helped to spur a great revival. In past revivals both gospel proclamation and social ministry converged, whereas today they are too often seen as rivals. Revival separates our preferences from unchanging truth.

John Piper

PRAYER PROMPT: *God, you are so creative! Everywhere we look we see evidence of your work. Even in the revivals you reveal yourself as an artist. It won't be hard to spot true revival as long as we look for your presence and the moving of your Spirit. Send it Lord! We're waiting and watching.*

God's VISION = (to expect) REVIVAL River's in desert

JANUARY 16

The Enemy of Revival

*When the enemy comes in like a flood, The Spirit of
the LORD will lift up a standard against him.*
ISAIAH 59:19 (NKJV)

As much as we desire revival, we have a bitter enemy who opposes our prayers and seeks to undermine our faith that God will indeed move in revival. Our prayers must focus on God's willingness to bring revival, but we must also firmly counterattack Satan, the resister of revival. When the enemy comes in like a flood, we must depend on the Spirit of the Lord to lift a standard against him. We must know that God—and his breath of fresh revival—will prevail.

Behind the present world iniquity, chaos, and unrest is Satan. He is the enemy who has come in like a flood. He is at work within the church seeking to prevent revival. He it is who makes Christians worldly and prayerless, and who introduces strife, division, false teaching, unbelief, etc. He has great power today because there is less prayer among God's people. Our prayer meetings have died out because we are so busy rushing about; organizing when we should be agonizing.

MAJOR ALLISTER SMITH

PRAYER PROMPT: *Father, the enemy has come into the church and the nation like a flood. Lord, raise up a standard against his demonic work. Prevail, Lord, over the enemy!*

JANUARY 17
Joy Unspeakable!

*Whom having not seen, ye love; in whom, though
now ye see him not, yet believing, ye rejoice
with joy unspeakable and full of glory.*
1 Peter 1:8 (kjv)

One of the greatest blessings that accompanies revival is joy. To quote Peter, it's pure "joy unspeakable and full of glory"! To receive revival is to receive the joy of the Lord—our strength and our hope!

Revival is a great releaser of God's joy. If there is no joy in the meeting, it isn't revival.

A genuine revival without joy in the Lord is as impossible
as spring without flowers, or day-dawn without light.

Charles Spurgeon

PRAYER PROMPT: *O God as we pray for revival, visit us with joy unspeakable. Fill us until we overflow. Allow our lips to praise you and set our feet a' dancing. Give us joy that is contagious, dependent not on our circumstances but on your presence. Joy, joy, joy!*

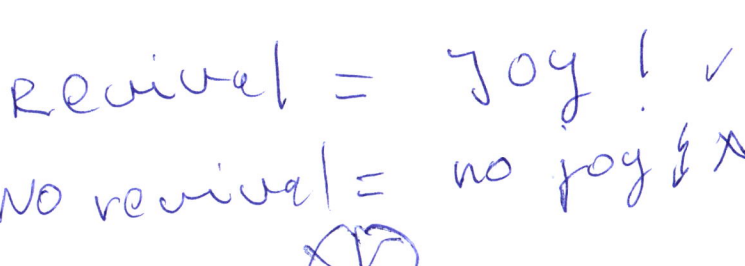

JANUARY 18

God's Alarm Clock

*Let us not sleep, as others do, but let
us keep awake and be sober.*
1 THESSALONIANS 5:6

Revival is God's divine alarm clock. The operative word is *alarm*. While evil advances in the world, many men and women, including Christians, are fast asleep.

As revival is ushered in by the Holy Spirit, the church awakens. People are saved, healed, and delivered from sinful lifestyles and obsessions.

Be assured, God's alarm clock has no snooze button. As the alarm goes off, it's time to move forward.

———

Many do not recognize the fact as they ought, that Satan has got men fast asleep in sin and that it is his great device to keep them so. He does not care what we do if he can do that. We may sing songs about the sweet by and by, preach sermons and say prayers until doomsday, and he will never concern himself about us, if we don't wake anybody up. But if we awake the sleeping sinner he will gnash on us with his teeth. This is our work: to wake people up.

CATHERINE BOOTH

———

PRAYER PROMPT: *Lord, may we listen hard for your divine alarm clock to sound the warning. The coming revival should and will shake us from our slumber. God, the hands of the clock are advancing. Allow the alarm to sound!*

JANUARY 19
Examine Yourselves

Examine yourselves, to see whether you are in the faith. Test yourselves. Or do you not realize this about yourselves, that Jesus Christ is in you?—unless indeed you fail to meet the test!
2 Corinthians 13:5

What is the church but a gathering of God's "called-out ones"? Each of us who has been called out has been guaranteed a home in eternity. But until that final day we have work to do. We must undergo frequent self-examination. We must know of a certainty that Christ dwells in us. Our church fellowship must also be tested. Are we cold, lacking the zeal of the Lord? Or are we hot with passion for the things of God? After all, revival begins with us and extends to our local church and throughout our community.

> The truth should be realized that all revival and spiritual quickening in the church, must come through individual hearts. We deplore the coldness of the church, its languishing devotion, its diminishing fervor and zeal, its spiritual deadness and lethargy. We sing revival songs. We pray revival prayers. We preach revival sermons. Yet we wonder why revival never comes. But how is it in the individual hearts? Has the revival begun there yet?
>
> J. R. Miller

PRAYER PROMPT: *God, hear us as we examine our hearts and test our faith. May we come alive to the reality of Christ in us. Bring light into our lives and into our churches. May every gathering of believers find room for one more . . . then another . . . and another. Thus, revival is born.*

#Truth/word based emotions

then **JANUARY 20** *1st* *TRUTH*
Emotions and Revival

> *A glad heart makes a cheerful face, but by sorrow of heart the spirit is crushed.*
> PROVERBS 15:13

To be sure, our emotions are touched during revival. The presence of the Lord overwhelms us. Tears may follow or any other emotional manifestation of revival. However, we must never be *led* by our emotions. Emotions express our inner feelings, but most of us have learned what happens when we rely on our emotions as a gauge of truth or error. Our emotions are, then, valid outlets when we're touched by the Holy Spirit. But they are no measurement of revival or even a lack of revival.

———

> What is really valuable before God is not how we emotionally feel the presence of the Lord or how we even feel love towards him; rather is it how we follow the Holy Spirit and live according to what he has revealed to our spirit. Not emotion but communion with the Lord in the spirit is what is valuable before God.
>
> WATCHMAN NEE

———

PRAYER PROMPT: *Lord, may my emotions be moved by your presence, but guard me from making my emotions the sole measurement of your revival. Give me the strength not only to feel your love in my heart but also to demonstrate it my actions.*

Revival ⇒ [cheerful] 100% ⊕ both/a (smile) maybe

Revival is God's Willlll
(intimate
fellow-ship) *(for us)!!!*

JANUARY 21

God's Will Is for Revival

> *This is the confidence that we have toward him, that if we ask anything according to his will he hears us.*
> 1 John 5:14

Sometimes it seems like we're uncertain if it's God's will to bring revival. We may reason (wrongly) that there isn't more revival because God doesn't will it or that it's become too late in history for another revival. But in doing so, we underestimate God's heart for his people.

God is for anything that draws us closer to him. But he wants us to desire his presence as much as he desires ours. This is why we pray. We pray passionately for revival, desperate for his intimate fellowship, and he responds in divine love.

> Our prayers must not be efforts to bend God to our will but to yield ourselves to his.
> CATHERINE MARSHALL

PRAYER PROMPT: *Father, we know revival is your will. We also know that when we pray according to your will, you will answer. In the prayer that Jesus taught us, we are told to pray that your will be done on earth. And so we continually knock on heaven's doors with persistence and by faith, trusting your positive reply. Soon, Lord, soon.*

God's heart for His pp!.|||
is His will for revival

"I experience the gospel and God's love for sinners afresh tod...

JANUARY 22
It's All About Jesus

"For God so loved the world, that he gave his only Son, that whoever believes in him should not perish but have eternal life."
John 3:16

Revival is all about the gospel and God's love for sinners. At the center of the gospel is our Lord Jesus Christ. When we experience revival, we experience the gospel afresh. We recall the joy of salvation, the wonder of God's love in Christ, and the fullness of his Holy Spirit in our life. If we keep the exaltation of Christ at the forefront of revival, it need never end.

Revival, above everything else, is a glorification of the Lord Jesus Christ, the Son of God. It is the restoration of Him to the center of the life of the Church. You find this warm devotion, personal devotion, to Him.

Martyn Lloyd-Jones

PRAYER PROMPT: *Father God, keep me ever mindful that in revival I'm "reviving" the joy of my salvation and the glorification of my Savior. Let not my motives be anything else. May my focus always remain on Jesus Christ. Help me experience the gospel afresh today.*

[If I keep the exaltation and glorification of my Lord JC at the forefront of revival, it need never end.]

JANUARY 23

God Is Enough!

The grace of the Lord Jesus Christ and the love of God and the fellowship of the Holy Spirit be with you all.
2 CORINTHIANS 13:14

God wants every believer to know he is trustworthy. He wants them to know he is enough for their every need. He proves this time after time, and yet when trouble threatens, we're slow to believe.

In revival, as we sense the nearness of God, we are once again convinced he is indeed enough. He is enough for our past (no matter how good or bad), our present, and for our eternal future. Revival is a celebration of the God who is enough.

> [God] loves people, loves to be in their midst, loves
> to look after them. Nothing can separate you from
> God's love, absolutely nothing. . . . God is enough for
> time, God is enough for eternity. God is enough!
> HANNAH WHITALL SMITH

PRAYER PROMPT: *Lord, you are enough! You are able to more than meet any needs I might have. You are enough for all my days!*

JANUARY 24

True Revival

Put off your old self, which belongs to your former manner of life and is corrupt through deceitful desires, and to be renewed in the spirit of your minds, and to put on the new self, created after the likeness of God in true righteousness and holiness.
Ephesians 4:22–24

No one leaves unchanged in a true revival. That's why we'll often hear old-timers recall past revivals with tears in their eyes. We enter revival one way, and we exit revival a new person, not unlike our conversion to Christ. In fact, many Christians count their revival experience as their conversion experience.

One danger is that when revival has waned, we are tempted to go back to our pre-revival selves. God's intent in revival is in changing lives that will stay changed. Revival life becomes the new norm. We only lose the joy when we harken back to pre-revival days.

> Beware of harking back to what you were once when
> God wants you to be something you have never been.
>
> Oswald Chambers

PRAYER PROMPT: *God, I love the newness your Spirit brings! Revival reminds me of the future you have for me, both here and in eternity. Lord, may I never be the same after revival!*

JANUARY 25

No Celebrities but Jesus

*"Everyone who exalts himself will be humbled,
and he who humbles himself will be exalted."*
LUKE 14:11

Revival is first, last, and always about God. It's never about us. We benefit but only as we humble ourselves at the majesty of God. We empty ourselves so that we can be filled with him. Pride keeps us full of self. Leaders may emerge during a revival, but such will be humble, always aware that this revival is the Lord's doing, not man's.

Be prepared to be brought low—very low during times of revival. Pride must die so that humility may have its way.

I am no longer my own, but yours. Put me to what you
will, rank me with whom you will; put me to doing,
put me to suffering; let me be employed for you or
laid aside for you, exalted for you or brought low for
you; let me be full, let me be empty; let me have all
things, let me have nothing; I freely and wholeheartedly
yield all things to your pleasure and disposal.

JOHN WESLEY

PRAYER PROMPT: *Lord, you know me better than I know myself. You know the places I need to be brought low in humility. You know my pride must give way so that you are exalted in my life. Offer me practical ways today to lower myself so that you and others may be elevated.*

JANUARY 26
Revival Brings Light into Darkness

*You are a chosen race, a royal priesthood, a holy
nation, a people for his own possession, that you
may proclaim the excellencies of him who called
you out of darkness into his marvelous light.*
1 Peter 2:9

All Christians belong to the same nation—a holy nation. We have been brought out of darkness into the light. We're a people of God's own possession, called out among the earth's nations to proclaim God's great excellency. Never is this distinction more apparent than during revival. Earth's national boundaries fall way as believers from all localities unite for God's glory. Revival is a special visitation of light in a dark world.

> All Christians, wheresoever they be, compose one holy nation. They are one nation, collected under one head, agreeing in the same manners and customs, and governed by the same laws; and they are a holy nation, because consecrated and devoted to God, renewed and sanctified by his Holy Spirit. It is the honor of the servants of Christ that they are God's peculiar people. They are the people of his acquisition, choice, care, and delight.
>
> Matthew Henry

PRAYER PROMPT: *O God, that you have called me out to be part of your holy nation amazes me. I am your possession, living now in the light and renewed by your Holy Spirit. Praise you, Lord, for including me in your eternal plan, and now make me a light for others.*

"Today, and forevermore, I proclaim the excellencies of Him!!!" #Revival

JANUARY 27

No Room for Racism

There is neither Jew nor Greek, there is neither slave nor free, there is no male and female, for you are all one in Christ Jesus.
GALATIANS 3:28

Racism finds no room at the revival altar—or anywhere else in the body of Christ. Racial prejudice still exists in the world, but it is not God's intent that this sin be part of his work. Thus, repentance of personal or churchwide racism is necessary for the blessing of revival. God will not bless the demeaning or exclusion of any of his born-again children. Not only must racial prejudice be left at the revival door; it must never be picked up again. One fruit of true revival is loving brothers and sisters who differ from us. For they and we are all fashioned by the same divine hands.

> We are seated with Christ in heavenly places, and from this rampart we look out upon life conscious that we are free from its petty strife. Race prejudices can no longer affect us. Class distinctions have been swept away.
> F. J. HUEGEL

PRAYER PROMPT: *Lord, bring an end to any racism that exists in your church. May we all see one another as brothers and sisters in the Lord, absent our earthly distinctions of class, race, and status. And may fresh revival follow this repentance!*

JANUARY 28

Do Not Hinder His Visit

*He did not do many mighty works there,
because of their unbelief.*
MATTHEW 13:58

What hinders revival? Surely prayerlessness and lack of faith contribute. Nor will revival come to people who feel no need to be spiritually revived. We can only wonder at the lost potential for miracles in Nazareth because of their unbelief. Likewise, we can wonder what our churches, communities, and nation would look like if there were no revival for lack of faith—for obstinate disbelief.

Revival requires a rising up of intercession on the part of God's followers. God will come in revival where needy people are praying in faith.

If we believe not with faith divine and
supernatural, we believe not at all.
JOHN OWEN

PRAYER PROMPT: *O Lord, how I pity the people of Nazareth who lacked miracles because they lacked faith. Forgive us in the places we've made the same mistake in our generation. We welcome you, and we believe in your "many mighty works."*

"God, I need you. I need revival. I need faith. Amen."

T.y!

JANUARY 29

Holding Fast to God's Purpose for Revival

*The counsel of the LORD stands forever, the
plans of his heart to all generations.*
PSALM 33:11

God has his purposes in revival. These purposes are often hidden, only to be seen perhaps years after the event. For every one of man's sins and ills, God has a remedy that will be found through seeking God. There are strongholds to be broken, both personal and national, and during revival, many people see those strongholds fall by the wayside.

Revival is not an entertainment. It always has a purpose—God's purpose.

This revival is not of man—God's finger is in
it, and by it he is developing his secret purposes
of mercy, wisdom, and righteousness.
OCTAVIUS WINSLOW

PRAYER PROMPT: *Father, in bringing revival, bring the fulfillment of your divine purposes. May we never thwart what you want to accomplish. Give us your vision for what you would have each of us do.*

JANUARY 30

The Contagion of Revival

"You are the salt of the earth, but if salt has lost its taste, how shall its saltiness be restored? It is no longer good for anything except to be thrown out and trampled under people's feet."
MATTHEW 5:13

When revival breaks out, it is as though our saltiness becomes seasoning to others. Our revival spreads like a forest fire. People come and see and then carry home the fire of revival. It then affects households, neighborhoods, and even former enemies. Many bars have closed their doors due to lack of business after a revival. When people are touched by the contagion of revival fire or have tasted the salt we bear, nothing stays the same.

> We are the salt that is to season others. . . . Shall the salt be unused until it loses its savor? . . . There are souls who, if they do not hear of Jesus from us will perhaps be never spoken to respecting him. If we do not seek their salvation, perhaps no one will. O, that the Holy Spirit would so come down upon us, that we may feel as if we could not rest—could not live—but as we seek the salvation of souls! May his Word be as a fire in our bones, that we may be weary with withholding, and unable longer to delay the work. It is our duty but may we feel it our privilege!
>
> JAMES SMITH

PRAYER PROMPT: *Father, may I be salt to those around me. May the joy of personal revival abound in me. May I become contagious to those who need to encounter your joy.*

JANUARY 31

God Intends a Great Mercy

*Let us then with confidence draw near to the
throne of grace, that we may receive mercy
and find grace to help in time of need.*
HEBREWS 4:16

One of God's intentions for his people is that they may draw near to his throne with confidence and thus receive mercy and grace. Revival releases a fresh rainfall of divine mercy and grace. We are aware of mercy as our not receiving the penalty for our sins and of grace as receiving what we don't deserve.

So as we pray for revival, let us dare to draw near to God's throne of grace, for great is our need.

> When God intends a great mercy for His people,
> the first thing He does is set them a praying.
> MATTHEW HENRY

PRAYER PROMPT: *Lord, I draw near your throne of grace with confidence that through Christ you welcome me into your presence. Send revival, Father. Rain mercy and grace on us, your people. For great is our need.*

FEBRUARY 1

Your Circle of Influence

"What man of you, having a hundred sheep, if he has lost one of them, does not leave the ninety-nine in the open country, and go after the one that is lost, until he finds it?"
Luke 15:4

We don't often think of our spiritual responsibilities other than as they relate to ourselves. But the truth is that every believer has a circle of acquaintances, including family, who are influenced by us. Do we take our influence over those circles seriously?

Revival is meant to bring repentance to believers and, many times as a result, saving faith to unbelievers. Who is on our prayer lists? Are we trusting God for their salvation? God has given this circle of influence to us as a gift and a responsibility. Part of revival praying is intercession for the lost.

Pray and believe for your lost friends. Give God thanks for setting them in your circle.

This generation of Christians is responsible
for this generation of souls on the earth!
Keith Green

PRAYER PROMPT: *Father, you have set certain people in my life for me to influence. I pray for this circle of influence—my family, friends, neighbors, coworkers, fellow students, and social groups. Every person in this circle has a purpose in my life. May I be sensitive to their needs. May your Holy Spirit prompt me when I should speak up and when I should shut up. Create a hunger in them to know you.*

FEBRUARY 2

There Will Be Mockers

"Blessed are you when others revile you and persecute you and utter all kinds of evil against you falsely on my account."
MATTHEW 5:11

Every revival will have its critics. It's lamentable when the rebukes come from unbelievers but more painful when the arrows fly from fellow brothers and sisters in Christ. Every self-appointed critic will have his own reason for disparaging a move of God. It's not important for us to know those reasons.

Our response is not to rebut the accusations but to pray and let God handle it. We are promised a blessing when reviled or persecuted. Even now as we pray for future revival, we may face the fiery darts of the enemy through the lips of skeptics: "It's too late for revival"; "Revival is too messy"; "Revival is just a show"; and on and on.

Pray. And remember that some of revival's antagonists are often won over by the events they once maligned.

If we find a revival that is not spoken against, we better look again to ensure that it is a revival.
ARTHUR WALLIS

PRAYER PROMPT: *Lord, silence the mockers of revival or bring them in to experience that which they've decried. Bring blessing, not cursing to those who defend themselves against a fresh move of your hand.*

FEBRUARY 3

He Is Worthy!

> "Worthy are you, our Lord and God, to receive glory and honor and power, for you created all things, and by your will they existed and were created."
> REVELATION 4:11

The revelation of God's greatness during revival cannot be overemphasized. Sensing the beauty and majesty of God is perhaps the greatest aspect of revival. Is it any wonder praise is such a major feature of revival?

We must never waver on the beauty, excellence, and worthiness of God. Circumstances and trials come and go, but God's worthiness is forever.

> If you had a thousand crowns you should put them all on the head of Christ! And if you had a thousand tongues they should all sing his praise, for he is worthy!
>
> WILLIAM TIPTAFT

PRAYER PROMPT: *O Lord, you are worthy of all praise! You alone are the majestic One! We bow before you in adoration, proclaiming your greatness. All glory and honor belong to you!*

"I sense God's beauty and majesty."

FEBRUARY 4

God's Grace Manifested in Revival

Give ear, O LORD, to my prayer; listen to my plea for grace.
PSALM 86:6

What is at the root of revival? Is it not the grace of God seeking those needing grace? A revival is God's grace manifested by his presence.

One can almost hear the voice of the Holy Spirit beckoning us to come and drink freely from his living waters. May we, even now, fully realize our own need of God's grace and fall to our knees in gratitude. For there is grace enough for all our needs. Drink deeply then!

> Come and drink from the infinite fountain of the
> Savior's priceless love! Drink freely and abundantly.
>
> OCTAVIUS WINSLOW

PRAYER PROMPT: *Father, your grace toward me is my anchor. Without grace I am lost. Hear my plea for grace. I'm humbled that your grace extends toward even me. I drink freely from your fountain of love.*

FEBRUARY 5

Hatred for Our Pet Sins

*We have all become like one who is unclean, and all our
righteous deeds are like a polluted garment. We all fade like
a leaf, and our iniquities, like the wind, take us away.*
ISAIAH 64:6

Who among us has no sin? We all have become unclean by our own doing. But regretfully, we cannot reverse the process and become clean by our own efforts. We must have a savior and a deliverer, and that Savior is Christ, our Lord.

We can, through faith, develop a hatred for the sins that so easily beset us. It's often difficult to rid ourselves of those seemingly small pet sins, but those small sins rarely remain small. In revival, we're brought low by the remembrance of our sinfulness. But, praise God, in revival a fresh flow of God's forgiveness causes us to shed our pet sins like a snake sheds its skin.

If your actions still show your love for your sin, deal harshly with them. Allow the deliverance wrought for you at Calvary to have its full delivering effect. You can, and must, live without your pet sins.

That one sin, whatever it is, while indulged, will hold
you back! You cannot make progress in holiness, until
it is mortified. Even its partial indulgence, though it
may be considerably weakened, will hinder you!

JOHN ANGELL JAMES

PRAYER PROMPT: *Lord, you know my tendencies toward sin, even the so-called small sins. I accept your forgiveness for my confessed sins and take deliverance from them as well. No sin shall take root in my life.*

FEBRUARY 6

Confess Your Sins

*Confess your sins to one another, and pray for
one another, that you may be healed.*
JAMES 5:16

Yesterday we explored how important it is to personally confess our sins, as this is an important aspect of revival. It cleanses our souls and makes us ready to receive a fresh experience of God's presence. But personal, private confession is only one side of the coin when it comes to sin. Even more blessing and healing abounds when we confess to one another, culminating in praying for one another. Happy is the Christian who has someone with whom to confess his sins and receive prayer. This is not usually done with casual acquaintances but is more likely among brothers and sisters with whom we have enjoyed a mutual deepening relationship. Brothers pray for brothers and sisters for sisters to avoid any awkwardness or misunderstanding. Faithful are the prayers of a genuine friend.

Christians are directed to acknowledge their
faults one to another, and to pray one for another,
and the efficacy of prayer is proved.
MATTHEW HENRY

PRAYER PROMPT: *Lord, praying alone is important, but having a prayer partner is also beneficial. Would you send me a prayer partner? Someone to whom I can bare my soul, confess my sins, and even share my aspirations. Such a person would be a great sounding board for sharing ideas and insights.*

FEBRUARY 7

An Undivided Heart

> *"Let your heart therefore be wholly true to the LORD our God, walking in his statutes and keeping his commandments."*
> 1 KINGS 8:61

Those Christians who will benefit most from revival—and are most likely to hasten it—are believers with an undivided heart. All our idols must be demolished, whether actual idols or imaginary idols of the heart. Holding fast to a precious idol is to rob God of the glory due him.

Check your heart today. Is there an idol that you hold dear? Is it an ambition, money, a car, fame, or even another person you can't bear to lose, though you know this relationship is wrong? God wants all of us. Let's give him all.

> God will have the whole heart.
> We must not divide our love between him and sin.
> The true mother would not have the child divided,
> nor will God have the heart divided;
> it must be the whole heart.
>
> THOMAS WATSON

PRAYER PROMPT: *God, you have my whole heart. I do not divide my allegiance to you and the world. It is all yours.*

Revival is knowing that:

FEBRUARY 8
Fully Equipped!

I'm *for every good work!*

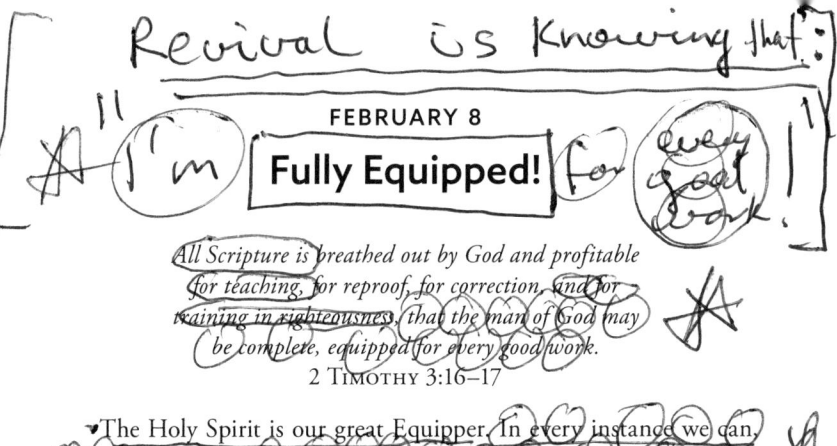

> *All Scripture is breathed out by God and profitable for teaching, for reproof, for correction, and for training in righteousness, that the man of God may be complete, equipped for every good work.*
> 2 TIMOTHY 3:16–17

The Holy Spirit is our great Equipper. In every instance we can, by faith, know that we have all we need to meet whatever our current situation may be. Paul told Timothy that the goal of "breathed-out" Scripture is that he (and we) might be equipped for every good work.

Revival is a time for an awareness of our equipping. What we think we lack for our divine assignments we either don't need or we can claim by faith. God does not send out his soldiers unequipped for battle.

> Each of us may be sure that if God sends us on stony paths he will provide us with strong shoes, and he will not send us out on any journey for which he does not equip us well.
> ALEXANDER MACLAREN

Quote

PRAYER PROMPT: *Lord, I lay down my useless self-made armor that the enemy so easily penetrates. Instead, I put on your equipping armor, tools, and weaponry so that I will be equipped for every good work you assign me.*

Boom

FEBRUARY 9

Revival Tears
Godly

Those who sow in tears shall reap with shouts of joy!
PSALM 126:5

There is a story about two Salvation Army officers who were failing in their newly established work. For advice, they contacted William Booth, the founder of the Salvation Army, whose brief reply was "try tears." They followed his suggestion and prayed with tears of anguish and petition, and a mighty revival followed.

Revival often comes with tears. Where there is prayer for coming revival, there will also be tears. If our prayers are the seeds of revival, our tears are the rain that waters the seeds. If we pray with tears, we shall reap with shouts of joy.

Tears come in two categories: sorrow for our sins and lack of faith and the tears of joy, born out of our true happiness in the Lord.

God sees both kinds of tears. He listens to the words that come from a tearful pray-er. Our tears for revival will produce the desired harvest, and we shall respond with shouts of joy.

Perhaps if there were more of that intense
distress for souls that leads to tears, we should
more frequently see the results we desire.

HUDSON TAYLOR

PRAYER PROMPT: Lord, break my heart for the lost and for the weakened church. May my heart show its passion through godly tears for your work on earth.

FEBRUARY 10

Overcoming Addictions

"If the Son sets you free, you will be free indeed."
JOHN 8:36

True revival sets captives free. In the presence of the Lord, earthly attractions fade into meaninglessness. Addictions fall as deliverance casts out the darkness of soul hunger. Into each person flows a work of the Holy Spirit of God.

God, however, is not restricted to delivering us from our addictions only when revival moves in. The Holy Spirit can set any captive free during a personal revival, whether instantly or over time with the aid of a support group and godly counsel.

To be set free from addiction is one of God's most joy-filled gifts.

> Man cannot live without joy; therefore when man
> is deprived of true spiritual joys it is necessary
> that he become addicted to carnal pleasures.
>
> THOMAS AQUINAS

PRAYER PROMPT: *Lord, I pray for those enslaved by addiction. I pray for my own tendency to become entangled with potentially addictive actions, substances, or attitudes. Bring freedom to my own heart, and to all who struggle.*

FEBRUARY 14
Revival and Our Inner Self

Though our outer self is wasting away, our inner self is being renewed day by day.
2 CORINTHIANS 4:16

Many of our avoidable problems spring from our outer man or woman.

The remedy is to deal with the outer self by strengthening the inner self—the spiritual self. Our behavior is a reflex or outworking of what's going on inside. For us to change our behavior, we must first change—or exchange—our inner self. We must feed the inner person with spiritual food in the form of meditating on the Word, learning from great Christians of the past or present, and deep prayer.

Pondering the greatness of our salvation and the immense love of God reminds us of the vast provision we have in the inner self to enable us to live victorious revived Christian lives.

You cannot lack any real good, since you have the fountain of all good dwelling in you. You cannot be finally overcome of any spiritual evil, since you have the Conqueror of sin and Satan and the world enthroned upon your affections. Your life, the inner, divine and spiritual life, can never die since Christ, who is essential life, lives and abides in you.

OCTAVIUS WINSLOW

PRAYER PROMPT: *Lord, sometimes I try to take the easy option of changing myself on the outside by giving up habits or adding new positive behaviors. As good as those might be, the real changes I need are on the inside. Help me, Father, as I take stock of the state of my inner life. By the power of your indwelling Spirit, transform me from the inside out.*

"In faith, fresh wind surely comes!"

FEBRUARY 12

"If You Have Faith"

> "Whatever you ask in prayer, you will
> receive, if you have faith."
> MATTHEW 21:22

God is looking for men and women who will pray in faith for a coming revival. Will he find them? Will we be the ones who ask earnestly in prayer? For if we ask according to his will and have faith in his plan and purposes, fresh wind must surely come.

Such has been the case in previous generations. Massive revivals have changed the world in which they occurred. All because Christians prayed in faith.

As I ponder Spurgeon's words below, I wonder, Is our faith "large enough"? Is our love for the lost "fiery enough"? If so, may God appear among us and do marvelous things.

> Oh! men and brethren, what would this heart feel if I
> could but believe that there were some among you who
> would go home and pray for a revival—men whose faith
> is large enough, and their love fiery enough, to lead them
> from this moment to exercise unceasing intercessions
> that God would appear among us and do wondrous
> things here, as in the times of former generations.
> CHARLES SPURGEON

PRAYER PROMPT: *Lord, may you find faithful followers who pray for revival. Send the rain, Father. Our wells are nearly dry.*

"God, find a faithful follower in me who prays for revival unceasingly, fiercely."

FEBRUARY 13

The Sovereignty of God in Revival

> *"I am the LORD, your Holy One, the Creator of Israel, your King."*
> ISAIAH 43:15

God's sovereignty is often a mystery. Why should we pray for revival if God desires it? Can't a fresh experience of his presence come without our prayers? Perhaps one reason is the desperation that leads us to pray also leads to revival. Would we see the need for revival if we weren't desperate?

It's a bit of a paradox, but God's sovereignty works through the prayers of his people.

Revival is always a work of God, but it is also the fruit of the prayers of Christians. Through prayer, we yoke ourselves to the sovereignty of God. Then revival comes.

> Revival is not something that human hands or wills can produce; it is something that only God can provide, according to his own good pleasure.
> JOHN SALE

PRAYER PROMPT: *Father, your sovereignty is a mystery. But I know you call your people to pray for that which you desire to give. Hear then our prayers for the revival you want to bring.*

"God is my King!"

FEBRUARY 14

God's Secret Work

> *"The secret things belong to the LORD our God, but the things that are revealed belong to us and to our children forever, that we may do all the words of this law."*
> DEUTERONOMY 29:29

Where does revival begin? From our point of view, it begins in the prayer room. But as we pray—perhaps even before we pray—God is at work behind the scenes, preparing for the events that will bring the revival we're praying for.

God has his plans for revival. We pray without knowing how or when God will unleash the miracle of revival. For that reason, we must not despair when it seems like nothing is happening in response to our prayers. Indeed, much is happening. We must believe it is so because we are counting on the faithfulness of God to fulfill his promises.

What is secret now will soon be manifest.

The Christian world will say that there is nothing going on when God is accomplishing most. Ask him for his eyes to see behind and deep down, and you will stand amazed at his working. God begins his revivals deep down, out of sight.

J. C. METCALFE

PRAYER PROMPT: *Father, I believe you are working even now, deep down and out of sight, for the revival for which we're praying. Soon, please make manifest what is now hidden from view, Lord.*

"I'm counting on God to fulfill His promises."
"Much is happening!"

FEBRUARY 15

Prayers for More Laborers

"The harvest is plentiful, but the laborers are few. Therefore pray earnestly to the Lord of the harvest to send out laborers into his harvest."
Luke 10:2

One fruit of revival is the voluntary enlistment of new recruits to the work of God. Laborers are always needed in the harvest of souls, and every Christian has a place of service. As we pray for revival, we also pray for more laborers. We offer ourselves as recruits to God's service and will gladly pay the cost to serve the Lord, knowing he is debtor to no one.

When we give to God, he gives back lavishly in the way of new harvest workers.

> It's true that (many) are praying for a worldwide revival.
> But it would be more timely, and more scriptural, for
> prayer to be made to the Lord of the harvest, that
> He would raise up and thrust forth laborers who
> would fearlessly and faithfully preach those truths
> which are calculated to bring about a revival.
>
> A. W. Pink

PRAYER PROMPT: *Father, as you send revival, send men and women, boys and girls who will be laborers in your vineyard. Then bring forth a great harvest from the coming revival.*

FEBRUARY 16

Resisting the Devil

*Submit yourselves therefore to God. Resist
the devil, and he will flee from you.*
JAMES 4:7

Prayer for revival causes abject fear in our enemy. For that reason, he is constantly seeking to undermine our prayers, often by whispering that God does not listen to our petitions.

Another tactic is to discourage us when our prayers don't bring instant revival or aren't answered the way we think they should be. What enrages Satan the most are the prayer warriors who are long-haulers, the men and women who are not deterred by his attacks on their prayer life. Instead, they fiercely resist the lies of the enemy.

A prayer warrior who is submitted to God and resisting the devil will see his prayers answered in due time.

> Depend upon it, if you are bent on prayer, the devil will not leave you alone. He will molest you, tantalize you, block you, and will surely find some hindrances, big or little or both. And we sometimes fail because we are ignorant of his devices. . . . I do not think he minds our praying about things if we leave it at that. What he minds, and opposes steadily, is the prayer that prays on until it is prayed through, assured of the answer.
>
> MARY BOOTH

PRAYER PROMPT: *Father, I'm aware of the enemy's tactic to discourage me, to remove my focus from you and your plans, but his lies will not prevail. I will not allow the enemy to rob me of prayer nor of the revival for which I'm praying. I will pray through!*

FEBRUARY 17

The Church Is Christ on Earth

Now you are the body of Christ and individually members of it.
1 Corinthians 12:27

We know Christ is in heaven, sitting at the right hand of the Father. But is there evidence that Christ still moves on earth today? Yes! The evidence is you and me. We who believe are the body of Christ. We are his hands extended to the poor, his heart beating in compassion for the lost, his eyes seeking the wounded and brokenhearted.

Revival is a wake-up call for all Christians to intercede in a weary world. It's a recharging of our batteries, giving us the strength and energy to do on earth what Christ would do.

We are entrusted to do even greater things than the works of Christ (John 14:12). But we can only do these in the power of the Holy Spirit.

> The Church is the Body of Christ, and the Spirit is the Spirit of Christ. He fills the Body, directs its movements, controls its members, inspires its wisdom, supplies its strength. He guides into truth, sanctifies its agents, and empowers for witnessing. The Spirit has never abdicated His authority nor relegated His power.
>
> Samuel Chadwick

PRAYER PROMPT: *Father, as part of your work on earth, may I fully live out the destiny you have for me. Show me the unique role I have in being Christ's hands on earth. Increase, Lord, my sensitivity to the needs of others.*

FEBRUARY 18

Quietness and Confidence

*Thus said the Lord God, the Holy One of Israel,
"In returning and rest you shall be saved; in
quietness and in trust shall be your strength."*
Isaiah 30:15

Some revivals can be loud with praise. At other times, silence is just as powerful. For many Christians quietness is foreign. Resting silently before the Lord may seem a waste of time. We may even find it sleep inducing. But when God is with us in quietness, there is no less power than when the church is filled with hallelujahs. Isaiah tells us that in quietness and trust we shall find strength.

Practice being quiet before the Lord. Don't rush to get up from your knees because it seems like nothing is happening. God is always at work, even in the quiet times.

> Quietness never can come through the smoothing of circumstances, so that there shall be nothing to trouble or irritate the spirit. We cannot find or make a quiet place to live in and thus get quiet in our own soul. We cannot make the people about us so loving and sweet that we shall never have anything to irritate or annoy us. The quietness must be within us. Nothing but the peace of God in the heart can give it. Yet we can have this peace if we will simply and always do God's will and then trust Him. A quiet heart will give a quiet life!
>
> J. R. Miller

PRAYER PROMPT: *Father, teach me to be still. Let quietness be a strength in my spiritual life. Help me shut out the noises from without so I can sense you moving within.*

FEBRUARY 19

Family Salvation

*"Believe in the Lord Jesus, and you will be
saved, you and your household."*
Acts 16:31

In both the Old and New Testaments, we see God saving not just individuals but entire households. In the Old Testament, we see Noah, Rahab, Abraham; and, of course, during the Passover, a lamb was sacrificed for the entire household. In the New Testament the households of Zacchaeus, Cornelius, Crispis, Lydia, and others were saved by faith.

Most of us have unsaved relatives in our families. What a blessing it is to see entire households come to faith in Christ during revival. As we pray, we must remember our own households—even our extended families—and ask that God would produce faith in their hearts during revival and usher them into the kingdom.

All who are born into our homes according to the flesh
should also be born into our homes according to the Spirit.
Watchman Nee

PRAYER PROMPT: *Father, thank you for individual salvation. But also thank you for those miraculous moments you bring saving faith into each heart of an entire household! Lord, consider those in my family that need you. Create in them a hunger only you can satisfy. Bring us all home to be reunited in heaven.*

FEBRUARY 20

Press Forward!

Let your eyes look directly forward, and your gaze be straight before you. Ponder the path of your feet; then all your ways will be sure. Do not swerve to the right or to the left; turn your foot away from evil.
Proverbs 4:25–27

One of the blessings of being a Christian is letting go of a painful past. All our sins have been forgiven, and God does not remember them. We now have a positive Spirit-filled future to embrace. But we can't embrace our future if we won't let go of the past—not just the past hard things we've endured but also some of the good things. We can't park on the glories of yesteryear. We must look ahead, directly forward.

Revival is a time for pushing the reset button. Walk straight ahead to the Lord, no swerving to the left or right or backward to some bygone era.

———

Press forward. Do not stop, do not linger in your journey, but strive for the mark set before you.
George Whitefield

———

PRAYER PROMPT: *Lord, life moves forward, not backward or sideways. My future is therefore a good one as I live for you and turn my feet forward, away from evil.*

FEBRUARY 21

God's Affection toward His Children

"For the Lamb in the midst of the throne will be their shepherd, and he will guide them to springs of living water, and God will wipe away every tear from their eyes."
REVELATION 7:17

In the Scripture we often see the wrath of God displayed. But we also see the tender mercies of God displayed as well. He leads us lovingly like a shepherd leads his sheep.

Ultimately the Bible is a record of God's love for each of us. His love has no limits, as amply demonstrated by the sacrifice of Christ, God the Father's beloved Son on the cross.

The grasp of God's genuine affection for us is a life-changer. Often in revival some Christians first experience the love that may have previously been just an important point of doctrine. And behind every objective point of doctrine, there exists a deeper subjective truth about the love of our heavenly Father.

Nothing is more powerful to engage our
affections than to find that we are beloved.
HENRY SCOUGAL

PRAYER PROMPT: *Lord, I appreciate the tender fatherly affection you give your children. You know just how and when to display your love for us.*

FEBRUARY 22

The Forgiveness of Sins

*He has delivered us from the domain of darkness and
transferred us to the kingdom of his beloved Son, in
whom we have redemption, the forgiveness of sins.*
COLOSSIANS 1:13–14

It's not possible to overemphasize the importance of the forgiveness of our sins. The cost was Christ's; the benefit, ours. In revival, it's good to revel in God's forgiveness of sins. His forgiveness is so thorough, it's as if we had never sinned.

Revival is also a time to remember the reason we have been forgiven. Our sins were not left unpaid. Nor were they merely looked over. The full penalty of our sins was placed on Christ, enabling total forgiveness and voluntary forgetfulness on the part of God.

What a merciful and forgiving Father! What a loving and sacrificial Savior!

Sins are so remitted,
as if they had never been committed.
THOMAS ADAMS

PRAYER PROMPT: *Father, I'm grateful for the forgiveness of my sins. I do not take lightly the price paid that removes my sins from even your memory. As I'm forgiven, may I also be quick to forgive the sins of others.*

FEBRUARY 23

Tender Sympathy

If there is any encouragement in Christ, any comfort from love, any participation in the Spirit, any affection and sympathy, complete my joy by being of the same mind, having the same love, being in full accord and of one mind.
PHILIPPIANS 2:1–2

When we are touched by revival, we of all people should be most sympathetic to the needs and sufferings of others. A fresh wind of God's presence and power brings comfort to the hurting and sends them out to bring healing to others. But we must first allow revival to have this effect on us. Then we must be willing to show affection, sympathy, and love to all—especially when the Holy Spirit prompts us to minister love to someone we may not have considered needing or deserving our sympathy. It may surprise us to know who near us is in silent pain.

Who knows but that revival may be sparked by some random act of love.

When a great revival of religion is coming, we shall expect to see the hearts of the Lord's people touched with the tenderest sympathy, and stirred to their very depths.

JAMES SMITH

PRAYER PROMPT: *Father, touch my heart as yours is touched by the needs of the sheep you love.*

FEBRUARY 24

Desperation Hastens Revival

As for me, I am poor and needy, but the Lord takes thought for me. You are my help and my deliverer; do not delay, O my God!
Psalm 40:17

Jesus came for the needy. That's how he comes in revival too. We *must* be desperate for him and him alone. We must be willing to pay the price, to let everything else go in order to experience revival. It's costly for sure; but on the other hand, it's totally free!

———

When God is about to bestow some great blessing on His church, it is often His manner, in the first place, so to order things in His providence as to show His church their great need of it, and to bring them into distress for want of it, and so put them upon crying earnestly to Him for it.

Jonathan Edwards

———

PRAYER PROMPT: *Father, we are needy for your presence. We're parched! Lord, take thought of us in our sad state and deliver us. Do not delay revival, O my God! We are praying and we are waiting!*

FEBRUARY 25

Revival Brings a Youthful Spirit

*The glory of young men is their strength, but
the splendor of old men is their gray hair.*
Proverbs 20:29

Revival has something for everyone, male and female, rich and poor, young and old.

For the young believer, there is the robust strength required for the heavy lifting in life. For the older Christian, there is the wisdom that comes with gray hair. Neither old nor young should regret their age; each stage of life has its own rewards.

Young believer, take the enthusiasm from revival that will guarantee your usefulness in the coming decades. Older believer, glance back at God's goodness through the years, but don't settle into that recliner just yet. God still has a work for you to do. He will revive!

> Those who are growing old should show the ripest spiritual fruitfulness. They should do their best work for Christ in the days which remain. They should live their sweetest, gentlest, kindliest, most helpful life in the short time which they have yet to remain in this world. They should make their years of old age—years of quietness and peace, and joy—a holy eventide. But this can be the story of their experiences only if their life be hid with Christ in God. Apart from Christ, no life can keep its zest or its radiance!
>
> J. R. Miller

PRAYER PROMPT: *Father, you are the God who never ages. You are forever young while I grow older with each passing year. Renew a youthful spirit in me, Lord. Keep me forever young at heart, forever expecting and enjoying revival.*

FEBRUARY 26
Conformed to His Image

We all, with unveiled face, beholding the glory of the Lord, are being transformed into the same image from one degree of glory to another. For this comes from the Lord who is the Spirit.
2 Corinthians 3:18

Christ lives in every believer. We behold his glory as we allow a great transformation to take place over time. From one degree of glory to another, we are being changed into his image.

Though we will inevitably bless others through the life of Christ within us, the true goal is our own transformation into his likeness. How blessed we are to see our old self fade as it is replaced with the image of Christ as the Holy Spirit does his inner work in our lives.

The best evangelism happens when others see Christ in us.

> We are not saved in order to be a blessing to other people—you will be that inevitably—but primarily we are saved in order to be conformed to the likeness of Jesus Christ, God's Son.
>
> Alan Redpath

PRAYER PROMPT: *Lord, I lay myself on your potter's wheel. Mold me, Father. Transform me into the image of Christ. Just as he is, let me be light in a dark world.*

FEBRUARY 27

Revival and the Word of God

*"It is written, 'Man shall not live by bread alone, but
by every word that comes from the mouth of God.'"*
MATTHEW 4:4

We will not experience revival if we do not believe, honor, and obey God's Word. A revival—a special visitation from God—depends on the truth between the covers of our Bibles. If we are critical or disbelieving, we will not see revival.

The way to best appreciate the Bible is to know that it is a treasured gift from God to his people. In its pages, we're instructed on how to live and how to die. It is our spiritual bread. Every word is from the mouth of God.

If we read the Bible with eyes of faith, it won't be long before we are revived.

> Revival puts an end to Biblical criticism, and brings
> deliverance to those who are victims of doubt; it is a
> return to the simplicity which is in Christ, to the absolute
> authority of His Word in the lives of both individual
> Christians and Churches. They learn to tremble before
> the Word of God. They prove the reality and authority of
> the power of the Holy Spirit, and of the Word of God.
> HUGH E. ALEXANDER

PRAYER PROMPT: *Father, I believe your Word. It is my compass as I navigate through life. Open the truths of the Bible to me as I read, study, and meditate on your Word.*

FEBRUARY 28
The Advance of God's Kingdom

"This command I gave them: 'Obey my voice, and I will be your God, and you shall be my people. And walk in all the way that I command you, that it may be well with you.' But they did not obey or incline their ear, but walked in their own counsels and the stubbornness of their evil hearts, and went backward and not forward."
JEREMIAH 7:23–24

Even though we rightly detest the dry days when there is no revival, we can take heart that such a time is perfect for revival. Through revival we become infused with new life, and thus the church is likewise refreshed. But we must see our spiritual state for what it is, and we must invite the Divine Physician to bring us healing through revival. A healthy church is enabled to move ahead as she should. Without revival, we will continue to stand still, not pursuing our assignment of telling the nations of their Savior.

It is by revivals of religion that the Church of God makes its most visible advance. When all things seem becalmed, when no breath stirs the air, when the sea is like lead and the sky is low and grey, when all worship seems to have ended but the worship of matter, then it is that the Spirit of God is poured upon the Church, then it is that the Christianity of the apostles and martyrs, not that of the philosophers and liberals, keeps rising from the catacombs of oblivion, and appears young and fresh in the midst of the obsolete things of yesterday and the day before.
SIR WILLIAM ROBERTSON NICOLL

PRAYER PROMPT: *Lord, I pray for your church to move ahead, following your lead. Let us not lag behind or, like a mule, plant our feet where we are, unwilling to advance at your pace.*

"RN, I am looking for that blessed Hope!"

MARCH 1

The Blessed Hope = The promised Return of J.C.

For the grace of God that bringeth salvation hath appeared to all men, teaching us that, denying ungodliness and worldly lusts, we should live soberly, righteously, and godly, in this present world; looking for that blessed hope, and the glorious appearing of the great God and our Saviour Jesus Christ; who gave himself for us, that he might redeem us from all iniquity, and purify unto himself a peculiar people, zealous of good works.

Titus 2:11–14 (KJV)

For generations, the promised return of Christ is has been our "blessed hope." That hope prompts us to deny all ungodliness and worldly lusts—to live sober lives, even in this present world. It has also been the hope of generations of Christians to see worldwide revival precede the Lord's return. While we pray for revival, we must keep our soul anchored in the blessed hope of Christ's return.

That blessed hope, is the hope of blessedness. A Christian's hope is not in this life; then he would have forlorn hope. There is nothing here to be hoped for but vicissitudes. All the world rings changes but we are looking for that blessed hope. This is the difference between the seaman's anchor and the believer's anchor. The seaman casts his anchor downwards; the believer casts his anchor upwards in heaven, looking for that blessed hope.

Thomas Watson

PRAYER PROMPT: *Lord, I place my hope in Christ and the kingdom of God. Like others from past generations and those of future generations, I pray for the consummation of the age as Christ returns as he promised.*

I place my hope in Christ and Christ's return.

MARCH 2

Waiting on God

> *Wait for the LORD; be strong, and let your heart take courage; wait for the LORD!*
> PSALM 27:14

We will have to wait while praying for revival. God has his timetable and it's nothing like ours. We pray expecting quick results. But when God plants the seeds of revival in our hearts, he often allows time to pass before sending revival. Some revivals may have been the result of many years of prayer preparation.

The coming revival may be attributed to the prayers of seasoned believers, some of whom may even have passed on. If we're not willing to wait as we continue to pray, we may not be the intercessors God has appointed to pray.

> Waiting for God is not laziness. Waiting for God is not going to sleep. Waiting for God is not the abandonment of effort. Waiting for God means, first, activity under command; second, readiness for any new command that may come; third, the ability to do nothing until the command is given.
> G. CAMPBELL MORGAN

PRAYER PROMPT: *Father, your timing in all things is perfect. What we consider waiting, you must consider as preparation. Lord, give me patience and a waiting, prayerful heart until the day of revival comes.*

MARCH 3

Giving Ourselves in Worship

*Ascribe to the LORD the glory due his name;
worship the LORD in the splendor of holiness.*
PSALM 29:2

Revival *always* results in worship. Not just lip-service worship but a true immersion of worship that is both born of the Holy Spirit and exalting the Lord Jesus Christ. In such worship God is pleased. But why wait for revival? All of our daily worship should be exalting Jesus. All adoration should be prompted by the Holy Spirit.

We are right in knowing such worship pleases God, but the irony is that this true worship changes us. Many unhappy Christians could be lifted up by entering into worship, for just as revival always results in worship, so too does worship result in joy.

> A revived church is full of the life, joy and power of the Holy Spirit. With the Spirit's coming, fellowship with Christ is brought right to the center of our worship and devotion; the glorified Christ is shown, known, loved, served, and exalted. Love and generosity, unity and joy, assurance and boldness, a spirit of praise and prayer, and a passion to reach out to win others are recurring marks of a people experiencing revival.
>
> J. I. PACKER

PRAYER PROMPT: *Lord, I worship you. I give glory to your name. You are Lord of lords and King of kings. All praise and honor belong to you. You are the giver of life, the source of my joy, and my hope for eternity where your praises shall ring forevermore.*

MARCH 4

God Keeps His Promises

My eyes are awake before the watches of the night,
that I may meditate on your promise.
PSALM 119:148

Every Christian is rich with the promises of God. The great mystery is why more believers don't avail themselves of God's promises. Even God must wonder at the lack of prayer that calls on the mighty promises in his Word.

Revival depends on those of us who are praying, holding God to his Word. If there is no revival, it will be due to our prayerlessness, not to God's lack of provision. As we pray for revival, let's do so by claiming the promises of God by faith. Let's meditate day and night on his promises.

God has no greater controversy with his people today than this, that with boundless promises to believing prayer, there are so few who actually give themselves unto intercession.

ARTHUR PIERSON

PRAYER PROMPT: *Lord, I live by your promises. I pray for my needs and you supply. I pray for revival and, in faith, watch for the advent of the outpouring of your Holy Spirit. Revive the trustworthiness of your promises in your church.*

MARCH 5

Carrying the Light of the Kingdom

> *"In the same way, let your light shine before others, so that they may see your good works and give glory to your Father who is in heaven."*
> MATTHEW 5:16

Revival empowers our churches to become *living* churches. And as a result our services will never be the same. When we are spiritually revived, it will show in our church's passion for the Lord and his people. There *will* be good works, and there will be fruit. The question every church body should answer is: *Are we really ready for revival and its aftermath?*

A day is coming when four songs, a sermon, and an offering simply will not work anymore. Perhaps this model has been functional for a season, but in an hour of deep darkness, we need to be a people who carry the light of the Kingdom. This will only happen as Christians live revival lifestyles.

MICHAEL BROWN

PRAYER PROMPT: *Lord, I pray for my church. May we become a carrier of light to those in darkness. Give us the passion of revival that we might experience the fruit of revival.*

MARCH 6

A Sense of Wonder

> *When I look at your heavens, the work of your fingers, the moon and the stars, which you have set in place, what is man that you are mindful of him, and the son of man that you care for him?*
> PSALM 8:3–4

What we seek in revival is the experience of awe as we bow before God. There is wonder in contemplating God, and all the more so in revival. That which we've known of our faith as head knowledge becomes true heart knowledge during revival. We often find that we don't want to leave this sacred place of revival.

Even now, think on the things of God. Ponder the mystery of the gospel. Consider a God who makes himself known to mere men and women. A God who cares deeply for his children. Such contemplation is health to our spiritual life.

Let your soul comprehend as much as it can of the Infinite, and grasp as much as possible of the Eternal, and I am sure if you have minds at all, that they will shrink with awe.

CHARLES SPURGEON

PRAYER PROMPT: *Lord, pondering your greatness takes my breath away. I know that I have only a glimpse of your greatness, and even that is a marvel. I pray, Father, for more realization of your magnificence. It changes my life.*

MARCH 7

The Vine Life

*"Abide in me, and I in you. As the branch cannot bear
fruit by itself, unless it abides in the vine, neither can you,
unless you abide in me. I am the vine; you are the branches.
Whoever abides in me and I in him, he it is that bears
much fruit, for apart from me you can do nothing."*
JOHN 15:4–5

If we are to be fruitful Christians, we must abide in the vine that sends forth the fruit. We must live in Christ. We may attempt to bring forth pretend fruit, but the fruit we produce ourselves has no taste or sweetness. Not only is there no taste and no nutrition, but the work required in pretend fruit is tiring. We work hard only to produce nothing of value.

Not so with revival. A revival experience is an abiding-in-the-vine experience. The fruit—the *true* fruit—flows freely and is sweet to the taste.

Trying to do the Lord's work in your own strength
is the most confusing, exhausting, and tedious of all
work. But when you are filled with the Holy Spirit,
then the ministry of Jesus just flows out of you.

CORRIE TEN BOOM

PRAYER PROMPT: *Father God, may the sweet fruit of your Holy Spirit flow out of me as I abide in you, the vine from which heavenly fruit is produced. May I be a bearer of much fruit.*

MARCH 8

God Is Not Passive

*It is God who works in you, both to will
and to work for his good pleasure.*
PHILIPPIANS 2:13

We see God active in revival. But when there is no obvious sign of revival, it does not mean God has become passive. Revival, like the Christian life itself, is a combination of God's moving and our moving. We do what he has willed us to do, and thus is God blessed and so are we. For there is no greater blessing than having God work in us to will and work for his good pleasure.

> In efficacious grace we are not merely passive, nor yet does God do some and we do the rest. But God does all, and we do all. God produces all, we act all. . . . God is the only proper author and fountain; we only are the proper actors. We are in different respects, wholly passive and wholly active.
>
> JONATHAN EDWARDS

PRAYER PROMPT: *God, it is comforting to know that you are always at work in my life. Even now, though I may not see your part in today's events, you are there, working in me to will and do your good pleasure. May I respond in faith to do my part in accomplishing your will for me.*

MARCH 9

The Indwelling Word of God

*Let the word of Christ dwell in you richly, teaching
and admonishing one another in all wisdom,
singing psalms and hymns and spiritual songs,
with thankfulness in your hearts to God.*
COLOSSIANS 3:16

Revival rekindles a love for God's Word. Not just reading the chapters. Not just doing a Bible study, but internalizing the Word. How else can we employ Paul's admonition to let the "word of Christ dwell in [us] richly"?

Taking in God's Word is like taking medicine. When we're sick and refuse medicine, we won't get well. God's Word, hidden in our hearts, keeps us spiritually well.

Let God's Word dwell within. The results will be seen within and without.

The Word of Christ does its work from within. Hence it must get into our heart and we must let it dwell in us. We can shut it out if we will. It cannot enter into our life unless we let it enter, nor will it stay with us unless it is hospitably entertained. It will not do anything for us either if we keep it out. A Bible lying on our table will not make known to us any of the wonderful revealings it contains. We must receive its words into our heart.

J. R. MILLER

PRAYER PROMPT: *O Lord, how I love your Word. I love the changes it brings to my life. Father, I pray for an even deeper understanding of your Word as it dwells within me.*

MARCH 10

A Divine Invitation

> *"Then the master of the house became angry and said to his servant, 'Go out quickly to the streets and lanes of the city, and bring in the poor and crippled and blind and lame.' And the servant said, 'Sir, what you commanded has been done, and still there is room.' And the master said to the servant, 'Go out to the highways and hedges and compel people to come in, that my house may be filled.'"*
> LUKE 14:21–23

Who is revival for? It's not for those who consider themselves to be part of the spiritually elite, for they consider themselves fully fed, not in need of reviving. Some of these "elites" might even sneer at revivals as being beneath them.

No, revival is not for those with a pharisaical bent. Revival is for whoever is eager for God. They crave his presence, his Word, his joy, his fullness. Revival is for the lowly and the hungry. May we always be in that number but never among those who disparage God's fresh presence rushing into the church and the world.

> Many times the gospel has the greatest success among those that are least likely to have the benefit of it, and whose submission to it was least expected. The publicans and harlots went into the kingdom of God before the scribes and Pharisees; so the last shall be first, and the first last. Let us not be confident concerning those that are most forward, nor despair of those that are least promising.
>
> MATTHEW HENRY

PRAYER PROMPT: *O Lord, I pray that you recognize my deep need for personal revival. I admit to not being all I'm meant to be. Fill me, Father, with yourself. Count me as one who is desperate for revival.*

MARCH 11

The Mighty Hand of God

*Fear not, for I am with you; be not dismayed, for I
am your God; I will strengthen you, I will help you,
I will uphold you with my righteous right hand.*
ISAIAH 41:10

The same right hand of God that is strong and righteous is also tender and full of compassion. In seasons of revival, we experience both in fresh and palpable ways. If we are weak, his hand is powerful. If we are wounded, his right hand is there to uphold us.

While some may fear the hand of God in judgment, we have only his tender touch to enjoy.

> His is a loving, tender hand, full of
> sympathy and compassion.
> D. L. MOODY

PRAYER PROMPT: *Father, I thank you that I never need to fear your hand in judgment. I pray for the gentle touch of a father's hand to comfort me when I am low and the powerful touch of your hand when I am weak.*

MARCH 12

Sanctified!

Know that the LORD has set apart the godly for himself; the LORD hears when I call to him.
PSALM 4:3

To be sanctified is to be set apart. All Christians are to be sanctified—set apart—for God's purposes. In a way, revival is a time of being set apart for a special work of God.

While we may have a more distinct sense of being set apart during revival, it does not need to be that way since God sets us apart for our unique work, revival or no revival.

When we, by faith, accept sanctification—being set apart—as God's will, it will change how we think, pray, and act. Each day may find us being used as a sanctified vessel fit for the Master's use.

What good work does God have for you to do today that only you can do? Take by faith God's call on your life. He has you set apart for himself. He will hear you when you call.

———

My first prayer in the morning when I awake is addressed
to the Holy Spirit, that He would take possession of my
thoughts, my imagination, my heart, my words, throughout
the day, directing, controlling, and sanctifying them all.

MARY WINSLOW

———

PRAYER PROMPT: *Father, it is enough that you have saved me. But to know that I am also set apart for your use is humbling. Thank you for using me, despite my many failings.*

MARCH 13

The Perfection of God's Plans for Me

> *The LORD will fulfill his purpose for me; your steadfast love, O LORD, endures forever. Do not forsake the work of your hands.*
> PSALM 138:8

God's love is made apparent in revival. His love is a personal matter for every believer. Because of his great love, he has tenderly created a unique plan for each of our lives. When we let him lead and we stay on the path of his choice, we are blessed. When we wander off the path, we suffer. Revival renews an awareness of God's perfect purpose for us. For example, during revival, some are clearly called to ministry or to be missionaries. Others are called to change jobs, get married, surrender an idol, or show up to the same life that's always been in front of them, but in a new way. Regardless of the specifics, the happiest Christians are those who know God's will and follow his path all the way to the doors of heaven.

> God's plans and purposes for me, and for you, dear reader, were all made and determined from the beginning. And as they are worked out day by day in our lives, how wise would we be if, with joyful certainty, we accepted each unfolding of his will as a proof of his faithfulness and love!
>
> SUSANNAH SPURGEON

PRAYER PROMPT: *Father, help me stay on the path chosen especially for me. When I've reached my final day on earth, may I come into your presence satisfied in having lived for your purposes.*

MARCH 14

The Rest of Revival

"Take my yoke upon you, and learn from me, for I am gentle and lowly in heart, and you will find rest for your souls. For my yoke is easy, and my burden is light."
Matthew 11:29–30

Many Christians carry burdens too heavy for them. Jesus invites us to find rest for our souls by taking on his light yoke. Many of our burdens are the result of misplaced loyalties. We have knowingly or unknowingly served Satan's plan for our lives by indulging in fleshly pleasures. We must accept Christ's offer to exchange burdens. If we are brave enough to take him at his word and make the exchange, we'll find it revives our weary soul.

> We have served Satan long enough. We have served diverse lusts and pleasures. We have served sin. Let us now break away from our old masters. Let us break their yoke and burst our bonds. Let us take the yoke of Jesus, engage in the service of Jesus, and make it our daily aim to please Jesus. Let us spread his truth, publish his fame, and bear testimony to his faithfulness and love.
>
> James Smith

PRAYER PROMPT: *God, I long to exchange my burden for your easy yoke. In receiving the rest of your gentle and lowly heart, I am revived. Keep me close to you, Lord, established in your rest.*

MARCH 15

Remember the Blood

*In him we have redemption through his blood, the forgiveness
of our trespasses, according to the riches of his grace.*
EPHESIANS 1:7

When we engage in revival prayer, we pray based on the blood of Christ, spilled for our redemption. All prayer is centered on the work of Christ and his blood atonement for our sins.

Many would-be disciples, past and present, turn away from the importance of the blood of Christ. They'd rather engage in prayer to God without any talk of blood. Yes, the spilling of his blood was awful, but we must remember it was necessary. Likewise, it was awful for an innocent lamb to be slain for each Hebrew household in order to be spared from the angel of death at the time of Passover, but it, too, had to be so. The saving was in the blood, for without it, there was (and is) no remission of our sins nor access to God through prayer (Heb. 9:22; 10:22–24).

Don't shrink back from the blood of Christ. When revival comes, it will be because blood was shed two thousand years ago.

All prayer is acceptable with God, and only so, as it
comes up perfumed with the blood of Christ; all prayer
is answered as it urges the blood of Christ as its plea: it is
the blood of Christ that satisfies justice, and meets all the
demands of the law against us; it is the blood of Christ
that purchases and brings every blessing into the soul.

OCTAVIUS WINSLOW

PRAYER PROMPT: *God, thank you that the blood of Christ has been shed for the remission of my sins, thereby giving me access to you in prayer. May I never forget that the innocent blood of Christ paid the debt of the guilty—me. Revival prayer isn't even possible without this precious blood!*

MARCH 16

Seek First the Kingdom

"Do not be anxious, saying, 'What shall we eat?' or 'What shall we drink?' or 'What shall we wear?' For the Gentiles seek after all these things, and your heavenly Father knows that you need them all. But seek first the kingdom of God and his righteousness, and all these things will be added to you."
MATTHEW 6:31–33

Do we want the blessings of God? If so, we will find them by seeking first the kingdom of God—no matter our earthly calling. During a season of personal revival, what else are we doing except seeking God and his kingdom and enjoying his presence?

If we would find revival, we must seek first the kingdom of God. When we seek, we shall find—abundantly so.

In whatever quarter of the world you may be, whatever your calling or profession: a soldier, a clergyman, a physician, a lawyer, a merchant, a tradesman; whether you may rise to a high position, or tread a humble path, put God first, and his presence and favor shall be as a crown of glory on your head.

GEORGE EVERARD

PRAYER PROMPT: *Lord, there is much in this life that I could seek before seeking for you. But I choose the wiser path—I choose to seek first your kingdom and your righteousness, knowing all I need shall be added by your hand.*

MARCH 17

Forgetting the Past

One thing I do: forgetting what lies behind and straining forward to what lies ahead, I press on toward the goal for the prize of the upward call of God in Christ Jesus.
Philippians 3:13–14

Many Christians suffer from a lesser spiritual life because they can't fully recover from a painful past. Perhaps they were a victim of someone else's anger or malice. Maybe they fell into sin. Maybe they committed some act they can't escape the memory of.

The apostle Paul had reason to be stuck in the sordid memory of consenting to the death of Christians, but he was able to set aside the past and move forward as he looked to the future "prize" of all Christians: resurrection day.

Revival is a time for just that: moving forward. Satan remembers your past. God does not. And to be useful, neither must we.

> We ought not to live in the past. We ought to forget the things that are behind and reach forward to the things that are ahead. "Forward, and not back," is the motto of Christian hope. The best days are not any days we have lived already but days that are yet to come.
>
> J. R. Miller

PRAYER PROMPT: *Father, it's encouraging to know that there are always better days ahead. The best is yet to come as you author the book that is my life. Help me as I set aside forever the painful memories of the past and press on toward the future you have promised!*

MARCH 18

The Cleansing Fear of the Lord

The fear of the LORD is clean, enduring forever.
PSALM 19:9

The importance of fearing the Lord is emphasized in both the Old and New Testaments. Though we are under grace because of God's new covenant with us, we must still fear God since it is the beginning of wisdom. And as the psalmist writes, the fear of the Lord endures forever. In times of revival, a fresh realization of who God is brings an automatic response of rightly fearing him. That godly fear is a cleansing fear in hearts that have grown cold because of a lack of revering God. The fear of the Lord brings renewed security. Fearing God removes all our other fears.

> The remarkable thing about God is that when you fear God, you fear nothing else, whereas if you do not fear God, you fear everything else.
> OSWALD CHAMBERS

PRAYER PROMPT: *God, I need the enduring fear of the Lord in my life. Too often I've taken you for granted, as though you were like a good pal. But you are Lord! You are holy and I am not! Father, establish my heart in the righteous fear of you.*

MARCH 19

Holiness

Since we have these promises, beloved, let us cleanse ourselves from every defilement of body and spirit, bringing holiness to completion in the fear of God.
2 CORINTHIANS 7:1

We must learn to see all of life's moments as holding a measure of holiness. For he who is holy is present in all our experiences. God's holiness is something we're to enjoy, not endure or resent. Revival invariably brings a renewed sense of God's holiness and our lack of holiness.

We are to embrace his holiness. After all, Christ's holiness and righteousness have been imputed to us as a gift! It is his holy record we stand on! We must then live out that promised holiness, becoming more like Christ as we grow.

Remember, however, that our feeble and foolish attempt at holiness through our own strength is nothing more than religious legalism. It must be *his* holy nature empowering us and working through us as we mature in our faith. All else is vain striving.

> It is my firm impression that we need a thorough revival of Scriptural holiness.
>
> J. C. RYLE

PRAYER PROMPT: *Lord, I desire your holiness in my life. Cleanse me from every defilement of body and spirit. Open my heart to discern the ways I can become more like you in righteous living.*

MARCH 20

God's Name

*"You shall not take the name of the LORD your
God in vain, for the LORD will not hold him
guiltless who takes his name in vain."*
Exodus 20:7

God's name is glorified in revival worship. How different that is to the daily hearing of God's name spoken in vain, even turning the name of Jesus into a curse word. This is the age we live in.

But as we cringe at such blasphemy, may we be reminded to praise God's name in that moment. Worship trumps cursing. We may also offer a short silent prayer for the person denigrating God's name, realizing he may be acting in ignorance. And may we also consider the small ways we, too, take our Lord's name in vain, whether by stealing credit due to him, blaming him for our poor choices, or carelessly using his gracious nature as an excuse to sin.

Does it grieve you my friends, that the name of God is being taken in vain and desecrated? Does it grieve you that we are living in a godless age. . . . But, we are living in such an age and the main reason we should be praying about revival is that we are anxious to see God's name vindicated and His glory manifested. We should be anxious to see something happening that will arrest the nations, all the peoples, and cause them to stop and to think again.

Martyn Lloyd-Jones

PRAYER PROMPT: *Father, I hallow your name. Blessed be your name. As I pray for revival, I pray for a turning back of the blasphemous use of your name by those who don't know you. May they be touched by revival and learn the true nature of the words they have used in ignorance or rebellion. I pray the same things for myself in the moments I'm unknowingly being careless with your name.*

MARCH 21

No Condemnation

> *There is therefore now no condemnation*
> *for those who are in Christ Jesus.*
> ROMANS 8:1

Revival is a time to be done forever with self-condemnation. To be a Christian and feel the weight of condemnation is to miss a key benefit of the gospel. In our flesh, before we knew Christ, our guilt over our sin and our knowledge of our deserved punishment was crippling. But having come to Christ, all our sins and self-condemnation were dealt with forever.

Think of it: if you are "in Christ Jesus," no condemnation can touch you. You are as justified before God as anyone else. There is no believer, past or present, who is more justified than you are.

Be done with condemnation forever.

> Justification is an act. It is not a work, or a series
> of acts. It is not progressive. The weakest believer
> and the strongest saint are alike equally justified.
> Justification admits no degrees. A man is either wholly
> justified or wholly condemned in the sight of God.
>
> WILLIAM PLUMER

PRAYER PROMPT: *Lord God, I once stood condemned at your feet. Thank you for dealing with that state of guilt by the sacrifice of your Son. You have removed forever the cause of my stumbling over my past. It is gone forever! Thank you for my justification.*

MARCH 22

Gratitude

> *Oh give thanks to the LORD, for he is good,*
> *for his steadfast love endures forever!*
> PSALM 107:1

In revival, the glory of the cross and our salvation from sin are magnified. We see our blessed lot with fresh eyes. We sense the steadfast love of God that endures forever. This love is unmoving, unchanging, unending.

In the cross we see the response of God to fallen mankind. That response is sacrificial love. Revival always brings us back to what happened at Calvary.

> This steadfast love of the Lord is never removed from his children. Since the believer is in Christ, nothing can separate him from the love of God. He has solemnly engaged himself by covenant, and our sins cannot make it void. . . . Calvary is the supreme demonstration of divine love. Whenever you are tempted to doubt the love of God, Christian reader, go back to Calvary.
>
> ARTHUR PINK

PRAYER PROMPT: *God, thank you for that awful but yet glorious event on Calvary and all it means to me. I pray that revival will increase the appreciation of Calvary for every believer.*

MARCH 23

The Ultimate Revival

> *You who have made me see many troubles and calamities will revive me again; from the depths of the earth you will bring me up again.*
> PSALM 71:20 (NRSVUE)

Revivals, though heaven-sent, fall short of the ultimate revival for each believer. This ultimate revival, to which all earthy revivals point, is resurrection revival—that day when we each pass over into the promised eternal life in heaven. The promise of a new incorruptible body is true evidence of God bringing back to life—*new* life—that which has died. So when we experience revival here, let it be a mere foretaste of that great revival awaiting us.

> Let us not be afraid to meditate often on the subject of heaven, and to rejoice in the prospect of good things to come. . . . Let us take comfort in the remembrance of the other side.
>
> J. C. RYLE

PRAYER PROMPT: *Lord, though I long for revival here on earth, I yearn even more for the revival awaiting me in eternity. May the foretaste of heaven fulfill me here, just as the reality of resurrection revival will fulfill me there.*

I meditate often on Heaven.
I rejoice in good things to come

MARCH 24

Living Stones

*You yourselves like living stones are being built up as a
spiritual house, to be a holy priesthood, to offer spiritual
sacrifices acceptable to God through Jesus Christ.*
1 PETER 2:5

Revival can be likened to a gathering of God's living stones, with the life-giver, Jesus, present. It, then, is a foretaste of heaven, where every living stone is in place, built on the chief cornerstone.

How are we made living stones? By partaking of the life-giving stone, Jesus Christ. A revival is a solemn yet joyous assembly of God's living stones. In the various seasons in this life, we struggle with hardened, stony hearts. Let us once again be "quickened by divine grace."

What are believers? They are living stones; each one being
quickened by divine grace, and made new creatures.
They are lively, made so by divine communications, and
kept so by fellowship with Jesus, the life-giving stone.

JAMES SMITH

PRAYER PROMPT: *Thank you for reviving me—for turning my heart from stone to flesh! Now that I am no longer a dead stone but a living one, Lord, I take my place in your spiritual house. I desire to be what you have created me to be and nothing more. I offer to you the spiritual sacrifices you find acceptable through Jesus, my Savior.*

MARCH 25

The Practical Results of Revival

Religion that is pure and undefiled before God the Father is this: to visit orphans and widows in their affliction, and to keep oneself unstained from the world.
JAMES 1:27

It would be a tragedy if, after a personal or widespread revival has ended, we go about our pre-revival days as if nothing happened. The expected results of revival should be the bearing of much fruit in the form of ministry to others.

We are henceforth to be givers of life. Reproducers of God's life. Givers to the hurting. Caring for orphans, widows, and others in need. We must leave the revival altar with an intent to use our energies to take Jesus to those in need.

God is pleased with no music below so much as with the thanksgiving songs of relieved widows and supported orphans; of rejoicing, comforted, and thankful persons.

JEREMY TAYLOR

PRAYER PROMPT: *Lord, when my path doesn't seem to lead me to others in need, change my direction. Let revival have its full effect of my assisting those in need. Do not let your life-giving power stop with me but flow through me to those who need it most.*

MARCH 26

Beware of Revival Wildfire

Let all things be done decently and in order.
1 Corinthians 14:40 (kjv)

What causes the death of revival? Of many things, "wildfire" is one unfortunate element. God begins and sustains the work of revival, but he surely withdraws his presence when man's fleshly nature asserts itself in the form of bizarre behavior, self-promotion, profiteering, or even sensuality. Thus, when we pray for or during revival, it's important to pray against the ungodly forces of wildfire. We may be surprised by who is the instigator or promoter of the disarray of wildfire. It could be the least likely among us.

> How often is a work of God marred and discredited by the folly of men! Nature will always, and Satan too, mingle themselves as far as they can in the genuine work of the Spirit in order to discredit and destroy it. Nevertheless, in great revivals of religion it is almost impossible to prevent wildfire from getting in among the true fire.
>
> Adam Clarke

PRAYER PROMPT: *Father, when you bring revival, it seems Satan also brings his cohorts to shut down revival, often through the spread of "wildfire." Lord, keep him at bay, along with any who would participate in your revival work with ulterior motives. Squelch the wildfire before it does damage to your work of revival. May all be done decently and in order.*

MARCH 27

All Our Needs Are Met

> *Oh, fear the LORD, you his saints, for those who fear him have no lack! The young lions suffer want and hunger; but those who seek the LORD lack no good thing.*
> PSALM 34:9–10

Only a poor or absent father refuses to meet the needs of his children—neither of which is our heavenly Father. Our God watches over us, surveying our daily needs, arranging circumstances to meet those needs. A child of God need not worry about daily bread. God has a table spread for us. He invites us to enjoy his provision. We shall lack no good thing. Every revival is likewise a spiritual feast, reminding us of our source for every need.

> Do not be afraid of need; in your Father's house there is bread enough. . . . I will care for your bodies. Do not worry about what you shall eat, drink, or put on. Let it suffice you that your heavenly Father knows that you have need of all things. . . . I will provide for your souls: food for them, mansions for them, and portions for them. . . . Behold, I have spread the table of My gospel for you, with privileges and comforts that no man can take from you. . . . I have set before you the bread of life, the tree of life, and the water of life. . . . Eat, O friends; drink abundantly, O beloved!
>
> JOSEPH ALLEINE

PRAYER PROMPT: *Lord, you are a good Father to your children. I have all my needs met, just as a child has his needs met by his loving father. Thank you for today's bread, both physical and spiritual.*

MARCH 28

A House Blessing

*The LORD's curse is on the house of the wicked,
but he blesses the dwelling of the righteous.*
PROVERBS 3:33

When we talk about revival, we usually envision a church setting—and understandably so. But God would have us invite revival into our homes, too. No child is too young to be exposed to the presence of God in revival. Nor is any believer too old to behold the glory of revival in the home. A Christian home is indeed a blessing, but a Christian home experiencing revival is a multiplied blessing. What might change in your home if you prayed for a family-wide revival to break out?

> [The Christian] fears the Lord, and therefore he comes under the divine protection even as to the roof which covers himself and his family. His home is an abode of love, a school of holy training, and a place of heavenly light. In it there is a family altar where the name of the Lord is daily had in reverence. Therefore the Lord blesses his habitation. It may be a humble cottage or a lordly mansion; but the Lord's blessing comes because of the character of the inhabitant, and not because of the size of the dwelling.
>
> CHARLES SPURGEON

PRAYER PROMPT: *Thank you, Lord, for my home. May we all daily worship and trust you. Renew our fervency and love for you. May visitors sense your presence as they enter. May my home be a home of revival.*

MARCH 29

Do All to His Glory

*Whether you eat or drink, or whatever
you do, do all to the glory of God.*
1 Corinthians 10:31

In revival, we are each brought low in the presence of God. Who can stand when God is with us? As we bow low, we're reminded that all we have is from and for the Lord. All we do is with his eye upon us. All is to be done for the glory of God. This means there are no mundane tasks in the life of the believer. Our lives in their entirety are submitted to God. Whether we eat, work, rest, or minister to others, it is all for the glory of God.

Forget the idea that God is only glorified by large or noteworthy deeds done in his name. His glory is to be present in all we do, large and small.

Remember always the presence of God. Rejoice always
in the will of God. Direct all to the glory of God.
Robert Leighton

PRAYER PROMPT: *Father, deliver me from the temptation of receiving glory that belongs to you. May my every deed, eating and drinking, working and resting, sowing and reaping be done for your glory.*

MARCH 30

Servants of God

*Have this mind among yourselves, which is yours
in Christ Jesus, who, though he was in the form of
God, did not count equality with God a thing to be
grasped, but emptied himself, by taking the form of
a servant, being born in the likeness of men.*
PHILIPPIANS 2:5–7

The apostle Paul urges us to have the mind of Christ, which results in emptying ourselves of selfishness, and, like Jesus, taking on the form of a servant.

We're also reminded of Jesus's words to his disciples that whoever would be great in God's kingdom must become the servant of all (Matt. 20:26). This mindset is opposed to our culture's self-exalting way of thinking, a mentality we must routinely throw off each time it crosses our mind.

Today, many carefully choose words to clarify their chosen identity. But few of us choose the word *servant* as our identifier. Yet through serving God exalts us. The road to greatness is marked "serve." A road too few of us travel.

Do you long for personal revival? Start serving. Fresh faith and spiritual fervor will soon follow.

We should always look upon ourselves as God's servants,
placed in God's world, to do his work; and accordingly labor
faithfully for him; not with a design to grow rich and great,
but to glorify God, and do all the good we possibly can.

DAVID BRAINERD

PRAYER PROMPT: *Lord, I know that with you the way up is down. You identify greatness with servanthood. May I then be no more than your servant, for such will make for a happy life.*

MARCH 31

Confidence in God

Some trust in chariots and some in horses, but we trust in the name of the LORD our God.
PSALM 20:7

To have true confidence in God means divesting ourselves of all confidence in ourselves. We have learned long ago not to trust in the chariots and horses of our own stables, for in light of life's bumps and rough patches, they have always failed. And yet God sees us through, urging us to put our full trust in him—to transfer our confidence from self to the Lord our God.

Retiring our chariots and setting our horses free may be painful, but until we do so, we will not experience the power of God in the rough patches of life.

The true confidence which is faith in Christ, and the true diffidence which is utter distrust of myself are identical.
ALEXANDER MACLAREN

PRAYER PROMPT: *Lord, I resign all trust in myself. When I became born anew by your Spirit, I learned that I must let go of my old self-confidence and rely on you. And in so doing, you have never failed, nor will you. Thanks be to you, O God.*

APRIL 1

Abandoning All

*"Any one of you who does not renounce all
that he has cannot be my disciple."*
Luke 14:33

Why are we so reluctant to renounce all for the sake of Christ? Do we fear being let down by him? What a poor expectation we have of God if we refuse to abandon all for him, fearing disappointment. The disciples, save Judas, did not regret leaving their old life for the new life Jesus called them to, even though they faced martyrdom as their earthly reward for abandoning all.

Neither will we regret renouncing all. We shall discover that renouncing self is not a loss but rather a gain. For those who give up everything for Christ now will inherit everything in the end.

Wherever there is true faith, there will also be self-sacrifice.

George Everard

PRAYER PROMPT: *Lord, revive my desire to abandon all in favor of your provision. Keep me looking ahead at my gain, not looking back to what I've abandoned. One is gold, while the other is dust.*

APRIL 2

Revival Worship

Let us lift up our hearts and hands to God in heaven.
LAMENTATIONS 3:41

In revival praying, any posture is suitable. But when there's an awareness of the nearness of God, hands are raised, knees bent, even lying prostrate can seem utterly natural. In Gethsemane, Jesus fell on his face in prayer. Several who begged Jesus for healing did so by kneeling before him. King David and the apostle Peter urged the lifting of holy hands in their biblical writings.

As we lift our hands, we must also lift our hearts, for posture means nothing if the heart is not engaged in worship. Allow yourself the freedom to assume the most natural position for your time of prayer. Whether your head is bowed or your hands are lifted high, allow the posture of your heart to focus on God.

When a man falls on his knees and stretches his hands heavenward, he is doing the most natural thing in the world.
A. W. TOZER

PRAYER PROMPT: *Lord, I lift my heart and my hands unto you. Receive my worship, hear my prayer, and accept my praise.*

APRIL 3

Kingdom Secrets

*Call to me and I will answer you, and will tell you
great and hidden things that you have not known.*
JEREMIAH 33:3

Revival can bring a fresh understanding of God and how he works in our life. Old truths we have forgotten become fresh again. The reality of God's love may be experienced in such a way that leaves us prostrate in worship. We may receive a personal prompting from the Lord that guides our ministry. We may even be compelled to pray for situations or people we're unaware of.

God doesn't hoard his secrets, but neither does he flaunt them. They are revealed to those who sincerely seek them.

> Revelation does not mean man finding God,
> but God finding man, God sharing His secrets
> with us, God showing us himself. In revelation,
> God is the agent as well as the object.
>
> J. I. PACKER

PRAYER PROMPT: *Father, yours is a secret kingdom, but it's an open secret to those who seek you and desire to know the great and hidden things not seen by unbelieving eyes. Lord, I call to you, knowing you promise to answer.*

APRIL 4

Beware of the Tongue

Set a guard, O LORD, over my mouth; keep
watch over the door of my lips!
PSALM 141:3

It is impossible to be changed by revival and have our tongue unchanged. A loose tongue is perhaps one of the surest signs that one does not fear God. Rumors, exaggerations, suspicions, and gossip are revival killers.

Perhaps worst of all is the damage done by offending others by undermining their worth. Our tongues are meant to bless, not curse. With the psalmist, we pray for God to set a guard over our mouth. May we only speak words that build up and never tear down, for we will be responsible for every idle word we utter (Matt. 12:36).

> God has given us two ears, but one tongue, to show that
> we should be swift to hear, but slow to speak. God has set
> a double fence before the tongue, the teeth and the lips, to
> teach us to be wary that we offend not with our tongue.
>
> THOMAS WATSON

PRAYER PROMPT: *Father, set a guard over my mouth. Watch over the door of my lips. May I be known as one who blesses with my mouth, not curses or condemns.*

APRIL 5

Guard Your Eyes

I will set no wicked thing before mine eyes.
Psalm 101:3 (kjv)

Jesus was blunt. He warned his disciples that eyes that offend must be plucked out (Matt. 18:9). How might we avoid eyes that offend? We can remove offending images from our view. In today's world, that's hard, but necessary, to do. The images we take in through our eyes can affect how we think and act. If we would be useful to the Lord, we must be good stewards of our eyes.

May we all bring revival to our eyes.

> There are some flowers which always turn toward the sun. There was a little potted rose-bush in a sick-room which I visited. It sat by the window. One day I noticed that the one rose on the bush was looking toward the light. I referred to it; and the sick woman said that her daughter had turned the rose around several times toward the darkness of the room but that each time the little flower had twisted itself back, until again its face was toward the light. It would not look into the darkness. The rose taught me a lesson: never to allow myself to look toward any evil but instantly to turn from it. Not a moment should we permit our eyes to be inclined toward anything sinful. To yield to one moment's sinful act is to defile the soul.
>
> J. R. Miller

PRAYER PROMPT: *Lord, I would not defile my soul by what comes into view through my eyes. May I stay alert to the temptations around me that would cause me to look away from purity and gaze at impurity.*

APRIL 6

Revival Overflow

*"Whoever believes in me, as the Scripture has said,
'Out of his heart will flow rivers of living water.'"*
JOHN 7:38

Who among us does not want to experience rivers of living water flowing from our heart? This wonderful experience is promised by Jesus to all who believe in him. Why then do we settle for dried-up riverbeds or trickles from a mere brook when the floodgates of God's Spirit are open for us?

Revival is a river-gushing experience with God. In revival we experience the reality of Jesus's promise. With no effort on our part, the river flows through us, bringing us great joy. But it must not stop with us. The joy we're given by the Spirit must overflow from us to others. God would not have us be stagnant pools when we're surrounded by souls thirsty for the joy of revival.

If the life of Christ is flowing through us, the water from the Rock turning the wheel, as it flows into the heart, it will fill us with joy; and if so, we cannot contain it, it must flow out.

G. V. WIGRAM

PRAYER PROMPT: *Lord, I want the rivers of living water to flow from my heart. Fill me, then, Father. Flow through me as a mighty river flows through the desert.*

APRIL 7

Nothing Is Too Hard for God

*"Behold, I am the LORD, the God of all
flesh. Is anything too hard for me?"*
JEREMIAH 32:27

At times, revival praying may seem like a lost cause. We pray and seemingly nothing happens. But are we asking too much of God in pleading for revival? Is God not able?

Of course, he is able. Nothing is too hard for God. He is the Lord of all flesh. The mighty Creator who brought forth this universe out of nothing. When we feel defeated and tired of waiting for God, remember to whom we are praying. In every matter, large or small, bring the hardest matters to the God for whom nothing is too difficult.

> We are sometimes placed in very trying circumstances; creatures cannot help us; our faith falters; our minds are agitated; our spirits droop; we give way to fear. But the Lord reproves us and asks, "Is anything too hard for me? Bring the matter to me, exercise faith in my Word, place yourself in my hand, wait upon me in my way. I will work and none shall hinder me!"
>
> JAMES SMITH

PRAYER PROMPT: *Father, I desire your work in my life unhindered. Overcome the times in my life—even my prayer life—when I feel discouraged. Be my divine encourager, Lord.*

APRIL 8

A Revival of Love

*God's love has been poured out into our hearts
through the Holy Spirit who has been given to us.*
ROMANS 5:5

If revival doesn't awaken in us a new and deeper sense of God's love, it must not be God's revival. One of God's goals in bringing revival is to rekindle our experience of his love.

The result, of course, is that we become messengers, even carriers, of God's love to others. Not just in words but in everything we do, God's love must be the motivating force.

God does not send revival without a purpose. If we miss the purpose of revealing God's love, revival will have been wasted on us.

> Oh, free, invincible, everlasting love!
> Overcome us! Melt us! Draw us!
> ANNE DUTTON

PRAYER PROMPT: *Father, melt me, draw me, overcome me with your love. Make me a conduit of your love to those I meet, especially those the world considers unlovable. Your love, Lord, overcomes every obstacle.*

APRIL 9

God's Ownership

Do you not know that your body is a temple of the Holy Spirit within you, whom you have from God? You are not your own, for you were bought with a price. So glorify God in your body.
1 Corinthians 6:19–20

Revival is all about the spiritual life. But we mustn't forget the physical component of the Christian life—the dedication of our body to God's service.

In revival we experience a call from God to surrender our entire lives—including our body, which has also been assigned to God's ownership. How then are we treating this body that belongs to the Lord? We treat it with care, nourishing it just as we nourish our spirit.

For some, revival may be the first time they've surrendered their body. For others, it's a renewed surrender. In either case, it will have ramifications on how we live—including the discipline of our body.

Discipline, for the Christian, begins with the body.
We have only one. It is this body that is the primary
material given to us for sacrifice. We cannot give our
hearts to God and keep our bodies for ourselves.

Elisabeth Elliot

PRAYER PROMPT: *Lord, I long ago committed my life to you. Today I want to affirm that commitment includes my body—the temple of your Holy Spirit. Help me treat your temple with care and consideration. It is, after all, a gift from you—and a stewardship to me.*

APRIL 10

"There Is No Secret!"

"Ask, and you will receive, that your joy may be full."
JOHN 16:24

For such an important move of God, we might expect a long to-do list in order to bring revival. Or there must be a secret known only to a few spiritually mature believers. But no, there is no secret to revival. It's simply to pray and believe. In the same way, we were each born again by faith in Christ, but God did the work in our hearts by his Holy Spirit.

Ask and receive. God does the rest. True of salvation. True of revival.

> In his book *In the Day of Thy Power*, Arthur Wallis relates the story of a Wiltshire evangelist who had just come to the town of Ferndale from Wales. The man stood up and said, "Friends, I have journeyed into Wales with the hope I may glean the secret of the Welsh Revival." In an instant, Evan Roberts was on his feet, and with an uplifted arm toward the speaker, he replied, "My brother, there is no secret! Ask and ye shall receive!"

PRAYER PROMPT: *Lord, along with thousands of others, I ask for your presence in revival. Come, Holy Spirit. Ignite us in holy fire!*

APRIL 11

Clean!

> *"Already you are clean because of the word that I have spoken to you."*
> JOHN 15:3

We rise from our revived knees as clean vessels for the Lord. God has spoken the word that cleanses. If there remains the spot of sin, or if the temptation of sin returns (as it surely will), we must resist as sanctified vessels. God's Word has made us clean. If we abide in his Word, we will stay clean. Sin cannot stand the light of the Word.

> The Word is both a looking-glass to show us the spots of our souls—and a laver to wash them away! The Word breathes nothing but purity; it enlightens the mind; it consecrates the heart.
>
> THOMAS WATSON

PRAYER PROMPT: *Father, I thank you for the cleansing Word that has set me free from sin and guilt. In times of temptation, may I always turn to the sin-repelling Word. When having sinned, may I once again be cleansed according to your Word.*

APRIL 12

A Mary Revival

Now as they went on their way, Jesus entered a village. And a woman named Martha welcomed him into her house. And she had a sister called Mary, who sat at the Lord's feet and listened to his teaching. But Martha was distracted with much serving. And she went up to him and said, "Lord, do you not care that my sister has left me to serve alone? Tell her then to help me." But the Lord answered her, "Martha, Martha, you are anxious and troubled about many things, but one thing is necessary. Mary has chosen the good portion, which will not be taken away from her."
Luke 10:38–42

A true revival begins with a "Mary" attitude, not a "Martha" attitude. It is sitting at the Master's feet, learning from him, fellowshipping with him, discerning his purposes in ushering in and sustaining revival. Man-inspired revivals may have admirable motives, but once a person has experienced true revival, the Martha kind of revival just won't do. Hold out for the real thing.

> People will talk about getting up a revival; of all things I do believe one of the most detestable of transactions. . . . The way to get the revival is to begin at the Master's feet; you must go there with Mary and afterwards you may work with Martha.
>
> Charles Spurgeon

PRAYER PROMPT: *Lord, forgive my Martha ways and instill in me a Mary heart. Allow me, like Mary, to sit at your feet and learn of you. Bring a Mary revival, Lord. We've had enough of Martha revivals.*

APRIL 13

The Touch of God

Moved with pity, he [Jesus] stretched out his hand and touched him and said to him, "I will; be clean." And immediately the leprosy left him, and he was made clean.
MARK 1:41–42

Revival is God touching his people, spiritually. In that singular touch we find healing, just as the leper was immediately healed when he was touched by Jesus. We may enter revival seeking many things—perhaps including some kind of healing—but if we experience nothing other than the touch of God reminding us anew that we are spiritually clean, it will be enough.

———

> In the midst of the awesomeness, a touch comes, and you know it is the right hand of Jesus Christ. You know it is not the hand of restraint, correction, nor chastisement, but the right hand of the Everlasting Father. Whenever his hand is laid upon you, it gives inexpressible peace and comfort, and the sense that underneath are the everlasting arms, full of support, provision, comfort and strength.
>
> OSWALD CHAMBERS

———

PRAYER PROMPT: *Lord, your fatherly touch is unmistakable. With your touch, I am cleansed, I am healed—made whole. Father, bring your divine touch to revive us, your church. We are in need of your hand of love upon us.*

APRIL 14

Hot or Cold or Lukewarm?

"I know your works: you are neither cold nor hot. Would that you were either cold or hot! So, because you are lukewarm, and neither hot nor cold, I will spit you out of my mouth."
REVELATION 3:15–16

Why is there so much time—often decades—between revivals? One possible reason is that many Christians are content with things the way they are. There is often little motivation to pray for revival until there's a shaking due to some event that disrupts our comfortable lives.

Dare we say that we are far too often simply lukewarm? Jesus says it would be better to be hot or cold than lukewarm.

As we pray for revival, pray for our churches. The unrest we feel prompting us to labor on our knees for revival must extend outward beyond ourselves, into the pews of our churches and the comfort of our homes.

As long as we are content to live without revival, we will.
LEONARD RAVENHILL

PRAYER PROMPT: *Father, hear our cry on behalf of half-hearted Christians and churches unaware of their dangerous lukewarm plight. May revival happen both inside and outside the church walls. Bring your holy and desired presence into our lives wherever we may be.*

APRIL 15

Welcoming God's Searchlight

"God opposes the proud but gives grace to the humble."
1 PETER 5:5

No matter how widespread revival is, there is always the deeply personal aspect. God searches every surrendered heart, providing conviction of sin when necessary. We must not toy with the hope for revival; it is a serious event. The wise Christian confesses known sin at once, always welcoming God's searchlight. Always receiving forgiveness and restoration personally *and* specifically.

Let no one pray for revival—let no one pray for a mighty baptism of power who is not prepared for deep heart-searchings and confession of sin in his personal life. Revival, in its beginnings, is a most humiliating experience.

JAMES A. STEWART

PRAYER PROMPT: *Lord, we are so desperate for revival, we willingly submit to the bringing down of our pride and sufficiency. Examine us with your searchlight. Give us the grace reserved for the humble.*

APRIL 16

Celebrating the New Nature

If anyone is in Christ, he is a new creation. The old has passed away; behold, the new has come.
2 CORINTHIANS 5:17

Sometimes it seems that those who are blessed the most by revival are longtime believers who have forgotten what it's like to be new creations. Life has a way of defaulting to the ordinary. But there is no such thing as an ordinary believer. The new creation of a believer is highly personal to each person—and far from ordinary. The Christian life is a miracle from start to finish. In revival, it is often the new creation within us that is revived.

> It is a miraculous thing to be a Christian, for real Christianity is the effect of a new creation! To make a Christian requires the same power as to make a world; nothing less can raise a sinner from a death in trespasses and sins! In every instance of real conversion, the almighty power of God is exerted!
>
> JAMES SMITH

PRAYER PROMPT: *Lord, I revel in my new creation. Remind me daily of the benefits of being born into your kingdom. Help me realize I'm no ordinary Christian, for no such thing exists. May I live fully day by day in my new creation.*

APRIL 17

Caution, Yes; Suspicion, No

"As for you, you meant evil against me, but God meant it for good, to bring it about that many people should be kept alive, as they are today."
GENESIS 50:20

Joseph, after undergoing years of unjust imprisonment, was able to declare to his offending brothers that what they had meant for evil, God was able to use to further his will. Many of us can look back at events that at the time seemed to work against us but later saw them as the hand of God working according to his perfect plan.

Similar to seasons of hardship, seasons of revival can often be misunderstood. Some of the people who approach revival with undue suspicion may be the ones to see most clearly what God was up to in bringing revival. It's okay to be cautious as revival approaches, but it's premature to allow caution to turn to suspicion. One clear test: Is man glorified, or is the Lord Jesus Christ exalted?

> We know not but that the events we so deeply bewail, are indispensably necessary to our salvation. We have reason to think that, if we saw the end as God does, we, instead of regarding our losses or bereavements as needless afflictions, would adore God for them as much as for the most pleasing of his dispensations. Let us then wait until he shall have revealed to us the whole of his designs; and be content to form our judgment of him when all the grounds of judging are laid before us.
>
> CHARLES SIMEON

PRAYER PROMPT: *Lord, when I'm doubtful as to your purposes during a troubling time, remind me of Joseph and reaffirm that in your sovereignty you are not only able to redeem any adverse situation but can turn it into the circumstance that revives my faith in you!*

APRIL 18

Delighting in God

*Delight yourself in the LORD, and he will
give you the desires of your heart.*
PSALM 37:4

We should always delight ourselves in God, but during revival our delight is heightened. This happens as we become aware of the presence of God in a way that's unlike our pre-revival days.

Our delight in God comes not so much from his many blessings but from a fresh understanding of his love, power, and majesty. So evident are these attributes of God that one can't resist the worship that comes from delight. Too, we find it easier to say yes to God in all things, having a deeper look into his heart through revival.

Don't wait for revival to delight in God. It begins now in our prayer closet and is only made stronger during revival.

Spiritual delight in God arises chiefly from his beauty
and perfection, not from the blessings he gives us.
JONATHAN EDWARDS

PRAYER PROMPT: *Lord, in you I delight. You are at the center of my life. All of me is encompassed by all of you. In your great love, you remind me that you also delight in me. What a wondrous love is this!*

APRIL 19

Revival Is a Taste of Heaven

The twelve gates were twelve pearls, each of the gates made of a single pearl, and the street of the city was pure gold, like transparent glass. And I saw no temple in the city, for its temple is the Lord God the Almighty and the Lamb. And the city has no need of sun or moon to shine on it, for the glory of God gives it light, and its lamp is the Lamb. By its light will the nations walk, and the kings of the earth will bring their glory into it, and its gates will never be shut by day—and there will be no night there.
REVELATION 21:21–25

Don't we all wonder what heaven is like? We have many clues in the Bible, but I suspect if we could see all of heaven's treasures through our mortal eyes, we couldn't bear the glory. But perhaps we have an additional glimpse of what heaven is like when we experience revival and we enjoy the heavenly oneness of all believers. We also taste the presence of the Lord and we worship in a way that seems to carry us closer to the gates of heaven.

No, we can't know the fullness of heaven now in our mortal frames, but we can have a foretaste of that eternal home we long for. It's called revival.

A revival means days of heaven upon earth.
MARTYN LLOYD-JONES

PRAYER PROMPT: *Father, thank you for my heavenly home. I long to be there for eternity. But until then, may I enjoy revival as a foretaste of heaven. Especially as I enjoy your revival presence.*

APRIL 20

Behold the Beauty of the Lord

One thing have I asked of the LORD, that will I seek after: that I may dwell in the house of the LORD all the days of my life, to gaze upon the beauty of the LORD and to inquire in his temple.
PSALM 27:4

During revival we may seek many things. The most important of which may well be to behold the beauty of the Lord. When most of us think about God, we don't often ponder his beauty. We don't take time to bask in his presence, gazing on him whom our souls adore.

If during revival we miss a sense of God's beauty and majesty, we have missed the truer and greater reward of revival.

God is infinitely beautiful in himself, and his
beauty ought to attract you like a magnet.
THOMAS GOODWIN

PRAYER PROMPT: *Father, what more can I ask than to dwell with you and gaze upon your beauty? This then is my goal. Revival gives me a preview of your glory, which I will one day enjoy fully. Give me eyes to see it!*

APRIL 21

"Not by Might, nor by Power"

> *"Not by might, nor by power, but by my
> Spirit, says the LORD of hosts."*
> ZECHARIAH 4:6

Oh, that men and women would enter our churches and say, "God is indeed among you!" Yes, that happens during revival, but what about postrevival? Will we carry revival to our home churches? What will be different about our church worship a year after revival has ended?

What about *now*? Must we wait for revival to have the fullness of God's Spirit at work in our congregations? Will the unsaved hear the gospel among us? Will strong relationships be built? Will forgiveness be instant? Will there be healing of body and soul? Will our worship be strong and Christ exalting? We must all ask of our churches: Is the revival presence of God still among us?

> We stand in need of those fresh, powerful manifestations
> from heaven. We are, alas! accustomed to go on with
> the service of God in human strength; praying, hearing
> and preaching in that way! We are so lukewarm, without
> the light and the power of the Spirit! We neither feel
> nor see others experiencing His powerful operations!
>
> JOHN ELIAS

PRAYER PROMPT: *Lord, it is not by might or power, but by your Spirit that we live as Christians. We have no power in ourselves. Bring your holy power to bear in your churches. Visit us with a great and lasting revival as in past times. Only you, Spirit, can change this decaying world.*

APRIL 22

Trials and Tribulations

"I have said these things to you, that in me you may have peace. In the world you will have tribulation. But take heart; I have overcome the world."
John 16:33

We are mistaken if we think revival removes all the trials in our life or there will remain no more obstacles to moving forward in the Lord. Jesus tells us otherwise. In this world, there will be tribulation, even when we're experiencing revival.

But Jesus didn't stop by predicting tribulations; he encourages us to "take heart" because he has overcome the world with all its trials and tribulations.

When we read about the lives of great Christians of the past, we're struck with the enormity of the trials they endured. No Christian who wants God's best will avoid the necessary trials of life. And those who seek revival as a means of avoiding trials are in for a disappointment. Revival is a heavenly strength that gets you *through* tests and hardships, not around them.

To learn strong faith is to endure great trials. I have learned my faith by standing firm amid severe testings.

George Mueller

PRAYER PROMPT: *Father, I'm not immune to the trials of life. I pray for two things: First, that I prevail through the trial by standing firm, and second, that you weave my trial into a lesson learned for my benefit. I pray that during revival my trials, though they will still exist, will diminish in their power to discourage my faith.*

APRIL 23

Overcome Evil with Good

Do not be overcome by evil, but overcome evil with good.
ROMANS 12:21

In God's kingdom we're struck by how opposite things are compared to this present earthly kingdom. We learn it is more blessed to give than to receive. The way to be exalted is to humble ourselves. The way to find ourselves is to lose ourselves. Forgive to be forgiven. Overcome evil, not with retaliation but with good. Revival life confirms this. If revival were of this present world, there would be much hoopla and fanfare. But with God, revival, though exciting, is almost hidden from this world. They don't understand how a revival can begin without much promotion or how it can spring from the prayers of just a few. But then they also don't understand how Jesus could choose unlearned men to take his message to the world. The résumé for becoming a disciple of Jesus has always been a blank sheet of paper.

To return evil for good, is fiendlike.
To return evil for evil, is beastlike.
To return good for good, is manlike.
But to return good for evil, is Godlike.
This is true practical Christianity.

JOHN ANGELL JAMES

PRAYER PROMPT: *Father, may I be dispenser of good, not evil. May my enemies know that my prayers are for them and that I bear them no animosity.*

APRIL 24

Willing to Be Invisible

"If anyone would come after me, let him deny himself and take up his cross daily and follow me. For whoever would save his life will lose it, but whoever loses his life for my sake will save it."
Luke 9:23–24

One of God's goals in revival is recruitment. Our Savior's words of invitation echo down through the centuries: deny self, take up the cross, and follow Jesus. Lose your life to save it.

It is a hard choice to make. Denying ourselves may mean loss of status among those whose opinions we value. It may mean deprivation. It may mean literal death, as many of God's martyrs would testify.

Who then can make such a choice? Who will say yes to God's revival recruitment? The answer is those who have seen God at work, who now trust him in all things, and who believe God's will for them will more than compensate for any supposed loss in this world.

The call is for those who are willing to proclaim the good news, pass through death on the way to heaven, and as far as earth's fickle memory is concerned, fade into oblivion.

Preach the gospel, die, and be forgotten.
Nikolaus von Zinzendorf

PRAYER PROMPT: *Lord, here I am. Send me! I'm willing to be recruited for your purposes. I expect nothing from this world in return.*

APRIL 25

A God-Directed Path

*In all your ways acknowledge him, and
he will make straight your paths.*
Proverbs 3:6

For many, revival is the opening of a door leading to God's will for their life. Decisions are made during revival that will take a lifetime to carry out. Revival marks a departure from our own will and acceptance of God's greater will, no matter where it leads. It's a surrender to God's directed path for the Christian disciple.

It's an experience defined by the popular hymn, "I Have Decided to Follow Jesus." That hymn is, ironically, the fruit of the great Welsh revival of 1904. The four stanzas begin with these words:

> I have decided to follow Jesus;
> Tho' none go with me, I still will follow,
> My cross I'll carry, till I see Jesus;
> The world behind me, the cross before me.
> Simon Marak (attributed)

Thy way, not mine, O Lord, however dark it be; lead me by thine own hand; choose out the path for me.

Horatius Bonar

PRAYER PROMPT: *Father, I do not trust the path for my life that I might choose. Guide my steps and light my path. Where you go, I will follow. "No turning back, no turning back."*

APRIL 26

The Fire That Is Revival

Let us be grateful for receiving a kingdom that cannot be shaken, and thus let us offer to God acceptable worship, with reverence and awe, for our God is a consuming fire.
Hebrews 12:28–29

Fire can be destructive or purifying. Both are true when it comes to revival fire. And like most fires, people flock to see the cause. When the Spirit of God sets the church aflame, impurities vanish like dross from silver in the furnace. But revival fire also emblazons people with Holy Spirit passion to live holy lives and be bold in their faith and their calling.

A revival without fire is no revival at all.

As Robert Owen testified of the Welsh Revival of 1904, "You just could not go into those revival meetings without catching fire."

> You'll know your heart's been set aflame by the fire of revival when nothing else matters to you as much as he does—and your love for him.
> Anne Graham Lotz

PRAYER PROMPT: *Lord, bring the fire that consumes our dross! Fan the flame that burns in our heart!*

APRIL 27

Fallow Ground

Sow for yourselves righteousness; reap steadfast love; break up your fallow ground, for it is the time to seek the Lord, that he may come and rain righteousness upon you.
Hosea 10:12

Are we truly ready for revival? Have we broken up the fallow ground in our own life? Are we aware of our sins? Contrite before God? Revival does not come to the proud. Humility is the highway that leads to a move of God. Self-examination may reveal the hard ground that calls for some serious plowing before we see revival. We cannot break up our brother or sister's fallow ground. We must tend to our own rocky soil.

> If we are to have revival, it must come from heaven, it must be the result of divine intervention; but how can we expect God to rain righteousness upon us before we have broken up the fallow ground? . . . To "break up the fallow ground" of our hearts means to bring them to a humble and contrite state before God, for this is the only state of heart that God can revive, the only state that is ready for the rain of revival.
>
> Arthur Wallis

PRAYER PROMPT: *Lord, where you find rocky soil in my life, break up my fallow ground. Plow my soul until the soil is ready for seeding a good harvest.*

APRIL 28

Dabbling in the Occult

*"Do not turn to mediums or necromancers; do
not seek them out, and so make yourselves unclean
by them: I am the LORD your God."*
LEVITICUS 19:31

Trusting in the occult practices—astrology, fortune-telling, divination, and such have always been off-limits to God's people. In the book of Acts, new converts eagerly burned their books of magic and other items offensive to God (Acts 19:19).

If we have any remaining interests—even casual forays into the world of the occult—they must be forsaken. During revival, our consciences should become sensitive to that which offends God—all the more so when the Word of God clearly calls out the evils of the occult. Let the Holy Spirit burn away all occultic interests as we repent of seeking knowledge beyond the scope of God's will. Revival cannot coexist with the occult.

When the word of Christ captures a person's mind
and heart, all involvement with magical arts goes. It
is Jesus versus the occult; you cannot have both.

JOHN PIPER

PRAYER PROMPT: *Lord, wherever I have been curious or tempted by darkness, I repent and claim your forgiveness. My I become dead to the things of Satan's kingdom.*

APRIL 29

The Day and the Hour

"Concerning that day and hour no one knows, not even the angels of heaven, nor the Son, but the Father only."
MATTHEW 24:36

Is the return of Christ near? There's no way to say with specificity. But if it is sooner than we realize, revival should become all the more meaningful as believers experience fresh fervency for Christ and more of the lost are drawn into God's family. Some Christians are reluctant to consider the Lord's soon return. What will it look like? Will I be scared? Am I ready?

The answer, of course, is that as we prepare for his return, God implants a yearning for home in his people. We should know that God's preparation includes reassurance that there is nothing to fear in the future if we're living as we should.

Take time to examine yourself, yes, but replace any fears or uncertainties with confidence (and invite the lost into that gospel confidence!). God knows what he's doing.

> The only way to wait for the Second Coming is to watch that you do what you should do, so that when he comes is a matter of indifference. It is the attitude of a child, certain that God knows what he is about. When the Lord does come, it will be as natural as breathing. God never does anything hysterical, and he never produces hysterics.
>
> OSWALD CHAMBERS

PRAYER PROMPT: *Father, I await the end of this present world, whether through my departure by death or by the return of your Son. May I live in light of his soon return. Come Lord Jesus!*

APRIL 30

God Has an Answer

If any of you lacks wisdom, let him ask God, who gives generously to all without reproach, and it will be given him.
JAMES 1:5

An unexpected fruit of revival is the newfound wisdom that compels us to trust God in all things. If we think we lack wisdom, James tells us to ask. God will then give us wisdom generously, without reproach. Though seasons of revival seem to enhance the level of heavenly wisdom we experience, we don't have to wait for revival to ask for wisdom. We can ask now for God's answer to our present burdens.

Know this: for our every situation or problem in life, God has the right answer. It's our privilege to seek the answer by asking God for wisdom concerning the matter. Having asked, look for God's answer. Do not take back the burden you have given to God.

> What is needed for happy effectual service is simply to put your work into the Lord's hand, and leave it there. Do not take it to him in prayer, saying, "Lord, guide me, Lord, give me wisdom, Lord, arrange for me," and then arise from your knees, and take the burden all back, and try to guide and arrange for yourself. Leave it with the Lord, and remember that what you trust to him you must not worry over nor feel anxious about. Trust and worry cannot go together.
>
> HANNAH WHITALL SMITH

PRAYER PROMPT: *Dear Lord, thank you for bearing my burdens. Each one I leave with you, I leave forever. You can bear them infinitely better than I can.*

MAY 1

Come!

> *"Come, everyone who thirsts, come to the waters; and he who has no money, come, buy and eat! Come, buy wine and milk without money and without price."*
> ISAIAH 55:1

Are we thirsty? Do we want the water God provides? Then come! God's provision is given freely. And who may come? God says, "Come, *everyone* who thirsts" (emphasis added). Thus, thirst is the only prerequisite. Do not bring money; do not bring gifts to God's table. He wants to provide all and at no cost to us. At times of revival, the table of God is spread before us. He offers plenty for all who will come. God will invite, but we must accept the invitation. At his table our thirst is quenched, our hunger is fed.

> Who does not thirst? Who has not deep needs burning in his soul? The blessing offered is precisely adapted to the need. . . . What water is to physical thirst, Christ is to men's spiritual needs. This world's vanities do not satisfy but what Christ gives, quenches all their thirst!
>
> J. R. MILLER

PRAYER PROMPT: *O Lord, I come! I'm thirsty and hungry. I desire to be fed at your table. I bring no gifts, no money, nothing to barter. I come empty-handed to receive from your fulsome hand.*

MAY 2

Hearing God's Voice

*Your ears shall hear a word behind you, saying,
"This is the way, walk in it," when you turn to
the right or when you turn to the left.*
ISAIAH 30:21

God guides us during revival. Each of us hears what we need to hear. Sometimes it's an urging in a new direction. Other times it's a call to rest. And sometimes it may just be encouragement. Always listen for the often faint voice of God. Make prayerful decisions in confidence, and you can't go wrong. Also, make space for God's Spirit to caution you on certain matters. Weigh whatever prompting you sense with what Scripture says, what the counsel of godly Christian friends say, and lastly, with circumstances.

> The path of life lies before you, but you are very liable to take a wrong turning. You may make a great mistake in the calling you follow, the situation you take, or any change that you make. But seek counsel from God and He will guide you aright. Commit your way unto Him, and He will make it plain. Watch His providential leadings. Avoid the rocks of self-will and self-confidence. Do not think you are wiser than anyone else. Honestly wish to do what is right and best before God, and you will not go astray.
>
> GEORGE EVERARD

PRAYER PROMPT: *Father, guide my steps, lest I wander off the path you've laid out for me. Lead me with your Word, the Spirit's leading, the counsel of trustworthy friends, and circumstances. Lord, my desire is to follow you wherever you lead me.*

MAY 3

Asking for the Burden

For while we are still in this tent, we groan, being burdened.
2 Corinthians 5:4

Praying for a burden the Lord has laid on our hearts is a joy. For when we pray as he directs, we have a part in the fulfilling of his will. If we ask God for the burden to pray for revival, he will surely give it. Our prayer burdens are from the Holy Spirit and keep us on our knees until revival comes and the burden is lifted.

The burden is light, but it is also weighty. It's light because we're praying for God's will. It's weighty in that prayer burdens often leave us wordless, groaning our prayers.

The common ministry of an intercessor is an example of being burdened in prayer.

A burden for revival is conceived in our spirits by the Holy Spirit. Our part is to ask for such a burden, submit to the person of the Holy Spirit, obey His promptings, and keep praying for revival. God causes the burden to increase until it is unthinkable not to pray.

Joy Dawson

PRAYER PROMPT: *Holy Spirit, lay a burden on my heart for revival. Allow my prayers to align with your perfect will. Bring forth such an intense desire for revival that I am left wordless, groaning in the Spirit for an outpouring of your Spirit.*

MAY 4

The Coming Tidal Wave

As they sailed he [Jesus] fell asleep. And a windstorm came down on the lake, and they were filling with water and were in danger. And they went and woke him, saying, "Master, Master, we are perishing!" And he awoke and rebuked the wind and the raging waves, and they ceased, and there was a calm.
Luke 8:23–24

When we look around at our surrounding culture, sometimes it feels like a great tidal wave of evil is approaching. We fear those caught in this powerful tsunami will be swept away. The only thing that can halt the approach of a disaster like this is a solid impenetrable wall of revival prayer. Picture the destructive wave as it approaches a city, ready to do its worst, only to be stopped and turned back by a brick wall we call revival praying. There is no tsunami that can breech the wall built with the bricks of believing prayer.

The time to build that wall is now. Pray for a revival wall that turns back the Satanic wave ready to crest, ready to destroy.

Christ's business is to lay storms, as it is Satan's business to raise them. He can do it; he has done it; he delights to do it: for he came to proclaim peace on earth. He rebuked the wind and the raging of the water, and immediately they ceased; not, as at other times, by degrees, but all of a sudden, there was a great calm.

Matthew Henry

PRAYER PROMPT: *Father, our surrounding world is in trouble—all because we have neglected your wisdom and turned to our own faulty plans for the way we think things ought to be. Forgive us, Lord, for our foolishness and, at times, apathy. May our prayers be the bricks in the wall holding back the tsunami of evil. Turn back any destructive wave that threatens to crash on our shores.*

MAY 5

Be Filled!

Do not get drunk with wine, for that is debauchery, but be filled with the Spirit, addressing one another in psalms and hymns and spiritual songs, singing and making melody to the Lord with your heart, giving thanks always and for everything to God the Father in the name of our Lord Jesus Christ.
EPHESIANS 5:18–20

There is an endless supply of God's new wine for every believer, and every believer must be filled at all times with this choice wine of God's Spirit. Just as the disciples were filled, so can we. To be sure, we do not do the filling. We are only empty vessels. It is God who fills. Our readiness to be filled is measured by our willingness.

> The disciples were completely surrendered to the will of God when they waited in the upper room, and they were all filled with the Holy Spirit. . . . We can give or yield, [but] God alone can consecrate by the filling. To be filled with the Holy Spirit is to be consecrated in the truest and fullest sense.
>
> JAMES SMITH

PRAYER PROMPT: *Father, your Spirit lives in me now, yet I pray to be continually filled and overflowing with the Holy Spirit. Bring a revival akin to the days of Pentecost. Empower your church with the consuming fire of revival.*

MAY 6

The Joy of Serving, Then Passing the Baton

O God, we have heard with our ears, our fathers have told us, what deeds you performed in their days, in the days of old.
Psalm 44:1

Children are not exempt from revival. As Jesus welcomed little ones, so must we. A child touched by revival will likely be a profitable adult for God. But revival must be maintained, and children must be taught the things of God. We know they will surely be exposed to much unrighteousness in their lives. Our prayers and our testimony must be evident to them. Do our children *know* our testimonies? Have we recounted the faithfulness of God to them? Is the Word of God alive for them as it is for us? God does not desire to skip generations. He wants the circle unbroken.

> We are rightly thankful when we propagate God's praises to posterity. We tell our children what God has done for us: in such a need he supplied us; from such a sickness he raised us up; in such a temptation he helped us. . . . By transmitting our experiences to our children, God's name is eternalized, and his mercies will bring forth a plentiful crop of praise when we are gone. . . . In the sense that when we are dead, we praise God because, having left the chronicle of God's mercies with our children, we start them on thankfulness and so make God's praises live when we are dead.
>
> Thomas Watson

PRAYER PROMPT: *Lord, I pray for the children affected by a fallen world. Protect them from any spiritual poison of this age. Raise up from among them soldiers in your army. Visit the coming generations with life-changing revival. May we who are adults raise the next generation to know and serve you.*

MAY 7

Limiting God

*You are the God who works wonders; you have
made known your might among the peoples.*
Psalm 77:14

The advent of a revival is a true wonder of God. He makes himself known through our praises and his presence. It is, therefore, fitting that we are awestricken by revival.

God reveals himself as the author of all our doings and dealings, a God who works wonders on our behalf. He is the God who knows everything about us, including our innermost thoughts and desires. Nothing about us is unknown to him. That, too, is a wonder.

When we are no longer filled with holy wonder for who he is and all he has done, revival has surely ended.

> Let this ever be deeply engraved upon the tablets of
> our heart: that all of God's doings and all of God's
> dealings, are doings and dealings to fill us with
> holy wonder, so that we may well say . . . with the
> Psalmist, "You are the God who works wonders!"
>
> J. C. Philpot

PRAYER PROMPT: *O Father! You are the worker of great wonders! I'm filled with awe at your love, creativity, and unfolding of your perfect will. I pray for a true revival that evidences your wonder. Bring it soon, Lord!*

MAY 8

Revival and Our Hands

> *God was doing extraordinary miracles by the hands of Paul.*
> Acts 19:11

Have you held up your hands lately and pondered their past use—and more importantly their future use? God has chosen to do many miraculous things through our hands—*your* hands.

Through Paul's hands God did extraordinary miracles. Now, consider the future miracles God will perform through your hands. It may be cooking soup for the sick, tending the wounds of a child, or comforting a grieving friend. God counts all of these as his miracles when done in his name.

It is our honor that God chooses our hands to do his work on earth—to revive the beloved souls he desires to comfort, help, and refresh.

> Here lies the tremendous mystery—that God should
> be all-powerful, yet refuse to coerce. He summons us
> to cooperation. We are honored in being given the
> opportunity to participate in his good deeds. Remember
> how he asked for help in performing his miracles: Fill the
> waterpots, stretch out your hand, distribute the loaves.
> ELISABETH ELLIOT

PRAYER PROMPT: *Lord, I hold up my hands and see that their past use has not always honored you. Thank you for forgiving me for neglecting the proper use of my hands. Bring revival to all of me, but especially to my hands. May their future use bring glory to you and refresh the hearts of others.*

MAY 9

Treasure in Heaven

"Do not lay up for yourselves treasures on earth, where moth and rust destroy and where thieves break in and steal, but lay up for yourselves treasures in heaven, where neither moth nor rust destroys and where thieves do not break in and steal. For where your treasure is, there your heart will be also."
MATTHEW 6:19–21

For many, the accumulation of wealth has come through hard work. But if wealth has become their treasure, then not only is it going to perish, but that hard labor has been in vain. God calls us to forsake all earthly treasures and make true deposits in our heavenly account because there is no more secure account than the one God watches over. If we could have a momentary glimpse of the true treasure awaiting us in heaven, we would surely give up all our trust in earthly treasures. May revival touch not only our hearts but also our bank accounts.

Has revival impacted the way you view your money and the way you spend it? ?

———

There are many who are uncertain about the future
life and the existence of God, because they cannot
see beyond this shell-like body of flesh, and their
thoughts, like delicate wings, cannot carry them beyond
the narrow confines of the brain. Their weak eyes
cannot discover those eternal and unfading treasures
which God has prepared for those who love Him.

SADHU SUNDAR SINGH

———

PRAYER PROMPT: *Lord, I have no lasting treasure here on earth. I put my trust in heavenly riches, not the fading fool's gold so many people accumulate here, to the neglect of their souls. Give me eyes to see the many opportunities to increase my heavenly bank account.*

MAY 10

Fear Not!

But now thus says the LORD, he who created you,
O Jacob, he who formed you, O Israel:
"Fear not, for I have redeemed you; I have
called you by name, you are mine."
ISAIAH 43:1

There is much to fear in this world. But the Christian has an antidote to all fears, and that's the declaration of God's ownership. We are *his*. Not just in heaven, but here and now we are experientially his. Nothing can touch us without passing through God's hands first. He created us, formed us, redeemed us. He calls by name, and he affirms his ownership of us. We are his trophies. Revival brings forth these promises like welcome rain on a parched desert.

"Fear not, . . . for you are mine!" In a sense I was
always his possession; but since he purchased me with
Christ's blood, I am among his jewels, his trophies,
his special possessions, his redeemed children!

Why should I be afraid? I am Christ's redeemed
child, and he owns and keeps me!

ALEXANDER SMELLIE

PRAYER PROMPT: *O Lord, I am yours! You have chosen me to be one of your jewels, one of your trophies. You own me now and will own me forever. Use me as you will, Father.*

MAY 11

Take Refuge

*The LORD is good, a stronghold in the day of trouble;
he knows those who take refuge in him.*
NAHUM 1:7

We bring our hard issues of life and submit them to God. Even if it will take a miracle for our remedy, we bring it anyway, for our God is a stronghold in our day of trouble. We take refuge in him and are forever safe. Our hard issues simplify as he brings his power to bear our burdens. He makes our bitter things sweet.

Today, take refuge in God. Bring your hard things and your bitter situations to the one who turned water into wine and who turns religion into revival.

> It is wonderful what miracles God works in wills that are utterly surrendered to him. He turns hard things into easy, and bitter things into sweet. It is not that He puts easy things in the place of the hard, but he actually changes the hard thing into an easy one.
>
> HANNAH WHITALL SMITH

PRAYER PROMPT: *Father, I take refuge in you during the day of trouble. Hide me; guide me. Turn the bitter to sweet and the hard to easy.*

MAY 12

Where Two or Three Are Gathered

> *"Where two or three are gathered in my
> name, there am I among them."*
> MATTHEW 18:20

Revival is not dependent on numbers. God can revive two or three—or even one. But it's a powerful element of revival when gathered believers pray, sing, and worship God.

Differences in minor doctrines wither away. Hands are joined with the hands of others or are outstretched in praise. The joy of corporate worship is contagious, and the sound of those united voices has the attention of angels.

In revival, let down your guard. Worship freely. Such is not just a hallmark of a revival season but necessary to the whole Christian life.

> To gather with God's people in united adoration of the
> Father is as necessary to the Christian life as prayer.
> MARTIN LUTHER

PRAYER PROMPT: *Father, I love to worship. When I'm alone in worship, I know I'm not really alone, for you are there. But I also love corporate worship when the voices of many proclaim your glory in song. I will love the revival worship here on earth but will also see it as a foretaste of heavenly worship.*

MAY 13

Revival Boldness

*When they had prayed, the place in which they were gathered
together was shaken, and they were all filled with the Holy
Spirit and continued to speak the word of God with boldness.*
Acts 4:31

The power of the believer rests in the abiding Holy Spirit. No power on earth is stronger than the Holy Spirit within us. For the disciples, the room they were in was shaken as they were filled with the Holy Spirit and spoke the word of God boldly.

Our prayer must be that out of the midst of revival there will come a generation of Christians who know the Word and preach it boldly, without shame.

What is holding you back from proclaiming God's Word this way?

God would have His children incorrigibly in earnest
and persistently bold in their efforts. Heaven is
too busy to listen to half-hearted prayers.

E. M. Bounds

PRAYER PROMPT: *Lord, I pray boldly for revival. I ask in earnest and with sincerity. Grant your church, and especially your intercessors, a Holy Spirit boldness that harkens back to the book of Acts.*

MAY 14

Mustard-Seed Faith

"With what can we compare the kingdom of God, or what parable shall we use for it? It is like a grain of mustard seed, which, when sown on the ground, is the smallest of all the seeds on earth, yet when it is sown it grows up and becomes larger than all the garden plants and puts out large branches, so that the birds of the air can make nests in its shade."
MARK 4:30–32

Do we have little faith? All we need is mustard-seed-sized faith. It's not the size of our faith that matters; it's the size of our God that matters. A church may plan and execute a revival event with no faith involved. But to believe God, even with mustard-seed-sized faith, for a true revival is to believe what is impossible with man. No amount of human planning will summon God's Holy Spirit to fall fresh on his people. So, when we pray for revival, we're praying for a supernatural intervention by God. Nothing less will do.

No faith is required to do the possible; actually only a morsel of this atom-powered stuff is needed to do the impossible, for a piece as large as a mustard seed will do more than we have ever dreamed of.

LEONARD RAVENHILL

PRAYER PROMPT: *O Lord, we need faith to believe you for the necessary revival to come. Even mustard-seed-sized faith will do! Help us, Lord, to have that faith, for we have a mountain that must be removed.*

MAY 15

The Simplicity of Revival

Now I commend you because you remember me in everything and maintain the traditions even as I delivered them to you.
1 Corinthians 11:2

God's revival requires no advance planning. Praying, yes; planning, no. Revival happens suddenly and simply. It often leaves the same way. In the wake of revival, we may find discarded traditions that once brought forth life but have long since become dead rituals. We must be willing to let that which gives life replace that which no longer breathes. We may find that some past traditions regain their life-giving ability and are worth keeping while others must go. When looking for revival, look low, not high. In revival, God moves beyond our understanding. It does not have the marks of man's hands on it.

Revivals in every case fall back on simplicity. They cut through the accumulated doctrines and subtle complexities of the schools until they arrive at some living message, some aspect of truth which has become forgotten, or has been so overlaid by tradition as to become lifeless.

James Burns

PRAYER PROMPT: *Lord, I thank you for the simplicity of the gospel and how that simplicity extends to your kingdom. So much so that even a child can have commendable faith. I thank you that revival is only complicated when we try to organize it or take control of what you're doing. Let us, Lord, enjoy the rest and the simplicity of faith and of revival.*

MAY 16

Awakening to Revival

"Stay awake at all times, praying that you may have strength to escape all these things that are going to take place, and to stand before the Son of Man."
Luke 21:36

Many Christians are, for all purposes, asleep, mesmerized by the glitter of this world. Revival, if Christians will have it, is a grand awakening call from God.

In revival, we cast off the stupor of sleep; we see past the hypnotizing glitter of the world and begin acknowledging our sin. We become invigorated by the things of God; and in the name of Jesus, we reject the strategies of Satan that have induced our sleep. In revival, we awaken, and we roust others from their dream state.

> The Christian world is in a deep sleep; nothing but a loud shout can awaken them out of it!
> George Whitefield

PRAYER PROMPT: *Lord, your alarm has gone off, and it is time for believers to awaken to a Christ-rejecting world. Keep us awake, Father, as we roust others to take up their armor and join the call for revival.*

MAY 17

The Sweetness of Revival

How sweet are your words to my taste,
sweeter than honey to my mouth!
PSALM 119:103

Of all that accompanies revival—repentance, cries for mercy, voices lifted in praise—we mustn't forget the sweetness of God's presence. That gift alone is worth every sore knee bent in prayer.

God's presence in revival *is* sweet. The more we bask in that sweetness, the sweeter it becomes. Of all that we take away from revival, his sweetness is what we most wish to remain with us forever.

O Lord, help me to watch and pray! I am afraid
of losing the sweetness I feel: for months past I
have felt as if in the possession of perfect love;
not a moment's desire of anything but God.

FRANCIS ASBURY

PRAYER PROMPT: *Lord, with Francis Asbury, I desire a lifetime of experiencing your sweetness to my soul. Your Word is like honey to me. Your presence exceeds the false sweetness of this earth.*

MAY 18

Receiving Revival as a Child

They were bringing children to him that he might touch them, and the disciples rebuked them. But when Jesus saw it, he was indignant and said to them, "Let the children come to me; do not hinder them, for to such belongs the kingdom of God. Truly, I say to you, whoever does not receive the kingdom of God like a child shall not enter it." And he took them in his arms and blessed them, laying his hands on them.
MARK 10:13–16

God loves it when we exhibit childlike faith when we pray. When we're praying for revival, let us come to our heavenly Father empty-handed, as a child sits on their father's lap, expecting his affection and blessing.

When parents brought their children to Jesus, what did he do? He took them in his arms and blessed them. If we would likewise be blessed, we must come to him as children.

We should go into his presence as a child goes to his father.
We do it with reverence and godly fear, of course, but we
should go with a childlike confidence and simplicity.

MARTYN LLOYD-JONES

PRAYER PROMPT: *Lord, may I approach you as a child approaches a father. Listen to my pleas as coming from a child, for I am your child. Bless me, Lord, as you bless all children who come to you.*

MAY 19

Revival as Antidote to the Evils of this Present Darkness

We do not wrestle against flesh and blood, but against the rulers, against the authorities, against the cosmic powers over this present darkness, against the spiritual forces of evil in the heavenly places.
EPHESIANS 6:12

The forces of darkness are always at work. There has never been a time when Satan has taken a break from his strategies to undermine God's plans. We must never forget that our battle, especially during a revival season, is spiritual warfare. As darkness descends, prayers must arise. There is no negotiating with evil. Our prayers must be forceful, faithful, and final. We must remind the enemy that there is no defeating God's church. We *will* see God move in response to our prayers. As we stand firm against the enemy who hates to see God's people fully alive and boldly on mission, so must we stand firm with God, claiming the promises, relentlessly recalling his faithfulness.

> The prayer of the feeblest saint who lives in the Spirit
> and keeps right with God is a terror to Satan. The
> very powers of darkness are paralyzed by prayer. . . .
> No wonder Satan tries to keep our minds fussy
> in active work till we cannot think in prayer.
> OSWALD CHAMBERS

PRAYER PROMPT: *Lord, you desire for us to be bold in believing you for revival. Therefore, I do not shrink back in my insistent prayers for a fresh outpouring of your Spirit, nor do I allow the enemy one inch of a foothold in my intercessions. I stand firm for revival and firm against Satan's strategies to thwart revival.*

MAY 20

A Christian's True Longing

He satisfies the longing soul, and the hungry
soul he fills with good things.
PSALM 107:9

Revival is satisfaction for our longing soul as God comes near. Though there may be many people in a revival, God is uniquely there for each one individually. Whatever the need, God is there, his supply at hand.

Those who are most satisfied in revival are the neediest and the hungriest for God. Such are vastly aware of their own lack before God and reach out in desperation for his presence to fill them. God will not leave empty the hungry, longing soul for long. Be willing to become desperate for him. It will be worth it.

I long to have my love to God a pure, fervent, solid,
lasting flame, that in spirit, soul, and body, I might be one
continual living sacrifice to his glory. But, oh! my little
grace is so pressed and annoyed with the body of sin, with
the body of this death, that I groan, being burdened. I
rejoice in hope of perfect holiness, of immortal glory. . . .
And, in the meantime, what do I long for? What do
I wait for? Surely it is this—an increasing knowledge
of Christ, conformity to him, and service for him.

ANNE DUTTON

PRAYER PROMPT: *Lord, the bottom line for all of us who believe is our deep longing for you, though I think many of us try to fill that longing with the world's offerings. Awaken us all to the blessing of revival for all who truly long for you.*

MAY 21

The Gift of Time

As each has received a gift, use it to serve one another, as good stewards of God's varied grace.
1 Peter 4:10

Revival is a time of surrendering all we are and all we have to the Lord's use. God has given each of us an allotment of time as a gift. Every minute is a gift we can rejoice in and give back to God according to his leading; or sadly, we can waste it. Though we often complain that we don't have enough time, God sees to it that we do have time for all that needs to be done, including time apart for rest and relaxation. Even Jesus and his disciples took time to rest.

Perhaps we're short on time because we've taken on responsibilities that aren't really ours in the first place. It never hurts to reassess our time commitments and revamp our busy schedules. Daily we receive this gift of time, and daily we must surrender it back to God.

> Your time is not your own, but the Lord's. If you waste it, or spend it unprofitably, you rob God; for it is one of the talents which he has entrusted to you as his steward. You are not at liberty even to employ it exclusively for yourself; but you must glorify God in the use of it, which you will do by employing it in the way that will be most beneficial to your whole being, and to your fellow-creatures.
>
> Harvey Newcomb

PRAYER PROMPT: *Father, my time here is limited. Help me make the best use of it. The expression "killing time" has an unfortunate ring to it. Let me not be guilty of that. Let me be an investor of my time.*

MAY 22

Our Battles

*Blessed be the LORD, my rock, who trains my
hands for war, and my fingers for battle.*
PSALM 144:1

When revival results in spiritual warfare against the enemy, it's important to know who trains us for our battles. We are not left to our own defenses. God is with us. He trains us. We may face many battles in life, but in not one of them are we unarmed and untrained. We are always winners, never losers in our battles with God at our side. All battles worth fighting are against giants. In fighting our giants, God brings even the mightiest down to size.

> David does not ascribe any honor to himself. Human strength is from within, from the nerves, and sinews, and muscles, but the believer's strength is from without. . . . Now, if Jehovah be our strength, then nothing can be too difficult for us, for he whose strength is the omnipotence of God can do all things. . . . [J]ust as the young soldier was, as it were, bound apprentice to the old warrior, went out to learn the drill, and afterwards was taken by him into the battle, so does the Lord by providence and by experience train his people's hands to war, and their fingers to fight.
>
> CHARLES SPURGEON

PRAYER PROMPT: *Lord, you train my hands for war and my fingers for battle. You arm me with spiritual weapons designed for any possible attack from the enemy. As you train my hands and fingers, also train my eyes so I can see the approach of the enemy. To be armed early is better than to be armed late.*

MAY 23

Revival During Adversity

If you faint in the day of adversity, your strength is small.
Proverbs 24:10

Our strength in times of adversity is revealed during revival. Then we are aware of the heavenly resources at our disposal during the most trying times. Revival may not end our adversity, but we are enabled to walk through the fire without getting burned.

In one sense, we should welcome adversity during revival. Truly, then, will we experience the divine inflow of strength we need to prevail through our adversity. We must not faint since the strength of God in us is indeed *not* small.

> It is only in the school of adversity that we really know what the Lord Jesus is. How much we learn from Him and of Him in one trial! Until the trial brought us sobbing upon His heart, how little we knew what that heart contained. Welcome, then, the grief that lifts you nearer to God, and that increases your acquaintance with, and your peace and joy in, the Lord Jesus.
>
> Octavius Winslow

PRAYER PROMPT: *Lord, though adversity seems insurmountable at the time, I see that it reveals our strengths and weaknesses. Father, strengthen me. Embolden me as I pass through adversity. Do not let me shrink back in fear but instead walk ahead in full faith.*

MAY 24

Recipe for Personal Revival

> *The LORD is near to all who call on him,*
> *to all who call on him in truth.*
> PSALM 145:18

Revival brings the nearness of God to each individual. We often think of revival in terms of large congregations and packed-out churches. And while revival does touch the crowds, it's also personal to each one present. Though God is Lord of all, he is also Lord of the individual.

We'll never see God desert the one lost lamb while the rest of the flock is safe. The Lord cares for the one as well as the ninety-nine. If we call on the Lord individually, he hears individually.

> God is as much concerned about every one
> of his redeemed people as though there were
> only that one in the whole universe!
>
> CHARLES SIMEON

PRAYER PROMPT: *Father, I praise you that when you see the need for revival, you see my need for revival. When I pray, you hear me as if I were the only one praying. Your full attention is on me, lest I wander, lest I forget my first love.*

"I call on God in truth; God is near! He hears me.

MAY 25

Weakness Is an Asset

*[God] said to me, "My grace is sufficient for you, for
my power is made perfect in weakness." Therefore
I will boast all the more gladly of my weaknesses,
so that the power of Christ may rest upon me.*
2 Corinthians 12:9

Who among us has not failed at some important task or made a wrong decision? Some of the most devastating failures are carved into our memories, reminding us how faulty we were and still are. But seldom do we realize how our failures and weaknesses are preparation for receiving the strength of God. In revival, we're often confronted by our own smallness in light of God's majesty. We should forget our past by destroying that looping tape and partaking of God's grace and the power of Christ, which, as Paul notes, rests on each of us.

> God is the God of those who fail. Not that he loves
> those who stumble and fall better than those who
> walk erect without stumbling; but he helps them more.
> The weak believers get more of his grace, than those
> who are strong believers. . . . When we are conscious
> of our own insufficiency then we are ready to receive
> of the divine sufficiency. Thus our very weakness is
> an element of strength. Our weakness is an empty
> cup, which God fills with his own strength.
>
> J. R. Miller

PRAYER PROMPT: *God, I thank you for my weakness! For through my weakness, I have access to your strength. The weaker I become, the stronger I become!*

MAY 26

Increased Sensitivity

Blessed be the God and Father of our Lord Jesus Christ, the Father of mercies and God of all comfort, who comforts us in all our affliction, so that we may be able to comfort those who are in any affliction, with the comfort with which we ourselves are comforted by God.
2 Corinthians 1:3–4

It's difficult to imagine experiencing revival with a hard heart. The tender presence of the Lord in revival has the effect of softening even the hardest of hearts.

Today's news often incites fear or brings our anger to a boil as we see the mounting injustices taking place with a hard heart as the result. But hard-heartedness doesn't win the spiritual battle taking place.

Once touched by revival, it's important to maintain that tender heart, despite news reports or adverse circumstances. Jesus faced the worst adversity the world has ever known and yet still had a tender heart all the way to the cross, into his grave, and in his resurrection. The same can be true of us as his tenderness fills us and flows through us.

What a desirable thing is a tender heart. How earnestly we should aspire after one. And when such has been graciously bestowed upon us, what diligence we should exercise in seeking to preserve the same.

Arthur Pink

PRAYER PROMPT: *Father, give me a tender heart toward you and others—the tender heart of Christ! Give me sensitive eyes to see, open ears to hear, and comforting words to speak to those in need.*

MAY 27
Transferring Kingdoms

Jesus answered, "My kingdom is not of this world. If my kingdom were of this world, my servants would have been fighting, that I might not be delivered over to the Jews. But my kingdom is not from the world."
John 18:36

A revival is a glimpse into God's kingdom. Though the glimpse is but seeing through a glass darkly, it is as near to heaven as we'll find on this earth. But to see this kingdom, to be part of it, we must let go of this present kingdom where sin is ever present. We must, by faith, remember that we are part of God's kingdom (and if we've forgotten, reenlist with fresh commitment!). We are to be ministers of his kingdom by tending the wounded, comforting the sick, and caring for the lonely. During revival, accept the glorious burden of being God's ambassador.

If you have not chosen the Kingdom of God first, it will in the end make no difference what you have chosen instead.
William Law

PRAYER PROMPT: *Father, I praise you for your glorious kingdom of which you've invited me to be a part. As an ambassador for your kingdom, may I reflect the goodness and compassion of my king.*

MAY 28

Transformation

*Do not be conformed to this world, but be transformed by the
renewal of your mind, that by testing you may discern what
is the will of God, what is good and acceptable and perfect.*
ROMANS 12:2

Transformation of the inner life is the way of the growing Christian. If there's no transformation, one must ask, Is there spiritual life at all? For divine life in the soul must by its nature and presence produce transformation. Is not our desire for the Lord and for revival a cry to be made new? Don't we all sense the need to be transformed into something greater than the things that have conformed us to this world? Isn't the key to evangelism an offer from God to *be* transformed? Transformation thus has its place in revival where we encounter the Great Transformer.

In all ages conformity to the world by Christians has
resulted in lack of spiritual life and a consequent lack
of spiritual vision and enterprise. A secularized or self-
centered Church can never evangelize the world.

JOHN R. MOTT

PRAYER PROMPT: *Lord, so many of us who are called by your name have been mesmerized by the attractions of this world. Revival is counter to all that is in this world. Bring those of us who yearn for revival a deeper desire for the transformation that can only happen through the working of the Holy Spirit.*

MAY 29
Don't Revive the Past

> *"No one who puts his hand to the plow and looks back is fit for the kingdom of God."*
> LUKE 9:62

God can't use us if our eyes are constantly looking back at the past, whether good or bad. No, we must put our hands to the plow and look straight ahead, lest the furrows be crooked and useless. For many, the past is being relived almost daily. We recall our mistakes with a regret that clings to us mercilessly. Or we remember past glorious victories and wish for those past days to return. Even the memory of past revivals may hinder us from future revival precisely because God has moved on and expects the same from us.

Remember that God has plans to use our past for a brilliant future. Past failures—and past victories—are the stepping stones to God's will for you, but they are not your ultimate destination. Move on. Become fit for the kingdom of God. Don't look back.

> Yes, repent of your past sins. But then be thankful
> that God will now be using them as stepping stones
> to a positive future. Praise God now for your past—
> not as your past—but as the raw building material
> for the man or woman you are meant to be.
> JOHN FLAVEL

PRAYER PROMPT: *God, sometimes it takes great faith to believe you can take past failures and turn them into future successes. But restoration is what you do—and do so well. Especially in revival do we sense a true ending to past miseries in favor of a redeemed future.*

I move on w/ God towards new future revivals!

MAY 30

The Healing Nature of Revival

*Bless the LORD, O my soul, and forget not all his
benefits, who forgives all your iniquity, who heals
all your diseases, who redeems your life from the pit,
who crowns you with steadfast love and mercy.*
PSALM 103:2–4

God is all about healing. Where God goes, so goes healing. In revival, emotions are soothed, broken spirits mended, and even physical healing is to be hoped for. After all, the psalmist lists the "benefits" of being a believer as forgiveness, healing, redemption, steadfast love from God, and mercy. Who among us will not claim such wonderful benefits by faith? Who among us will not share these benefits with those in need?

Beloved, come to Jesus and be healed!
Savior, I wait Your healing hand!
Diseases fly at Your command;
Now let Your sovereign touch impart,
Life, health, and vigor to my heart!
JAMES SMITH

PRAYER PROMPT: *Father, thank you for the many benefits of being your child. Help me as I claim every benefit as I need them. Each benefit claimed adds to my testimony of your gratefulness.*

MAY 31

No Turning Back

*Demas, in love with this present world, has
deserted me and gone to Thessalonica.*
2 Timothy 4:10

Make no mistake, we all have a bit of Demas in us. The attractions of this world are so numerous that there is literally something to love for everyone.

But when revival comes, the glitter of this present world diminishes; the attractions of heaven brighten. That part of us that sympathizes with Demas, we see for what it is—a robber of God's plan for our life. When we love the world, we're useless to God.

Every believer knows their inner Demas, and every believer must put that Demas to death and get on with their earthly assignment.

> It is an evil world, as it is a deadening world. It dulls and deadens the affections to heavenly objects. Earthly things choke the seed of the Word. A man entangled in the world is so taken up with secular concerns, that he can no more mind heavenly realities than an elephant can fly in the air! And even such as have grace in them when their affections are beslimed with earth, they find themselves much indisposed to meditation and prayer; it is like swimming with a heavy stone around the neck!
>
> Thomas Watson

PRAYER PROMPT: *Lord, put the spotlight on the Demas in me and empower me as I root out this usurper of revival. Replace the Demas in me with a Timothy or Lydia spirit, happily uprooted from this world and its glitz.*

JUNE 1

Revival: God's Intervention

*"I have heard the groaning of the people of Israel whom the Egyptians hold as slaves, and I have remembered my covenant. Say therefore to the people of Israel, 'I am the L*ORD*, and I will bring you out from under the burdens of the Egyptians, and I will deliver you from slavery to them, and I will redeem you with an outstretched arm and with great acts of judgment. I will take you to be my people, and I will be your God, and you shall know that I am the L*ORD* your God, who has brought you out from under the burdens of the Egyptians.'"*
Exodus 6:5–7

A revival can be God's way of intervening when church decline reaches a new low. Instead of judgment, God sends revival in response to our prayers. It can also be God moving in to protect his suffering children. When the Israelites were oppressed by the Egyptians, God heard their groaning and intervened. All these centuries later, God still hears the groans of his people and intervenes. When we were in eternal peril, the coming of Jesus was heaven's greatest intervention. Revival seasons are the way God intervenes to help his people remember their ultimate, eternal intervention in Christ.

It is most significant that since the Reformation revivals have recurred with increasing frequency. Again and again God has rescued that which had gone beyond all human aid . . . The need can but grow more urgent as the age draws to its close. When revivals cease to flow from the mercy of God, judgement must come.

David Panton

PRAYER PROMPT: *God, thank you for your merciful interventions. Our world is in dire need of the intervention of revival. Send a fresh outpouring soon, Lord.*

JUNE 2

What if We Had a Worldwide Revival?

*For the earth will be filled with the knowledge of the
glory of the L<small>ORD</small> as the waters cover the sea.*
H<small>ABAKKUK</small> 2:14

Someday we will experience the presence of the Lord permanently. Then, his glory will be known through all the lands of the earth. But what if we could get a foretaste of this here and now? Yes, it's up to God to bring revival, but it's up to us to ask. Why then should we not ask *big*? Why not ask and believe for a revival that circles the world? Why not have a glimpse of that future great, never-ending revival?

In reading the New Testament, I don't see Jesus rebuking anyone for asking too big. With God nothing is impossible. Let's ask big, not small.

There is a Divine mystery about Revivals. God's sovereignty
is in them. I may not live to see it, but the day will come
when there will be a great Revival over the whole earth.

A<small>LEXANDER</small> W<small>HYTE</small>

PRAYER PROMPT: *Father, you invite us to ask big, and so we do. We ask for a revival that touches every country around the world. May earth be filled with your glory as the waters cover the sea.*

JUNE 3

Overcoming Tragedy

*The LORD is near to the brokenhearted
and saves the crushed in spirit.*
PSALM 34:18

Perhaps the strongest testing of our faith is when we're aware of tragedy in our own life or we hear of unspeakable tragedy in the life of someone else. "Where was God?," we ask. As difficult as it may seem, we must believe that in some way unknown to us, God will redeem all our worst sorrows. It may be hard to believe the Lord is near when we're brokenhearted and crushed in spirit, but the truth is that he is closer than ever and our tragedy is a reverse Trojan horse in which dwells the presence of God.

One aspect of revival is that God's presence comes near to all, but especially to the brokenhearted. His nearness is a promise, and God cannot go back on even one promise.

Physicians in their rounds do not stop at the homes of the well, but of the sick. So it is with God in His movements through this world. It is not to the whole and the well but to the wounded and stricken, that he comes with sweetest tenderness!

J. R. MILLER

PRAYER PROMPT: *Lord, tragedies are so hard to bear. We often say things to those engulfed in tragedy, but our words can come across as clichés. It is your comfort that the hurting need. Your presence can bring hope beyond the days of tragedy. O, Father, bless the hurting today. Bring revival to restore what has been taken away.*

JUNE 4

Take Up the Whole Armor

*Therefore take up the whole armor of God,
that you may be able to withstand in the evil
day, and having done all, to stand firm.*
EPHESIANS 6:13

Useless is the soldier who goes into battle without armor or weaponry. Make no mistake, in revival there is always a summons to duty for God's soldiers. Our weapons are mighty but not carnal. Our armor is spiritual, not made of flesh. Our sword is the Word.

From now until we're summoned home to heaven, we're always to be ready for battle. No one goes AWOL in God's army. It's our destiny to serve in a war we cannot lose.

> In heaven we shall appear, not in armor, but in
> robes of glory. But here these are to be worn night
> and day; we must walk, work, and sleep in them,
> or else we are not true soldiers of Christ.
> WILLIAM GURNALL

PRAYER PROMPT: *Lord, I want to be a true soldier of Christ. I will take up the armor and withstand any evil day as it comes. My stance is firm. My heart resolute. Strengthen me, Lord!*

If I look for miracles in faith I will see them !!!

JUNE 5

Miracles Abound!

> *Now to him who is able to do far more abundantly than all that we ask or think, according to the power at work within us, to him be glory in the church and in Christ Jesus throughout all generations, forever and ever. Amen.*
> EPHESIANS 3:20–21

When we're not in revival, we often settle for an everyday sort of faith, with little or no expectation of miracles. But when revival awakens us, we become aware that even the smallest level of faith is capable of bringing forth miracles. If we look for miracles in faith, we will see them. If we don't look in faith, we will surely miss many acts of God.

Let us come to see that everything and every second is a miracle. This is key. For the revived Christian, there is no end to the miracles of life.

> *A Christian is a perpetual miracle.*
> CHARLES SPURGEON

PRAYER PROMPT: *Father, I often miss miracles because I'm not looking for them, or I take certain "coincidences" for granted. Open my eyes, Lord, to see that all of life is a miracle and worthy of my appreciation.*

(In Christ), I'm a perpetual miracle !!!

JUNE 6

Revival Is for Believers

The natural person does not accept the things of the Spirit of God, for they are folly to him, and he is not able to understand them because they are spiritually discerned.
1 CORINTHIANS 2:14

We may be surprised by the reactions of non-Christians as they observe revival. To the unbeliever, revival is perhaps a show, a sham, an emotional circus. Never will such a person discern the reality of revival until they are born from above.

Still, many who initially scoff at revival are eventually won when the Holy Spirit opens their eyes. But until then, both the gospel and revival are seen as irrelevant to unbelieving eyes. Our prayer is always for God to reveal himself to the mocker, convicting him or her of sin and the glory of grace that is the gospel and that Christ died for them.

> There is nothing attractive about the gospel to the natural man; the only man who finds the gospel attractive is the man who is convicted of sin.
> OSWALD CHAMBERS

PRAYER PROMPT: *Lord, I pray for a revival that will sweep many unbelievers into your kingdom. Use the obvious change happening within your church to open the eyes and hearts of those outside of it.*

JUNE 7

Temptations

*[Jesus] said to his disciples, "Temptations to sin are sure
to come, but woe to the one through whom they come!"*
LUKE 17:1

Though we're guaranteed to face temptations in this life, we're also able to overcome them by the power of the Holy Spirit within us. But must these temptations leave a scar? Or might they also leave us with a lesson learned?

For many, the continued presence of temptations also allows for the continued reliance on the Lord. Through the centuries, the strongest Christians have known the pain of temptations, many falling prey to those temptations, but then also the relief that forgiveness and grace bring.

It's lamentable that we're tempted—especially during revival seasons when Satan is especially keen to trip us up—but Jesus knew we would face fierce attempts from the enemy and from our own flesh. The secret about temptation is to learn its lessons early.

My temptations have been my Masters in Divinity.
MARTIN LUTHER

PRAYER PROMPT: *Father, you know my temptations and my triggers. I don't expect revival to remove my temptations, but as I'm in your presence, may I realize again the foolishness of sin and the benefits of victory over it.*

JUNE 8

Prayer and Revival

Be constant in prayer.
ROMANS 12:12

We know revival comes from prayer, but do we realize that revival empowers *more prayer*? The two—prayer and revival—are like the two sides of a coin. We can't have one without the other. If there is no prayer, there will be no revival. Where there is revival, there *will* be prayer. Revival prayer is power prayer, especially where there is a congregation of pray-ers. And as long as the saints are gathered in prayer, revival will thrive. When prayer ebbs, so does revival.

Prayer is not only key to bringing revival; it is key to maintaining revival.

True revival lives in prayer. Prayer draws power from
revival. We need only to follow the way-marks of their
remarkable history to be satisfied of their inseparable unity.

J. B. JOHNSTON

PRAYER PROMPT: *Father, let us not be content with just the arrival of revival. May we remember to sustain revival by being constant in prayer.*

"I sustain revival because I'm constant in prayer."

\#RevivalLife #Revived
\#Awakened #Leadership

JUNE 9

Infusing Our Daily Routine with Revival Life

*This is the day that the LORD has made;
let us rejoice and be glad in it.*
PSALM 118:24

Busyness with routine earthly duties can weaken our spiritual life and eventually kill it, but it doesn't have to be that way. God never withdraws his presence from us. Even at our busiest, he is always there.

Brother Lawrence, a lay brother in a Paris monastery testified of this in his classic book, *The Practice of the Presence of God*. His work in the monastery? He was no more than a helper in the kitchen, the last place one might expect to experience the presence of God. But not for Brother Lawrence. Daily he met God met there.

Where are you the busiest? Do you consciously experience God's presence during these times? It may even be possible to experience personal revival at the most unexpected times.

God is willing. Are we?

The most holy and important practice in the spiritual
life is the presence of God; that is, every moment
to take great pleasure that God is with you.

BROTHER LAWRENCE

PRAYER PROMPT: *Lord, surely the best blessing of revival is being in your presence. It's a fresh experience of Immanuel (God with us). I treasure your nearness to me, both now and in revival.*

JUNE 10

The God of Revival Never Sleeps or Slumbers

*He will not let your foot be moved; he
who keeps you will not slumber.*
PSALM 121:3

God is not passive in our lives. It's not like he's watching our life unfold on a TV screen and every so often sees something that needs his attention. No, he is always working in our lives, especially when we don't perceive his interest in us.

His care for us extends even to our beds. While we sleep, God doesn't take a break. He is as active on our behalf as when we're awake. His care knows no limits.

While we may be more vitally aware of his presence during revival, we are mistaken if we conclude that when revival has waned, God's presence has left us. That can never happen. God's attention is always "on" for each and every one of us.

> The Lord keeps his people as a rich man keeps his treasure, as a captain keeps a city with a garrison, as a sentry keeps watch over his sovereign. None can harm those who are in such keeping. Let me put my soul into his dear hands. He never forgets us, never ceases actively to care for us, never finds himself unable to preserve us.
>
> CHARLES SPURGEON

PRAYER PROMPT: *"O my Lord, keep me, lest I wander and fall and perish. Keep me that I may keep your commandments. By your unslumbering care prevent my sleeping like the sluggard, and perishing like those who sleep the sleep of death." (Charles Spurgeon)*

JUNE 11

Cherished by God

God shows his love for us in that while we were still sinners, Christ died for us.
ROMANS 5:8

The joy of the Christian is in living out what it looks like to be a person owned, cherished, and cared for by God. Revival only brings into focus what has always been true—the miracle not that God loves us now as his children but that he first loved us while we were yet sinners. It's always a good exercise to recall the early, radiant days of our Christian life as well as the later days when God astounded us with certain miracles we needed at just the right time. Such pondering changes us as we affirm his love for us. May we each reflect whose we are.

> Oh! what is in us that should cause the Lord to give such gifts to us as He has given? We were all equal in sin and misery; nay, doubtless, we have actually out-sinned thousands, to whom these precious gifts are denied. Oh! we were once poor wretches sitting upon the ash-heap, yes, wallowing in our blood, and yet behold the King of kings, the Lord of lords, has so far abounded in His love, as to bestow Himself, His Spirit, His grace, and all the jewels of His royal crown upon us! Oh! what heart can conceive, what tongue can express, this matchless love!
>
> THOMAS BROOKS

PRAYER PROMPT: *Lord, there is no greater experience than knowing I belong to you and that you have loved me in my most unlovable moments. In my sin you called me out. Now you keep me through the trials of life. You revive me when I'm low. For all of this, I give thanks and praise.*

JUNE 12

Quick to Repent

Bear fruit in keeping with repentance.
MATTHEW 3:8

Sometimes we become accustomed to the occasional sin in our life. We may think that because our sin is forgiven, it can be easily dismissed from our conscience.

If we continue with this attitude, it represents a forgetfulness about the hatred God has for our sin. Though forgiven, we are not given a license to continue in known rebellion against God's ways. We forget that we are called to a life of holiness, not to intermittent holiness interrupted by our pet sins. Sin robs us of the joy of the Lord. His presence remains, but there is a cloud that can only be dispelled by repentance.

Revival can bring our awareness of sins to the surface. We may find ourselves shedding tears of repentance, which are surely holy tears to God. Never let sin off the hook. Repent quickly.

True holiness in this life is but quick repenting.
THOMAS CHALMERS

PRAYER PROMPT: *Father, I hate sin. I hate that it seeks me out, trying to rob me of fellowship with you. Lord, strengthen me so that I may bear the fruit of repentance. Remind me to always keep away from the sources of sin. Holy Spirit, convict me early when I have sinned.*

JUNE 13

Revival Is Calling Out the "Called Out" Ones

"Come out from among them and be separate, says the Lord. Do not touch what is unclean, and I will receive you."
2 CORINTHIANS 6:17 (NKJV)

In establishing the church as "called-out ones," God has chosen people to represent him on earth. The problem is that we've not done a good job of living a called-out life. The ways of the world, designated as "unclean" by the Lord, still hold an attraction for many Christians. The result is the world sees no difference in us and finds no attraction to Christianity.

In revival, the distinction between the kingdom of God and the kingdom of this world is made far more apparent as believers are filled with boldness to step out of darkness and boldly associate with the Light.

During this current era, now more than ever, Christians must experience the stepping out that makes for a radiant and attractive church.

> The glory of the gospel is that when the church is absolutely different from the world, she invariably attracts it.
> MARTYN LLOYD-JONES

PRAYER PROMPT: *Father, make the distinctives of the Christian life obvious and attractive to unbelievers through the way I live my life. Fill me with boldness to be separate from the world, seeing Christ as more dazzling than the glitz of this present age. Help me step out for your name's sake!*

JUNE 14

Losing All

> *Whatever gain I had, I counted as loss for the sake of Christ. Indeed, I count everything as loss because of the surpassing worth of knowing Christ Jesus my Lord. For his sake I have suffered the loss of all things and count them as rubbish, in order that I may gain Christ.*
> PHILIPPIANS 3:7–8

Though we gain much through revival, we may also lose much. Are we willing to let go of even the good to gain the best? The apostle Paul both lost much and gained much in his encounter with Christ. But wisely, he understood what he lost—even the good things—were simply rubbish in comparison to what he gained.

Do you want personal revival? Revival for your family? Your church? Your community? Your nation? Be willing to lose all things in order to receive the better things. Surrender whatever God is prompting you to hand over, trusting that whatever he gives you in return is a surer reward. Start surrendering, and it won't be long before you experience a fresh wave of God's presence sweep through your heart and life.

> The shining of God's face upon His redeemed child is a substitute for every loss.
> JAMES EVANS

PRAYER PROMPT: *Lord, you have called each of us to a life of loss and a life of gain. May I embrace all that will mean in my life. Grant me a fully surrendered heart.*

JUNE 15

United to Christ

He who is joined to the Lord becomes one spirit with him.
1 CORINTHIANS 6:17

The union of the believer to Christ is a perfect one. We should expect nothing less from the One who initiated that union, the One preparing a bride for his Son. In eternity, our collective oneness with Christ is shown in the Bible as the unity between a bridegroom and his bride.

Today, if you are "in Christ," united to him by faith, your union with him is perfect. Live out that biblical truth in daily life. The engine of personal revival is our union with Christ.

Believers and Christ are one.
F. J. HUEGEL

PRAYER PROMPT: *Father, thank you for the union I have in Christ, a union you initiated and now sustain. This union is the driving force of my personal revival. In your Son, I have all I need.*

JUNE 16

Our Daily Needs

Everyone who has been born of God overcomes the world. And this is the victory that has overcome the world—our faith.
1 John 5:4

We have the life within us that can meet the daily needs we have, no matter what those needs are. Our inner life is more than equal to our daily tasks. This overcoming life is given to us freely, but it must be received and lived out by faith.

Revival is like a clinic where we who have ailed spiritually are brought before the Great Physician and made whole. Revival has a way of forever stamping the presence of God on our soul. That presence is both healing and life-giving.

> The healthy Christian is not necessarily the extrovert, ebullient Christian, but the Christian who has a sense of God's presence stamped deep on his soul, who trembles at God's word, who lets it dwell in him richly by constant meditation upon it, and who tests and reforms his life daily in response to it.
>
> J. I. Packer

PRAYER PROMPT: *Father, I have been born from above; therefore, according to your Word, I have overcome the world by my faith. Revival then becomes a celebration of Christ's victory and my victory in him.*

JUNE 17

Provision for Our Sins

*If we walk in the light, as he is in the light, we
have fellowship with one another, and the blood
of Jesus his Son cleanses us from all sin.*
1 John 1:7

Revival always brings to mind what happened on the cross. There full provision was made for all our sins. We have no need to agonize over our release from the guilt of our past sins. But know this: it is walking in the light that the blood of Jesus avails us. To claim Christ and to walk in darkness is incompatible.

May we be revived daily and allow the stream of total forgiveness to wash over us. When we find we have wandered, we must quickly return to the lighted path where we find fellowship with one another and experience the constant cleansing of our sin.

> All that God asks is that the heart should be
> cleansed from sin, full of love, whether it be
> the tender heart of a little child, with feeble
> powers of loving, or of the full-grown man.
>
> Duncan Campbell

PRAYER PROMPT: *Lord, thank you not just for forgiving my past sin but for making provision for any present or future sins. Thank you for the blood that cleanses from all sin. Reinvigorate my heart in this glorious truth today.*

JUNE 18

Gazing upon Our God

*Splendor and majesty are before him; strength
and beauty are in his sanctuary.*
Psalm 96:6

Ponder gazing upon God. No, we can't do that literally—not yet. But we can gaze upon him spiritually. We can, as the old hymn says, "look full in his wonderful face." To do so is to partake in revival. There, in God's presence, we're reminded that God is beautiful.

We often gaze at captivating sunsets, at children playing, or at beautiful flowers. We marvel at such beauty, but if we look beyond these evidences of God's beauty in creation, we will see the beauty of God himself.

> The man who gazes upon and contemplates day by day the face of the Lord Jesus Christ, and who has caught the glow of the reality that the Lord is not a theory but an indwelling power and force in his life, is as a mirror reflecting the glory of the Lord.
>
> Alan Redpath

PRAYER PROMPT: *Father, I look forward to the day when I shall gaze upon your majesty in person. But even now I ponder your beauty and marvel that you make yourself known to mere men and women, including me. May your beauty be reflected in my life as I live by faith in you.*

JUNE 19

Judging Others

Why do you pass judgment on your brother?
Or you, why do you despise your brother?
For we will all stand before the judgment seat of God.
ROMANS 14:10

When I see a Christian who is judgmental toward others, I often wonder if this is a Christian who has not yet dealt fully with his or her own sin. Has the person not owned his sin and then laid it at the foot of the cross in true confession and repentance?

In revival we have no time or desire for judging others, for as we bow our knees to the Lord, we're reminded that God's rightful judgment against us was laid on Christ. Instead of condemning others in our mind, we are freshly impassioned to see them come to know the only One who can take their condemnation away.

The very faults we condemn in our neighbors often exist in ourselves in even graver form! Jesus teaches this when he says, "Why do you behold the mote that is in your brother's eye but do not consider the beam that is in your own eye?"
While we are finding little specks of fault in others and judging and condemning them on account of these motes we ourselves have greater faults! We are not fit to be judges of others, because we have the same faults which we see in them. Besides, while we are looking after the faults of others we are in danger of neglecting the care of our own life!

J. R. MILLER

PRAYER PROMPT: *Father, I'm so busy removing the beams from my own eye I have no time or desire to pass judgment on others. Instead, may I offer the same mercy to others that you have granted to me.*

JUNE 20

Clearer Vision

[Jesus] took the blind man by the hand and led him out of the village, and when he had spit on his eyes and laid his hands on him, he asked him, "Do you see anything?" And he looked up and said, "I see people, but they look like trees, walking." Then Jesus laid his hands on his eyes again; and he opened his eyes, his sight was restored, and he saw everything clearly.
MARK 8:23–25

Our creative God finds fresh ways to intervene in the affairs of his creation. In bringing revival, God may act in a way we expect or in an entirely new and different way. We may miss revival if we insist on it looking as we think it should. The Jewish people missed their coming Messiah because Jesus didn't meet their expectations. Many times, God answers our prayers in unexpected ways. The wise Christian gives God room to bring revival *his* way.

> Christ never doeth his work by the halves, nor leaves it till he can say, It is finished. He put his hands again upon his eyes, to disperse the remaining darkness, and then bade him look up again, and he saw every man clearly, Now Christ [did it] this way because he would not tie himself to a method, but would show with what liberty he acted in all he did. He did not cure by rote . . . but varied as he thought fit. Providence gains the same end in different ways, that men may attend its motions with an implicit faith.
>
> MATTHEW HENRY

PRAYER PROMPT: *Lord, you are the creative God with your own methods and plans to accomplish your will. Give us eyes to perceive revival and eyes to discern what is not revival.*

JUNE 21

Ask, Seek, Knock

*"Ask, and it shall be given you; seek, and ye shall find;
knock, and it shall be opened unto you: For every one
that asketh receiveth; and he that seeketh findeth;
and to him that knocketh it shall be opened."*
MATTHEW 7:7–8 (KJV)

One aspect of prayer that causes many Christians to fail is a lack of *persistent* praying. We may pray for a certain matter a few times, but when the answer is slow in coming, our prayers—if they continue at all—become dull to our own ears and, worse, also to God's ears. We are instructed by Jesus to ask, but then to add seeking to our asking, then to add knocking to our asking and seeking. Prayer for revival includes all three aspects, but especially importunity in our prayers.

Let us be importunate, God loves importunity, and
the importunate are sure to succeed. We must not
only ask, but seek; not only seek, but knock; not only
knock, but continue knocking, until the Lord opens
the windows of heaven, and pours out his blessing.

JAMES SMITH

PRAYER PROMPT: *Lord, open the windows of heaven! Pour out the promised blessing. I will ask, seek, and knock until you visit me anew!*

JUNE 22

Our Natural Life

His divine power has granted to us all things that pertain to life and godliness, through the knowledge of him who called us to his own glory and excellence, by which he has granted to us his precious and very great promises, so that through them you may become partakers of the divine nature, having escaped from the corruption that is in the world because of sinful desire.
2 PETER 1:3–4

God will either change aspects of our natural life, or he won't. And when he doesn't, the conclusion we must reach is that we are called to glorify God in the natural and unchangeable aspects of our life. In every case, his grace is sufficient, and his power trumps our natural weakness. Many of us berate ourselves about what we wish we could change about ourselves. But if change is really called for, we change through partaking of the great promises and living out the divine nature given to us at our new birth.

> Precious faith lays hold on Precious promises, and so raises the soul beyond mere nature into the highest conceivable condition, making it like to God in holiness and virtue. The phrase, "partakers of the divine nature," is a very remarkable one; we cannot become divine, but we can be partakers of his holiness.
>
> CHARLES SPURGEON

PRAYER PROMPT: *Father, you know all about it, including those natural aspects of my being that can't be changed. I pray then that in my natural weakness you manifest your strength. I pray that by your precious promises I partake of your victory and your holiness.*

JUNE 23

Dwelling in God's Presence

You make known to me the path of life; in your presence there is fullness of joy; at your right hand are pleasures forevermore.
Psalm 16:11

It's a blessing from God that we all have different assignments. Some, to be sure, are more perilous and trial filled than others. But because God knows our path, we can rejoice at whatever lies ahead. If severe trials be our lot, we rejoice as if our pathway has no mountains or valleys. When revival comes, many will be going through hard times. For them, revival brings extra strength to bear present and future trials. It brings an awareness of the secure refuge available to every believer. That refuge can never be penetrated by the enemy.

> The secret of his presence is a more secure refuge than a thousand Gibraltars. I do not mean that no trials come. They may come in abundance, but they cannot penetrate into the sanctuary of the soul, and we may dwell in perfect peace even in the midst of life's fiercest storms.
>
> Hannah Whitall Smith

PRAYER PROMPT: *Father, I know there will always be trials this side of heaven. But as I dwell in your presence, all trials are diminished or turned into a blessing unknown to me. I pray for the ability to weather any severe trial that comes my way, confident you're in the trial with me.*

JUNE 24

Resurrection Power

If the Spirit of him who raised Jesus from the dead dwells in you, he who raised Christ Jesus from the dead will also give life to your mortal bodies through his Spirit who dwells in you.
ROMANS 8:11

One of the most remarkable truths in Christianity is that we who believe have the same power in us that raised Christ from the dead. Resurrection power. Revival power. Power to move the mountains in our lives. The greatest tragedy in Christianity is that so few Christians avail themselves of this mighty power, thus missing out on the remedies to their troubles. What distracts you or hinders you from walking in this power today?

> Prayer is the risen Jesus coming in with his resurrection power, given free rein in our lives, and then using his authority to enter any situation and change things.
>
> OLE HALLESBY

PRAYER PROMPT: *Thank you, Father, for filling me with the same resurrection power that raised Christ from the dead. May I never miss the chance to pray through—and walk through—my troubles with this power.*

JUNE 25

Containers of God's Word

*I have stored up your word in my heart,
that I might not sin against you.*
Psalm 119:11

A revived Christian is a Christian who loves and feeds on God's Word. We find life in the pages of the Bible. We study it, but we shouldn't stop there. We must memorize it, pray it, ponder, and meditate on it. We mine it for the golden promises by which we live. We become containers of God's Word. And then we live it out as we walk in this world. We are thus enabled to live the revival life.

> We must not only know God's word, we must live
> it. To live it, we must meditate on it. The promises
> may be compared to a gold mine, which only enriches
> when the gold is dug out. By holy meditation, we dig
> out that spiritual gold which lies hidden in the midst
> of the promise, and so we come to be enriched!
>
> Thomas Watson

PRAYER PROMPT: *Father, your Word is a gold mine. I love its wisdom. It truly is a lamp unto my feet. In taking your Word into my being by memorizing and meditating on it, I become a container of your Word. It is spiritual gold, and I am an eager gold miner.*

JUNE 26

The Treasure within the Believer

*We have this treasure in jars of clay, to show that the
surpassing power belongs to God and not to us.*
2 Corinthians 4:7

God deposits treasures in each of us in the person of the Holy Spirit. This treasure always works in accordance with our God-given personality. So the Holy Spirit and individual personality mesh perfectly to fulfill His will in us—the representation of him on earth to the lost.

Too often we forget this treasure. But God often uses revival to awaken us to our fortune within. He brings to life the truth that we, of all the people on the earth, have such riches inside our frame. Right this minute, as you read this, be aware that yes, even you, are a jar of clay, filled with treasure, all to demonstrate that the surpassing power belongs to God and not to us.

What an exalted character, and what an enviable man, is
the true Christian! All the resources of the Triune God
unite to replenish this earthen vessel. No angel in heaven
contains a treasure half so costly and so precious as that
poor believing sinner, who, getting near to the Savior's
feet, and bathing them with tears of penitence and love,
can look up and exclaim, whom have I in heaven but you?
and there is none upon earth that I desire beside you.

Octavius Winslow

PRAYER PROMPT: *Lord, thank you for the unspeakable treasure you've placed in me. Through your priceless Holy Spirit living within me, may my life be a display of your riches to the lost.*

JUNE 27

A Life of Expectancy

*"You also must be ready, for the Son of Man is
coming at an hour you do not expect."*
LUKE 12:40

God's revivals are like a line of dominoes falling onto one another, until the last domino falls. Revivals will continue as long as there are praying believers to be revived. But the last revival will surely be accompanied by the return of the Lord, and what a last revival that will be! There will be no need for any further revivals, for we shall all be rejoicing in God's presence.

The present domino of revival reminds us to expect the Lord's return, whether sooner or later. Revival readies us. It excites us as if it is a foretaste of heaven. How then can we not yearn for that last domino to fall?

The true Christian should not only believe in Christ, and love Christ; he should also look and long for Christ's second coming. If he cannot say from his heart, "Come, Lord Jesus!" then there must be something wrong about his soul.

J. C. RYLE

PRAYER PROMPT: *Lord, I praise you for the revivals you initiate on earth, but I long for that last great revival that shall culminate with the close of this fallen world's story. Come, Lord Jesus!*

JUNE 28

Nehemiah's Prayer

> *As soon as I heard these words I sat down and wept and mourned for days, and I continued fasting and praying before the God of heaven. And I said, "O LORD God of heaven, the great and awesome God who keeps covenant and steadfast love with those who love him and keep his commandments, let your ear be attentive and your eyes open, to hear the prayer of your servant that I now pray before you day and night for the people of Israel your servants, confessing the sins of the people of Israel, which we have sinned against you."*
> NEHEMIAH 1:4–6

Nehemiah had a burden from the Lord to repair the wall. This burden manifested itself through intense prayer and fasting. Nehemiah would not be denied. Neither must we. Our prayers for revival—for God to repair and rebuild and revive our hearts to burn for his glory and his work in this world—must be relentless. It must also be accompanied by confession of sin when necessary and by fasting whenever possible.

> We must continue in prayer if we are to get an outpouring of the Spirit. Christ says there are some things we shall not get, unless we pray and fast, yes, prayer and fasting. We must control the flesh and abstain from whatever hinders direct fellowship with God.
>
> ANDREW BONAR

PRAYER PROMPT: *Father, in seeking revival, I join with thousands of others who are praying and fasting for a great outpouring of your Spirit. Just as you did not refuse Nehemiah's request to repair the wall, we pray that you will not refuse our prayers for the repair and revival of our hearts.*

JUNE 29

Believing for Even the Most Hardened Sinners

*The saying is trustworthy and deserving of full
acceptance, that Christ Jesus came into the world
to save sinners, of whom I am the foremost.*
1 Timothy 1:15

Nothing is more surprising in revival than seeing the hardest of sinners bow at the altar of repentance. Men and women given to drugs and alcohol give way to their knees as the weight of God's glory rests on them.

We all know such people—the last ones we expect to see saved. But it is God's special delight to overshadow them with his presence.

Begin praying now for the hardest ones in your circle of influence to be softened by God's Spirit. Always remember the apostle Paul, who, as Saul of Tarsus was a chief opponent of Christians. He was swept into the kingdom in a way that astonished even him. May it be likewise with our unsaved friends.

Everything sprang into new life. Former blasphemers were the most eloquent in prayer and praise. These men appeared to be making up for lost time. . . . Drunkards forgot the way to the saloons, which in fact were empty in a few nights. All the former inebriates were busy worshiping.

David Matthews, *I Saw the Welsh Revival*

PRAYER PROMPT: *Dear Lord, soften hard hearts. Bring new life to those who know their need and even to those unaware of their need. Let no one be untouched by revival.*

JUNE 30

The God of All Creation

"'In him we live and move and have our being'; as even some of your own poets have said, 'For we are indeed his offspring.'"
ACTS 17:28

It boggles the mind to consider the vastness and greatness of God. It further amazes me that this great God knows each person on earth—past, present, and future—intimately. So often we're displeased at some aspect of who we are. We may dislike our appearance, our temper, or our placement in life, but in doing so, we take issue with God. Happiness is being true to who God says we are, not to who we think we should be. Revival brings appreciation for the creativity of God. What we previously disregarded in God's design, now we receive with gratitude.

———

> [God] has such multitudes to remember, and yet he knows me individually and intimately! The stars lie along the face of the sky like bright unnumbered dust; but he knows star from star. The flowers spring up in battalions; but not a single flower is born to blush unseen. He knows it, and rejoices in it. There are billions of people in the world today, and I cannot grasp the tremendous aggregate; but he is familiar with each beating soul.
>
> ALEXANDER SMELLIE

———

PRAYER PROMPT: *Father, you are Lord of all! Your greatness amazes me! Your creativity is beyond fault. I praise you that in revival, though it be corporate, you see every heart and pour out your blessing abundantly. I rejoice in you today, Lord!*

JULY 1

Modern Idols

*Those who pay regard to vain idols forsake
their hope of steadfast love.*
JONAH 2:8

We may mistakenly think idolatry, the enemy of revival, belongs only to faraway heathen populations. But modern society has its idols too. Whatever we allow to usurp God's plan for our life is our idol. The desire for money can reveal idolatry. The hunger for fame may keep us from God's will. We may even look in the mirror and find our most adored idol.

The irony, of course, is that idols have no life. They are dead in themselves, and they produce death in all who worship them. God, on the other hand, offers life to his worshippers. To see revival, we must all divest ourselves of any and all idols. To keep our idols is to forsake the hope of revival. It is to choose death instead of life.

Ask God to reveal any idolatry in your life, not so that you may be punished for years on end, but so you can return to God and the path of life.

---

*If revival is being withheld from us it is because
some idol remains still enthroned.*
JONATHAN GOFORTH

PRAYER PROMPT: *Father, I have discarded all my known idols. If any remain, please show me. My worship is only for you, the great Life-giver. Idolatry has only been a life-destroyer. Keep my heart from attaching to false gods.*

JULY 2
Pale Counterfeits of True Revival

*"That which is born of the flesh is flesh, and
that which is born of the Spirit is spirit."*
JOHN 3:6

Woe unto us if we're ever satisfied with an imitation of true revival, often marked by a strong personality presiding over the event and ushered into being by a lavish marketing campaign preceding the revival. The event may raise goose bumps, but little more than that.

The goal of true revival is twofold: the glorifying of God and a life-changing experience for the Christian. True revival may be lost in an age that celebrates human effort and applauds superficial achievements.

> Quite simply, it is a fact of history that the church of Christ has not experienced any major nationwide revival under the conditions of advanced modernity. On the other hand, modernity undercuts true dependence on God's sovereign awakening by fostering the notion that we can effect revival by human means. On the other hand, modernity makes many people satisfied with privatized, individualistic, and subjective experiences that are pale counterfeits of true revival.
>
> OS GUINNESS

PRAYER PROMPT: *Father, send true revival. We want no other.*

JULY 3

Revival and Fear

*I sought the LORD, and he answered me
and delivered me from all my fears.*
PSALM 34:4

Fear is the deadly enemy of faith and thus of the Christian. Faith is designed to overcome every fear. As the psalmist noted, in seeking the Lord we receive deliverance from *all* our fears.

Complacency is the deadly enemy of revival. Complacency desires no interruptions in one's comforts. But revival is just that: a disruption to our present comfort, and we thus become fearful of the changes revival might bring. But blessed is the Christian willing to be shaken out of his or her complacency. And if we seek the Lord, the promise for deliverance from fear is ours.

> If men will not fear God, they shall fear men; yes, they shall be made a terror to themselves. And indeed it is a dreadful punishment for God to deliver a man up into the hands of his own fears. I think there is scarce a greater torment to be found in the world than for a man to be his own tormentor, and his mind made a rack and engine of torture to his body.
>
> JOHN FLAVEL

PRAYER PROMPT: *Lord, when I fear, I will seek you and will be delivered from all my fears, including your plans to bring me to maturity—whatever that takes.*

JULY 4

Revival Touching Our National Leaders

First of all, then, I urge that supplications, prayers, intercessions, and thanksgivings be made for all people, for kings and all who are in high positions, that we may lead a peaceful and quiet life, godly and dignified in every way.
1 Timothy 2:1–2

What would our country look like if our government leaders experienced revival? What if national emergencies led us to prayer? What if we repented from our national sins? Many historians attribute the end of slavery to revival. The next revival could usher in an end to our current national sins. If that happened, we know there would be two results: critics of such a revival, labeling it "religious" interference with contemporary life. The other result would be God's blessing. Whenever there was repentance in the Bible, blessing and often restoration followed. In our prayers for revival, we must pray for our leaders as we pray for ourselves. Pray too for the naysayers, many of whom may be, like Paul, future champions of the faith.

We need a baptism of clear seeing. We desperately need seers who can see through the mist—Christian leaders with prophetic vision. Unless they come soon it will be too late for this generation. And if they do come we will no doubt crucify a few of them in the name of our worldly orthodoxy.

A. W. Tozer

PRAYER PROMPT: *God, revival is a tool you use to effect societal change. Revivals have blessed nations that were spiritually sick. Today many countries are in spiritual decline. Bring revival, Father! Change the course of our nation. Root out our spiritual laziness. Give us a vision for a land that honors you and leaders who govern in godly ways. For woe to nations that refuse to acknowledge you. Grant repentance and restoration!*

JULY 5

Awake, Sleepy Church!

You know the time, that the hour has come for you to wake from sleep. For salvation is nearer to us now than when we first believed.
ROMANS 13:11

Every passing day brings us one day nearer to either the Lord's return or our entrance into heaven through death. That being the case, the apostle Paul reminds the Roman believers and us that it is time to awake from sleep. If that was true for the Roman church two thousand years ago, how much truer is it for the twenty-first-century church?

God knows the seemingly perpetual need of the church to rise from our slumber and tend to the matters that require an awakened church. Thus, God sends revival at the appointed time in order that we overcome our narcolepsy.

> When is a revival needed? When carelessness and unconcern keep the people asleep. When may a revival be expected? When the wickedness of the wicked grieves and distresses the Christian.
>
> BILLY SUNDAY

PRAYER PROMPT: *Lord, I pray that we, the believers, are distressed enough by the surrounding wickedness that we now pray for revival with expectation. I pray, with others, against the onslaught of this world's evil.*

JULY 6

Seething Hot Prayers

*In these days he went out to the mountain to pray,
and all night he continued in prayer to God.*
LUKE 6:12

There are prayers, and then there are PRAYERS in all caps. These are the urgent, desperate prayers that come seething hot from the heart. They are the prayers Jesus prayed in the garden of Gethsemane. They are the prayers the apostle Paul wrote about in Romans 8 that are so intense, they come out in groans. These are the prayers of revival-praying Christians.

When we pray for revival, let's pray in all caps. Let's pray seething hot prayers.

> Those prayers God likes best which come
> seething hot from the heart.
> THOMAS WATSON

PRAYER PROMPT: *Lord, the prayers in my heart are seething hot—the prayers you like best. May that passion come seething hot out of my mouth and into your ears.*

JULY 7

Unity

*Finally, all of you, have unity of mind, sympathy,
brotherly love, a tender heart, and a humble mind.*
1 Peter 3:8

A few things can shut down revival quickly. One factor is division. During revival, all minor disagreements should be set aside or, better yet, resolved through mutual understanding. In John 17, we read of Jesus praying for his people to be unified. The apostle Peter urged the readers of his epistle to "have unity of mind."

For revival to have its desired effect, we must be willing to receive other born-again believers with a spirit of brotherly love. Unity, not division, is the essence of revival.

Preparing for revival is a perfect time to *practice* unity even as we also *pray* for unity.

Be united with other Christians. A wall with loose bricks
is not good. The bricks must be cemented together.

Corrie Ten Boom

PRAYER PROMPT: *Lord, I accept my brothers and sisters who aren't on the same page as me. If they love you and are born again, indwelt with your Holy Spirit, then they are my family. As I pray for revival, I pray also for unity in the body of Christ. During these troubling times, may we learn to care for one another with tender hearts and humble minds.*

JULY 8

Life-Giving Revival

The thief comes only to steal and kill and destroy. I came that they may have life and have it abundantly.
JOHN 10:10

Jesus came to give us not just life but *abundant* life. The entrance of that abundant life usurps the thief's destruction. God's life always trumps Satan's destruction of life in the same way Christ's death was trumped by his resurrection. We have life set before us, but to partake of this life, we must empty ourselves. We must become weak in order to become strong.

Revival is a time of regaining our promised abundant life. It's a time when Satan's tactics fall flat. In our imagination, we can see Satan flee from the presence of revival. For as we are revived and strengthened, he is weakened and defeated.

The abundant life—the revival life—is ours to live. Don't settle for less!

Before he furnishes the abundant supply, we must first be made conscious of our emptiness. Before he gives strength, we must be made to feel our weakness. Slow, painfully slow, are we to learn this lesson; and slower still to own our nothingness and take the place of helplessness before the Mighty One.

A. W. PINK

PRAYER PROMPT: *Lord, I see my own emptiness, but at the same time, I see your strength in me. Surely the antidote to my lack is an awareness of your abundance. For this you came—to give me that abundant life.*

JULY 9

Sowing the Seeds of Revival

> *Whoever sows sparingly will also reap sparingly, and whoever sows bountifully will also reap bountifully.*
> 2 CORINTHIANS 9:6

To reap revival, we must sow the right seeds. The sowing is prayer. The seeds are desperation, repentance, hunger, grief over personal or national sin. Like most gardens, one more thing is needed: rain from heaven. Since revival is a blessing from God, the needed rain must come from him as well. Thus, three requirements for revival are prayer, need, and divine blessing. A constant supply of all three will surely bring the revival harvest.

> As God has pledged himself by his Word to bless, his blessing must come down direct from Heaven, as the former and latter rain upon the earth, and, as the effect of the Divine blessing, a glorious revival would take place. Then the drooping, dying plants in the garden of the Lord, would revive and flourish; then the seed of the kingdom, long since sown, would germinate and spring up; then the dry bones lying in the open valley of this world, would be clothed with flesh and quickened into life; then this bleak desert, this barren land, would become like Eden, clothed with beauty, pervaded with power, and crowned with blessing. This, this is the revival that we need!
> JAMES SMITH

PRAYER PROMPT: *Father, where there are seeds of revival, recruit the sowers—men and women of believing prayer. Send rain from heaven that we might reap a bountiful revival harvest.*

JULY 10

The Lord, My Strength

I love you, O LORD, my strength.
PSALM 18:1

To bring the kind of revival God sends, we need to seek the Lord's strength and his presence. There can be no revival without God's presence. Neither can there be God's presence without revival. Our seeking must not be meager. It must be constant; it must be continual. How then is this possible? We accept the burden to set our hearts and minds on revival. Even though we must attend to many outer duties, the prayer for revival is always in our mind. When we are not consciously praying, we are subconsciously praying.

The intercession is always there, either verbal, thoughtful, or an inner groaning in the spirit.

> It is the Spirit that gives light and power to speak. The manifestation and power are needed by us. O that we might have more of the communion and fellowship of the Holy Ghost . . . and may we sincerely shun those things that grieve Him; and may we not be content to go on with the great work without Him! And let us never imagine that we can do anything in our own strength.
>
> JOHN ELIAS

PRAYER PROMPT: *Lord, send your presence. Send your strength. All we need can only come from you. Hear my prayers, both conscious and subconscious.*

JULY 11

Craving God's Presence

> *You will seek me and find me, when you seek me with all your heart.*
> JEREMIAH 29:13

It takes seeking God with all our heart to find him. When he is found, we realize all the searching was worth it. In fact, the seeking brought a joy of its own.

Craving his presence is required to find him. Once found, we never want to be out of the Lord's presence. And though he is found by our seeking, we don't stop the search. The more we grow in Christ, the more we realize that the joy of continual seeking will last the rest of our lives. The knowledge of God is like a well that never runs dry.

Seeking revival is primarily seeking the presence of God.

What solemn feelings are produced in the mind under a sense of God's presence! How the Lord's presence turns night into day, makes every crooked thing straight and every rough place plain! How it banishes all the gloom, melancholy, and despondency which hang over the soul! How it clears up every difficulty and like the shining sun, it drives away the damps and darkness of the night. If there is one thing to be coveted more than another, it is that the Lord's presence might be more felt in our hearts!

J. C. PHILPOT

PRAYER PROMPT: Lord, how wonderful is your presence. Your nearness is the nearness of revival, which we crave. Father, we have sought you and have found you, but we still seek more. The knowledge of you is a well that never runs dry.

JULY 12
The Will of God

> Blessed be his glorious name forever; may the whole earth be filled with his glory! Amen and Amen!
> —PSALM 72:19

During our short time on earth, we will put our hands to many tasks. We may work as a farmer, type on a computer, run an assembly line, or wait tables in a diner. But to whatever we put our hand, we are to do so for God's glory and to fulfill his will for us. No matter what our hands do, we are aware that doing the will of God works to his glory. A Christian may enter the revival as just another worker doing a day job, but that same Christian leaves the revival with a renewed awareness that he is working out God's will in that job. And there is no greater occupation than that.

> Whatever man may stand, whatever he may do, to whatever he may apply his hand—in agriculture, in commerce, and in industry, or his mind, in the world of art, and science—he is, in whatsoever it may be, constantly standing before the face of God. He is employed in the service of his God. He has strictly to obey his God. And above all, he has to aim at the glory of his God.
> —ABRAHAM KUYPER

PRAYER PROMPT: *Lord, whatever I do, I do in your name. Guide me, therefore, into the places where I can best glorify you. Keep me from idle distractions that waste my precious years on earth.*

JULY 13

Going Forward in Revival

*Commit your work to the LORD, and
your plans will be established.*
PROVERBS 16:3

Even though revivals are often thought of in terms of large numbers of people, we must remember that God doesn't see each person in revival as merely a face in the crowd. Revival with God is an intimate, personal experience. God is there not for the crowd but for the individual Christian. The takeaway is that this sense of God's intense interest in us individually follows us home after revival. Follows us to our families, our churches, and our workplace. All our future endeavors, both large and small, are watched over by God with care.

Just as Christ died for us individually, so now he lives to care for us one by one.

> From low thoughts of God, we are apt to fear that he
> will not exert himself for us. But he will attend to us,
> if we trust in him, as much as if there were not another
> creature in Heaven or on earth to attract his notice.
> Nor is it in great things only that he will interpose for
> us, but in the smallest that can possibly be imagined.
> In fact, there is nothing great or small with him; nor
> indeed is there anything small as it respects us.
>
> CHARLES SIMEON

PRAYER PROMPT: *Lord, you are my God. I have no others. And though you do have others besides me, you see me, love me, and treat me personally. Indeed, Christ died for me as if I were the only sinner needing redemption. Thank you for your single-eyed care for me.*

JULY 14

God's Timing in Revival

For still the vision awaits its appointed time; it hastens to the end—it will not lie. If it seems slow, wait for it; it will surely come; it will not delay.
HABAKKUK 2:3

Though revival may seem slow in coming, do we really think God is late in sending it?

Never! God's revival is always on time and always timely. Though it is slow by our timetable, it is in accordance with God's best plans. We must always remember that God is the Creator and thus the dispenser of time. There is an appointed time for revival, and it will surely come; it will not delay.

> Set no time to the Lord the creator of time, for his time is always best.
> SAMUEL RUTHERFORD

PRAYER PROMPT: *You, O Lord, are the author of time. You are, therefore, not constrained by time. We pray for revival, but you choose the season for its arrival. We pray soon, though Lord. Let it not delay for long.*

JULY 15

Revived Through Trials

Though I walk in the midst of trouble, You will revive me; You will stretch out Your hand against the wrath of my enemies, and Your right hand will save me.
PSALM 138:7 (NKJV)

As odd as it may seem, revival can be a means of sanctifying our trials. In such a case, those with heavy burdens or who are walking through deep valleys may have the most to gain in revival. God stretches out his hand to save us—not *from* but *through* the trial. Those who lose the most during revival are those who will not bring their every burden to the Lord. Though God outstretches his hand, we must outstretch our prayers.

Among the most fruitful means of spiritual revival, overlook not the hallowed results of sanctified affliction. Times of trial are times of restoring and growth in the history of spiritual life. The cloud of sorrow may be upon your heart, the shadow of death upon your tabernacle, but this may be the appointed way of quickening your soul to more spiritual sensibility, of recalling the truant affections, and of drawing you nearer, and still nearer to God. Oh blessed discipline of trial that quickens, revives, and strengthens the life of God in the soul!

OCTAVIUS WINSLOW

PRAYER PROMPT: *Lord, sanctify my trials. I ask that you deliver me, not from them, but through them. May my every trial have a redeeming end.*

JULY 16

Spiritual Pride

*When pride comes, then comes disgrace,
but with the humble is wisdom.*
Proverbs 11:2

If any among us believe we are more spiritual or deeper than others, that is surely pride, pure and simple. And when pride comes in, so does disgrace.

We may all be different and have varying gifts from other believers, but that's not a mark of spiritual depth. To perceive oneself as deeper than others is a prideful display of our shallowness. The truly spiritual among us are often the ones least likely to acknowledge it. They're too busy fulfilling their calling of service to others. Their time in prayer is unseen by others. Their humility is a sign of their maturity.

Revival has a way of leveling the playing field. The proud will be humbled, and the humble shall be blessed.

Pride comes from not knowing yourself and the world. The older you grow, and the more you see, the less reason you will find for being proud. Ignorance and inexperience are the pedestal of pride; once the pedestal is removed pride will soon come down.

J. C. Ryle

PRAYER PROMPT: *Father, I have no cause for earthly pride. Anything worthy of praise in my life is simply a fruit of knowing you. Lord, I desire the wisdom Solomon found in humility.*

JULY 17

Secret Sins

He knows the secrets of the heart.
Psalm 44:21

Secret sins are killers of revival. We likely take the time to repent of the "big" sins in our life, but we may think God doesn't care about our small sins. We tell ourselves *I can experience revival and not deal with my secret sin.* But that's like saying because my cancer is small, I can neglect it; it will either just go away on its own accord or stay the same small tumor. But we know cancer isn't like that. Neither is secret sin. It will grow into a larger sin, perhaps even a deadly sin.

Keep revival alive. Deal with every known sin, big and small.

Secret sins commonly lie nearest the heart.
Thomas Brooks

PRAYER PROMPT: *Father, may I not tolerate any secret cancerous sins in my life. Cleanse me wholly and deliver me from the potential for sin that resides in me.*

JULY 18

Revival and Our Sin

"Come now, let us reason together, says the LORD: though your sins are like scarlet, they shall be as white as snow; though they are red like crimson, they shall become like wool."
Isaiah 1:18

Revival reminds us of our how complete God's forgiveness is. God invites us to reason with him regarding past sins. He declares our scarlet sins are now white as the snow. Though red like crimson, now they are as wool. In short, our sins have been forever dealt with. There is nothing more to be done. Jesus's words from the cross, "It is finished," marked the ultimate payment for the sins of the repentant believer. Why then do so many of us continue to replay our past failures with sin? Accept now the absolute forgiveness God extends and carry past sins no longer. The more distance we put between ourselves and our sin, the safer we are, and the closer we are to revival.

God ordains forgiveness absolute, unbounded, unrestricted, unlimited, unfenced by boundaries, unconfined by barriers. He erects a lofty throne, on which this grace supremely reigns.

Henry Law

PRAYER PROMPT: *Lord, I distance myself today from any remaining sins I've not fully dealt with. I will embrace not only your forgiveness but also your infinite forgetfulness.*

JULY 19

Revival Power

The kingdom of God does not consist in talk but in power.
1 CORINTHIANS 4:20

We don't often think of what causes Satan to fear, but surely revival among God's people tops the list. When he sees churches on their knees praying for revival, he surely trembles and does his best to bring such intercessions to a halt. In short, Satan is fully aware of and terrified by the power of prayer. Satan can deceive, depress, and even murder. But the kingdom of God comes with power to obliterate Satan's work.

As we pray in revival power, Satan will flee.

> Have we Holy Spirit power; power that restricts the devil's power, pulls down strongholds and obtains promises? . . . What has hell to fear other than a God-anointed, prayer-powered church?
>
> LEONARD RAVENHILL

PRAYER PROMPT: *Lord, it's amazing and wonderful that you have given me revival power over the enemy through my prayers. Through intercession, Satan stumbles, instead of him causing me to trip up. Thank you, Father, for revival power.*

JULY 20

Dedication to the Lord

*I appeal to you therefore, brothers, by the mercies of
God, to present your bodies as a living sacrifice, holy and
acceptable to God, which is your spiritual worship.*
ROMANS 12:1

God accepts certain sacrifices from us. Such sacrifices include praise, prayers, and even our bodies. But what he cannot accept or delight in is our old self—our fallen nature. We dare not bring our old nature into God's presence and dedicate it to him. How can we possibly submit our condemned flesh to a holy God.

God's remedy for the fallen self is not sacrifice but death. We are to reckon our old self dead to sin. Nothing but death is fitting for our "old man." It is the new self we offer to God, and the new self he delights in. Once we are a new creation we may then offer up our new life to him in thanks—and *that* he delights in.

Have you surrendered the old self? Have you dedicated to him all parts of the new self?

The first condition of consecration, must always be entire
readiness to accept God's will for our life. It is not enough to
be willing to do Christian work. There are many people who
are quite ready to do certain things in the service of Christ
who are not ready to do anything he might want them to do.

J. R. MILLER

PRAYER PROMPT: *Father, you have provided a wonderful way of dealing with the "old man" all Christians have known in themselves. You command us not to sacrifice our old man but to reckon it dead. What I can sacrifice is my body as a living sacrifice, holy and acceptable to you.*

JULY 21

Sing for Joy!

Let all who take refuge in you rejoice; let them ever sing for joy, and spread your protection over them, that those who love your name may exult in you.
Psalm 5:11

Joy is one hallmark of revival. When we experience the presence of God, we're filled with joy. How then can we not sing of our joy? Though joy comes with revival, we should be singing joyful songs even when revival is absent. God's presence is always with us, even when revival has yet to come or has come and gone. Joy is always the Christian's song, delighting not only us but pleasing God as well.

> Unless heard, the singing is unimaginable, and when heard, indescribable. There was no hymnbook. No one gave out a hymn. Just anybody started the singing and very rarely did it happen that the hymn started—no one knew by whom—was out of harmony with the mood at the moment. Once started, as if moved by a simultaneous impulse, the hymn was caught up by the whole congregation almost as if what was about to be sung had been announced and all were responding to the baton of a visible human leader. I have seen nothing like it. You felt as if the thousand or fifteen hundred people before you had become merged into one myriad-headed but single-souled personality. Such was the perfect blending of the mood and purpose that it bore eloquent testimony to a unity created only by the Spirit of God.
>
> R. B. Jones, a leader in the Welsh revival

PRAYER PROMPT: *Lord, I pray you will keep my heart full of heaven's melodies. I pray you might even ignite revival through the singing of your praises. What a mighty force is found in singing!*

JULY 22

We Are Children of Light

*You are all children of light, children of the day.
We are not of the night or of the darkness.*
1 Thessalonians 5:5

Revival brings more light to the children of light. Revival is a temporary respite from the spiritual darkness surrounding us. It brings even more of God's radiance—or awareness of it—to the children of the day.

The light of revival heightens our ability to see darkness for what it is and to repel it, bringing the light of Christ to bear on our circle of influence. Those who are still in darkness are exposed to light through our witness as we interact with this world. Letting our line shine is a true result of living in revival.

> Who are the children of light? These are God's children, who were once darkness but are now light in the Lord. They are enlightened to see the nature, value, and preeminent excellency of spiritual things. The natural man discerns not the things of the Spirit of God, but these do. They know that spiritual blessings are the chief blessings, and therefore prize them, seek them, and enjoy them. They love the Father of lights from whom comes every good and perfect gift. They are in union and communion with Christ, the great luminary, the light of the world. They live to enlighten others, being constituted the light of the world.
>
> James Smith

PRAYER PROMPT: *Father, thank you for the light you shine for me. May that daylight scatter the night all around me. Bring, Lord, a revival of your radiance to those stumbling in darkness.*

JULY 23

Expecting the Impossible

> *"Ah, Lord GOD! It is you who have made the heavens and the earth by your great power and by your outstretched arm! Nothing is too hard for you."*
> JEREMIAH 32:17

In the spiritual battle we face, we must be bold in faith, expecting the impossible. And in this present day, we may think revival is impossible—all the more reason to cast out doubt and believe God by expecting revival. We are like the man who carried his umbrella to the prayer meeting to plead for rain. Whatever obstacles we face—impossible as they may seem—are to be overcome by faith. We are warriors in an army that cannot be defeated, but we must soldier on through every obstacle to secure our victory.

> Christ wants not nibblers of the possible, but grabbers of the impossible, by faith in the omnipotence, fidelity, and wisdom of the Almighty Saviour who gave the command. Is there a wall in our path? By our God we will leap over it! Are there lions and scorpions in our way? We will trample them under our feet! Does a mountain bar our progress? Saying, "Be thou cast into the sea," we will march on. Soldiers of Jesus! Never surrender!
> CHARLES STUDD

PRAYER PROMPT: *Lord God, nothing can stop my prayers from reaching your ears. In the battle for revival, I will not give up, retreat, or lay down my arms until the glorious day of your outpouring.*

JULY 24

Give and Receive

> *"Give, and it will be given to you. Good measure, pressed down, shaken together, running over, will be put into your lap. For with the measure you use it will be measured back to you."*
> LUKE 6:38

Is it possible to outgive God? No! God is ready to disburse all we need in return for all we give. We worship in revival, glorifying God, but we receive back innumerable blessings. Whether we're talking about money, time, or work, if we give abundantly, we will likewise receive abundantly. If we will invest our prayers in revival praying, we may well see the greatest revival in the history of the church.

> [Give and] God, in his providence, will recompense it to you; it is lent to him, and he is not unrighteous to forget it but he will pay it again. Men shall return it into your bosom; for God often makes use of men as instruments, not only of his avenging, but of his rewarding justice. If we in a right manner give to others when they need, God will incline the hearts of others to give to us when we need, and to give liberally, good measure pressed down and shaken together. They that sow plentifully shall reap plentifully. Whom God recompenses he recompenses abundantly.
> MATTHEW HENRY

PRAYER PROMPT: *Father, may I be a channel of blessing with whatever blessings you send my way. Remind me that the chief reason for material blessings is to pass them on. May revival result in my giving in good measure, pressed down, shaken together, running over.*

JULY 25

Our Sufficiency in Christ

Not that we are sufficient in ourselves to claim anything as coming from us, but our sufficiency is from God.
2 CORINTHIANS 3:5

One of the first and best lessons we learn as Christians—often through trial and error—is our own insufficiency. Though our failures frustrate us, they're doing us a favor in exposing our need for a sufficiency not of ourselves. We thus are forced by our failures to turn to God not to make us sufficient but for him to become our sufficiency. The road to success as a Christian is the highway of brokenness.

Revival is the place where God visits us with an awareness of his all-consuming sufficiency on our behalf.

> Let us live by faith, and in the obedience thereof shroud
> ourselves under the shadow of Jehovah's wings, and
> cry unto him continually, under a deep sense of our
> utter insufficiency—and of his all-sufficiency to guide
> us by a right way all through this valley of misery,
> until he has brought us unto himself in glory!
>
> ANNE DUTTON

PRAYER PROMPT: *Father, may my insufficiency be a gateway to your sufficiency. And may the sufficiency of revival leave us able and ready to meet every need among your people.*

JULY 26

Restoration in Revival

*Restore to me the joy of your salvation, and
uphold me with a willing spirit.*
Psalm 51:12

Who among us has not needed an occasional restoring of our fellowship with God? We too easily fall into routines that have become acceptable imitations of the living faith we know we should be experiencing.

Revival is a visitation from God that brings a refreshing and restorative oil of gladness to our spirit. It reminds us from where we have come and to where we are headed in eternity. Sin is confessed, repented of, and forgiven, thus lifting the burden of guilt that so easily crushes our spirit.

Revival is the visitation of God which brings to life
Christians who have been sleeping and restores a deep
sense of God's near presence and holiness. Thence springs
a vivid sense of sin and a profound exercise of heart in
repentance, praise, and love, with an evangelistic outflow.

J. I. Packer

PRAYER PROMPT: *Lord, bring an abundance of peace and restoration during revival. Awaken us with a deep sense of your near presence.*

JULY 27

Accepting Our Divine Assignment

We are his workmanship, created in Christ Jesus for good works, which God prepared beforehand, that we should walk in them.
Ephesians 2:10

All of our past has been preparation for the work of God we're called to do. Every Christian has his or her role to play in God's work here on earth. For many, their assignment is easily known. Others struggle to know their unique usefulness to God. But it need not be. God not only prepares us for our work; he also leads us to it. Prayer, in which we confess our willingness to follow God's lead, *will* be answered. His leading is always in agreement with his Word. It's determined by our passions, talents, circumstances, and guidance from others who know us best. Our role may also be revealed during revival. Or what we thought was God's will may be shown as the wrong path. Trust God and take that next step of faith.

> God has foreordained the works to which He has called you. He has been ahead of you preparing the place to which you are coming and manipulating all the resources of the universe in order that the work you do may be a part of his whole great and gracious work.
>
> G. Campbell Morgan

PRAYER PROMPT: *Lord, I bow before you as I consider the privilege of being part of your good work as I obey your call on my life. Give me breath until my assignment is complete.*

JULY 28

Divine Rain on a Dry and Weary Land

O God, you are my God; earnestly I seek you; my soul thirsts for you; my flesh faints for you, as in a dry and weary land where there is no water.
Psalm 63:1

Revival is often compared to rain, especially in the dry and weary land we wander today. But do we really thirst for downpours from heaven? God won't send rain when the land is not dry. His help is not offered when no one is seeking it. His power is reserved for the powerless. When there is no revival, we must ask ourselves, Are we thirsty for revival?

> We lose sight of these blessed realities and get into a dry and weary land where there is no water. But the Lord in mercy again revives his work upon the heart, and then springs up afresh the longing desire to see his power and his glory. If we have once seen it, we shall long to see it again—if we have once enjoyed it, we shall desire to enjoy it again. Nor will the Lord deny the earnest desires or turn a deaf ear to the cries of his people. Every visit of his presence is a pledge for another; for whom the Lord loves, he loves to the end, and the grace that he gives he will most certainly crown with glory.
>
> J. C. Philpot

PRAYER PROMPT: *Yes, Lord, we are thirsty for revival! Send the rain to our dry desert. Bring your power and your glory. Allow us to rejoice in your presence and worship you in truth.*

JULY 29

Breaking Chains

Behold, an angel of the Lord stood next to [Peter], and a light shone in the cell. He struck Peter on the side and woke him, saying, "Get up quickly." And the chains fell off his hands.
Acts 12:7

Acts 12 opens with the apostle James dying by the sword at Herod's command. Also at Herod's command, Peter is put in chains only to be rescued by an angel who tells him: "Get up quickly." As he does so, his chains fall off. Why didn't an angel also come to James's rescue? One probable answer is that James's assignment on earth was finished, but Peter's was not. Peter went on to have a great ministry, including the writing of two New Testament letters. What we can take away from this is that we, like Peter, are invincible until our assignment here on earth is complete. Like Peter, we must "get up quickly" and see our chains fall off. Chains of fear, rejection, failure, our past. Whatever has been our chains, we cannot finish the race in them. Revival is an angel arriving to bid us to "get up quickly" and get on with our assignment.

> God will open a back door for his people to escape out of sufferings. . . . Thus he did to Peter [whose] prayers had opened heaven and God's angel opens the prison! God can either prevent a snare or break it. . . . He who can strengthen our faith can break our fetters.
>
> Thomas Watson

PRAYER PROMPT: *Father, I hear your call for me to "get up quickly" and be about your business. Prepare the way. Open back doors and front doors. Send angels, if needed. Open the prison; break the chains!*

JULY 30

Glorious Preaching!

Preach the word; be ready in season and out of season; reprove, rebuke, and exhort, with complete patience and teaching.
2 Timothy 4:2

When revival comes, it's accompanied by bold preaching that reaches the heart of the hearers. Bold preachers such as Jonathan Edwards, George Whitefield, and Evan Roberts are good examples. Their preaching strengthened believers and convicted sinners. The weakness of the contemporary church may be due to the weakness of preaching that doesn't change the lives of the congregation. Even more evidence for the need of revival.

Powerful preaching is a hallmark of true revival. Revival preachers demonstrate their commitment to the authority and sufficiency of the Scriptures, with bold, urgent, and uncompromising preaching, as they set before God's people the way of life and death. Powerful, Spirit-filled sermons concerning sin, Christ and the cross penetrate the hearts of the saved and lost alike with the realities of eternity.

Henry Blackaby

PRAYER PROMPT: *God, I pray you will raise up powerful men and women who will carry your Word to the lost. As you bring these warriors in, anoint them with the power of the Holy Spirit. Use them to capture more souls for Christ.*

JULY 31

Great Intercession for the Nations

> *"You will receive power when the Holy Spirit has come upon you, and you will be my witnesses in Jerusalem and in all Judea and Samaria, and to the end of the earth."*
> Acts 1:8

It's understandable that our intercessions are mostly focused on our own church or city. But we must pray for even greater than local revival. Our prayers must extend around the globe. Our prayers must be for the persecuted church in Asia, for the poverty-stricken churches of Haiti, and certainly to the pockets around the world where the gospel has never been heard. Ask God to give you a burden for a specific country and follow through, interceding for the furtherance of the gospel and the establishment of life-giving churches. Pray for the coming of many witnesses. Make this a long-term commitment, not a one-time prayer. What area of the world is he setting upon your heart?

> O that the rulers of some nations did but know that a free Bible is the grand secret of national prosperity; and that the surest way to make subjects orderly and obedient, is to allow a free passage to the living waters of God's Word! O that the people of some countries did but see that a free Bible is the beginning of all real freedom, and that the first liberty they should seek after, is liberty to have a Bible in every house, and a Bible in every hand!
>
> J. C. Ryle

PRAYER PROMPT: *Father, extend your outpouring to faraway lands. Bring revival to nations that have never known your presence in this way. Bring peace to warring nations, bring food through us to hungry peoples everywhere. Bring Christian education to young men and women around the globe. Leave no country unaffected by revival.*

AUGUST 1

Revival Is Not about Us

*Now to him who is able to keep you from stumbling and
to present you blameless before the presence of his glory
with great joy, to the only God, our Savior, through
Jesus Christ our Lord, be glory, majesty, dominion, and
authority, before all time and now and forever. Amen.*
Jude 24–25

It's not about what we do in revival; it's what God does. It's always first about God. Our praises, our worship, our preaching are all Christ centered. Revival eyes are singular eyes, focused on him.

As for us, who we are and what we do after revival are simply overflow. Our postrevival lives now have a renewed purpose: to give him glory, majesty, dominion, and authority now and forever.

―――――

> If we expect a great revival of religion, it seems
> to us that the eye must be taken off self entirely,
> and be fixed on the glory of God alone.
>
> James Smith

―――――

PRAYER PROMPT: *O Lord, unto you be all praise, for you are worthy! Revival is a celebration of you. We are blessed in blessing you!*

AUGUST 2

The Mystery of Revival

*This is how one should regard us, as servants of
Christ and stewards of the mysteries of God.*
1 Corinthians 4:1

Though God has revealed much to us through his Word and through nature, much remains a mystery that we assume will be revealed in eternity. But for now, God has given us enough to live our God-appointed lives. And what he has shown us is ours to steward. What we know of prayer, heaven, the church, evangelism, or any other aspect of our faith is to be shared in the arena in which we are placed. We all are different and have differing stewardships. We must be faithful in what we've been given and prayerful for our brothers and sisters as they minister their gifts.

God is not fully explainable. If he were, he would not be God. Sometimes no answers will resolve our questions. At such times we should just enjoy pondering the mystery of God and of the revival seasons he brings at various times in various ways.

There is no wonder more supernatural and divine in
the life of a believer than the mystery and ministry of
prayer . . . the hand of the child touching the arm of
the Father and moving the wheel of the universe.

A. B. Simpson

PRAYER PROMPT: *Father, so much of who you are remains a mystery. In Christ we see much about you, but it's a blessing to consider the mystery behind all the things we do not know this side of heaven, including revival. Someday all will be revealed, and we long for that day.*

AUGUST 3

God Is Not Containable

*As the heavens are higher than the earth, so are my ways
higher than your ways and my thoughts than your thoughts.*
Isaiah 55:9

We are welcome to bring our weighty problems to the Lord at any time, especially as we seek him in revival. As we lay our issues at his feet, we can know that he will tend to every situation with his answer. It may not be the answer we expect, but it will be the right answer. His ways are higher than our ways and thus can always be trusted.

No matter how serious or how numerous our problems, they will be solved as we submit them to God. The God of revival is the God who removes obstacles from our path.

As God is exalted to the right place in our lives,
a thousand problems are solved all at once.

A. W. Tozer

PRAYER PROMPT: *Father, I've seen you come through in the past when I've come to a dead end with my problem. I've learned that you are so far above any problem I have, you can solve it to my benefit. So I trust you, Lord. Your ways are higher than my ways.*

AUGUST 4

Revival Is a Worldwide Need

> *This gospel of the kingdom will be proclaimed*
> *throughout the whole world as a testimony to*
> *all nations, and then the end will come.*
> MATTHEW 24:14

Will there be an end-times revival before the return of the Lord? Or is the close of the age so near it precludes a worldwide revival?

No one knows. Even Jesus doesn't know the day or the hour of his return. But we do know that when the gospel has been proclaimed throughout the whole world, then the end will come. And right now many missionaries are helping fulfill that prophecy in parts of the world that have never been reached for the gospel.

So as we pray for revival, we pray for those tireless workers, and we pray for a hastening of that final day.

> The extension of vital Christianity through the world is not more incredible than the establishment which it has already gained in the earth; especially when we consider, that, what has been already done, is, under God, the work of a few unlettered fishermen. O that that day may appear! O that God would hasten it in his time!
>
> CHARLES SIMEON

PRAYER PROMPT: *Father, you desire all to hear the gospel, and then the end shall come. I pray today for that approaching day; may it come soon! I pray, too, for the workers in distant places, proclaiming the good news. Bring revival to their ministries; use them to awaken your church and to birth more souls into your kingdom.*

AUGUST 5

One Accord

*All these with one accord were devoting themselves
to prayer, together with the women and Mary
the mother of Jesus, and his brothers.*
Acts 1:14

God loves it when his people are in one accord. The doorway to revival is open when Christians lay aside their differences and, as in the book of Acts, devote themselves to pray. Discord can halt or even prevent revival. The time for unity is now; we don't wait until revival happens to be one with our brothers and sisters.

Love is what makes for unity. Love trumps all minor differences. If we can't say we love *all* who name Christ as Savior, we're not ready for revival.

They did this with one accord. This intimates that they were together in holy love, and that there was no quarrel nor discord among them; and those who so keep the unity of the Spirit in the bond of peace are best prepared to receive the comforts of the Holy Ghost.

Matthew Henry

PRAYER PROMPT: *Lord, my prayer echoes the prayer of Christ that your people may be in one accord, united in our love for you, resolute in praying for revival. Father, whatever it takes, bring us into unity.*

AUGUST 6

The Militant Church

We know, brothers loved by God, that he has chosen you, because our gospel came to you not only in word, but also in power and in the Holy Spirit and with full conviction.
1 THESSALONIANS 1:4–5

One of the most thrilling fruits of revival is the recharging of the church. Never was the church meant to be as weak and declining as it is today. God's church is to be on the march, in the heat of battle, winning souls, defeating the enemy. Militancy is called for.

Revival is a calling up the troops of God, enlisting and training new recruits as well as a hospital for wounded soldiers—all directed and empowered by the Holy Spirit in every case.

> The Church of God is called to be a militant Church, not a Church passive, nor a Church awake with the energy of the flesh, but a Church militant in the power and energy of the Holy Spirit.
>
> JESSIE PENN-LEWIS

PRAYER PROMPT: *Lord, what has happened to your church? Where there are divisions, end them. Where there is hurt, bring healing. Where there is timidity, bring boldness. Restore your church to the force it has been before and the force it can be again.*

AUGUST 7

Order out of Chaos

By him all things were created, in heaven and on earth, visible and invisible, whether thrones or dominions or rulers or authorities—all things were created by him and for him. And he is before all things, and in him all things hold together.
COLOSSIANS 1:16–17

All we see of creation tells us God brought it all forth. Scripture tells us that all in heaven and on earth was created *by* Christ and *for* him. Though revival in some cases may seem disorderly, the result of revival is not chaotic. God is a God of order, and the most successful believers are those who allow order in their lives. The disorderly Christian installs his or her own obstacles to success. Living the Word through the power of the Holy Spirit brings artistry and order into your life. Order brings bountiful fruit.

> What a sad world this would be, were it governed by Fate! Were its blended lights and shadows, its joys and sorrows, the result of capricious accident, or blind and wayward chance! How blessed to think that each separate occurrence which befalls me is the fulfillment of God's own immutable purpose!
>
> JOHN MACDUFF

PRAYER PROMPT: *Dear God, you are the God of order, not chaos. I pray that revival might set your church straight again by setting each of your children aright again. May we, the body of Christ, be well ordered, under your command, not disorderly or undisciplined.*

AUGUST 8

Seeing God in Life's Circumstances

We know that for those who love God all things work together for good, for those who are called according to his purpose.
ROMANS 8:28

We must see that God is sovereign in this universe. Nothing escapes him. He speaks through every life event, but we must be able to hear him above the noise surrounding those events. What may seem random to us now will be understood in eternity.

God in his wisdom determines our steps. All matters, large or small, are of his design for us. Even when the enemy charges in, God has ordained the strength we need to get through.

The life of faith is a life of trusting God in all things.

Oh, we shall see, when we arrive in heaven, how wonderful has been the wisdom that has guided us in all our journey through! You may be quite certain that all that takes place, small or great, is in that covenant that is ordered in all things and sure. Nothing is uncertain with God.

MARY WINSLOW

PRAYER PROMPT: *Father, help me see you in all things pertaining to my life. Let nothing come my way that you have not planned to work for my good. Revive in me the reality that you will see to my path and remove the boulders in my way or turn them into stepping stones leading to where you want me to be.*

AUGUST 9
Revival Changes Everything

"As I was on my way and drew near to Damascus, about noon a great light from heaven suddenly shone around me."
Acts 22:6

The coming of revival can surprise us. We pray, go about our day, time passes, and then, seemingly out of nowhere, comes revival. Revival is a divine interruption in the normal day-to-day affairs of this world. When revival comes, everything changes. The affairs of men and women subside as the affairs of God prevail. Saul of Tarsus, persecutor of Christians, found out just how suddenly God can change a person's direction. The great light that appeared to Saul came suddenly, and the change was severe. So it is with the advent of revival. Though we may be surprised by revival, we can still be ready. We can be praying. We can employ our spiritual gifts. We can be part of a thriving revival-seeking fellowship. Most of all, we can be expectant of revival, faithfully watching for the divine interruption from on high.

Revival . . . is God revealing Himself to man in awful holiness and irresistible power. It is such a manifest working of God that human personalities are overshadowed and human programs abandoned. It is man retiring into the background because God has taken the field. It is the Lord making bare His holy arm and working in extraordinary power on saint and sinner.

Arthur Wallis

PRAYER PROMPT: *Lord, come and breathe life into your church. Turn hearts toward you. Bring with revival a great wave of evangelism that sweeps multitudes into your kingdom. Overshadow our meager plans with your perfect will for revival.*

AUGUST 10

Created for Divine Love

> *In all these things we are more than conquerors through him who loved us. For I am sure that neither death nor life, nor angels nor rulers, nor things present nor things to come, nor powers, nor height nor depth, nor anything else in all creation, will be able to separate us from the love of God in Christ Jesus our Lord.*
> ROMANS 8:37–39

Do we really grasp the full impact of the gospel we believe? We learn from Paul in his epistle to the believers in Rome that we're *more* than just conquerors. We are in such a secure place that we cannot be separated from the love of our God by death, angels, rulers, things present or things to come, powers, height or depth, *nor anything else in all creation!* In revival, we stand in awe of our exalted position, seated with Christ in heavenly places. Revival is like a huge magnifying glass that enlarges the reality of the glorious gospel.

In revival the love of God is made manifest.

> The love of God to his people was as eternal as the eternity of his being, as everlasting as his uncreated nature. . . . It panted, it yearned for an outlet. It sought and found it in Christ.
> OCTAVIUS WINSLOW

PRAYER PROMPT: *Lord, as you bring revival, may we comprehend more fully the extent of your love for us. It will surely change us.*

AUGUST 11

God Keeps His Promises

God is not man, that he should lie, or a son of man, that he should change his mind. Has he said, and will he not do it? Or has he spoken, and will he not fulfill it?
NUMBERS 23:19

The promises in the Bible are gold and can be trusted. God does not offer promises he doesn't intend to keep. The Christian life is made possible by God's promises. John 3:16 and other verses guarantee our salvation.

Eternal life for those who believe is a promise, not a probability. As we go through life, we live by the sure promises of God, not one of which will fail.

The assurance of God's keeping his promises is what emboldens us to ask for and expect revival. Get hold of the promises of God for your life and for revival.

God must be true to himself. Is there any power that can possibly prevent him from fulfilling his word and oath? Surely not. . . . God *will not*, and Satan *cannot* reverse the blessing.

C. H. MACKINTOSH

PRAYER PROMPT: *God, you have put yourself out there to be trusted and tried, and you have been found faithful. You will not lie, nor will Satan prevent revival. To do so would undermine your promises.*

AUGUST 12

Our Unique Calling

As in one body we have many members, and the
members do not all have the same function.
ROMANS 12:4

We all have different callings. Happy is the Christian who accepts his or her calling with joy, even if that calling is less dramatic than others. Some are brave missionaries, leaving the comforts of home to serve in foreign lands. Others are called to stay home and work to support the workers in God's vineyard.

Nicolaus Zinzendorf, leader of the Moravian revival, said, "Preach the gospel, die, and be forgotten." But few of us want to be forgotten. Zinzendorf, despite his motto, has not been forgotten. He is remembered not so much for who he is but for the faithful work he left behind. Serve the Lord gladly whatever your post in life.

Blessed the man and woman who is able to
serve cheerfully in the second rank.
MARY SLESSOR

PRAYER PROMPT: *Father, forgive me if I've ever aspired to be something other than what you've called me to be. I am still a soldier in your army, no matter my post. Some are called to be generals, others to sergeants, and still others to privates. Let me be brave enough to assume the highest rank you have for me but content if my assigned rank is low.*

AUGUST 13

The Holy Spirit

> *He saved us, not because of works done by us in righteousness, but according to his own mercy, by the washing of regeneration and renewal of the Holy Spirit.*
> TITUS 3:5

Christ is honored in revival, but God the Son is not the only one. God the Father and God the Holy Spirit are also honored. The advent and sustaining of revival are the works of the Holy Spirit. We must never let revival fall into the hands of mere man. The Holy Spirit tends to the inner work we experience in revival. It is the Holy Spirit who renews us. Honor the Son, but do not neglect the Spirit. He is the Comforter, Teacher, and Guide into all truth. Even as we pray for revival, the Holy Spirit inhabits our prayers.

> Do not fail to honor the Holy Spirit in this great work of revival. The work is all his; beware of taking it out of his hands. . . . Pray much for his anointings; go to him as the Glorifier of Christ, as the Comforter, the Sealer, the Witness, the Earnest of his people: it is he who will apply the atoning blood, it is he who will revive your drooping graces, it is he who will fan to a flame your waning love, by unfolding the cross, and directing your heart into the love of God. Take not your eye off the love of the Spirit; his love is equal with the Father's and the Son's love. Honor him in his love, let it encourage you to draw largely from his influences, and to be filled with the Spirit.
>
> OCTAVIUS WINSLOW

PRAYER PROMPT: *Lord, as I worship you, I worship you as my heavenly Father, my Savior, and my Helper and Comforter in the person of your Holy Spirit. I implore you to send Holy Spirit-inspired revival to your people.*

AUGUST 14
Life through Spiritual Eyes

> *Having the eyes of your hearts enlightened, that you may know what is the hope to which he has called you, what are the riches of his glorious inheritance in the saints.*
> —EPHESIANS 1:18

As unbelievers, we saw and interpreted the world through our natural eyes. God, through the indwelling of his Holy Spirit, retrains our eyes so we see and interpret life's events and world events through spiritual eyes. In revival, our eyes are opened to greater spiritual realities than before. We see with a fresh compassion, a stronger sense of God's leading and a renewed passion for the Word of God. This is all the work of God, done for our benefit and for his use as we love others with the love of Christ.

> The distinctive mark of a Christian is that his eyes are upon God. On his bed by night, in his room by day, in business or at market, when his soul is in trouble, cast down, and perplexed, his eyes are upon God. From him alone all help must come; none else can reach his case. All other but the help of God is ineffectual; it leaves him where it found him, it does him no good. We are never safe except our eyes are upon God. Let our eyes be upon him, we can walk safely; let our eyes be upon the creature, we are pretty sure to slip and stumble.
>
> J. C. PHILPOT

PRAYER PROMPT: *Lord, may I see through eyes that are open to the many daily opportunities to praise you or offer help to others. I must remember that when I was born again, so too were my eyes born again.*

"My eyes are upon God!"

AUGUST 15

A Heart for the Poor

[Jesus] sat down opposite the treasury and watched the people putting money into the offering box. Many rich people put in large sums. And a poor widow came and put in two small copper coins, which make a penny. And he called his disciples to him and said to them, "Truly, I say to you, this poor widow has put in more than all those who are contributing to the offering box. For they all contributed out of their abundance, but she out of her poverty has put in everything she had, all she had to live on."
Mark 12:41–44

Revival reminds us that we live in a needy world. And what is often needed most is what we must give. Let revival awaken in each of us to give, not out of our abundance—anyone can do that—but out of our own poverty if that be our lot, remembering the widow, who by giving less than the others, gave more and enjoyed the notice of the Lord.

Feed on Christ, and then go and live your life, and it is Christ in you that lives your life, that helps the poor, that tells the truth, that fights the battle, and that wins the crown.

Phillips Brooks

PRAYER PROMPT: *Lord, when I see the needy, I see you. The poor widow who gave out of her poverty is a reminder to me that giving is more important that getting. Help me live generously. Remind me to ask, "What would the widow do?"*

AUGUST 16

Flee!

*Flee from sexual immorality. Every other sin a
person commits is outside the body, but the sexually
immoral person sins against his own body.*
1 CORINTHIANS 6:18

What God creates for humanity is for good. Satan, working through the desires of our flesh, perverts it. Christian sexuality is good. The marriage bed is undefiled. But for many, both unbelievers and Christians alike, sex has become an obsession. As with any sin, God calls us to repent of our sexual immorality. Revival has a sanctifying effect on us. We may walk away from revival free from any besetting sin, including all the perversions of sexual immorality. No one would knowingly sin against their own body, but we do so when we indulge in sexual sin.

Revival is a time to come clean with God not just about our sins in general but about any specific and personal sexual sin.

Society has become so obsessed with sex that it
seeps from all the pores of our national life.
BILLY GRAHAM

PRAYER PROMPT: *Father, you created sexuality for good, not for evil. If there is any hint of sexual immorality in me, I repent. In revival, I reject all temptations to sexual immorality.*

AUGUST 17

Take No Thought

Do not be anxious about tomorrow, for tomorrow will be anxious for itself. Sufficient for the day is its own trouble.
Matthew 6:34

Happy is the Christian who can fully entrust tomorrow to the Lord and live off of grace for today. Anxiety is the enemy of faith, constantly seeking to undermine our resolve to trust God.

When we pray for coming revival, we're not seeking to avoid tomorrow's woes, we're seeking God's power to meet tomorrow fully strengthened against whatever the day brings.

Pray first for today and leave tomorrow to God.

> Indulge no needlessly anxious thoughts. Do not allow life to degenerate into a round and vortex of weary care. God gives no prevenient store of grace. He provides no program of tomorrow's evils and trials, its needs and necessities. But when the morrow comes, the promised strength comes with it, and the traveler pursues his way with the words which the great Rest-Giver whispers in his ear, "I will make My grace sufficient for you."
>
> John MacDuff

PRAYER PROMPT: *Dear Lord, urge me to take one day at a time. You are fully trustworthy. I lay today's burdens and concerns on your altar, and I leave them there.*

AUGUST 18

Neglecting Our Gift?

Do not neglect the gift you have, which was given you by prophecy when the council of elders laid their hands on you.
1 Timothy 4:14

Every Christian has at least one spiritual gift. A gift is not something we earn. A gift of any kind is given freely but with a purpose. God gives us our gifts to use in his service. Timothy learned of his gift through the council of elders. Some believers learn of their gifts by meeting the needs they see. Others learn of their gifts through pastoral counseling. Some may learn of their gifts through revival. How we receive our gift or gifts is not important. Employing our gifts as God leads is what matters. Just as we receive freely, so must we give freely. Most important is that we not neglect our gift or gifts.

To neglect our gifts is to reject our gifts.

> Lord, quicken my faith, give me to see how deep and
> wide, and full and free is the unspeakable love which
> spared not your own Son, and therefore can spare
> every other gift, to me, your undeserving child!
>
> Susanna Spurgeon

PRAYER PROMPT: *Father, you are the Giver of many gifts, many of which are surely unclaimed by unaware believers. I pray for a renewed knowledge among your people of their gifts. Revive in each of us an awareness of our gifts and give us the courage to step out in faith and use them.*

AUGUST 19

Revival and Our Deepest Pain

*O Lord my God, I cried to you for
help, and you have healed me.*
Psalm 30:2

Is God's power great enough to heal our deepest pain? Emphatically yes! It's an insult to God to say otherwise—to underestimate his concern and power as "not enough." We must always remember that God knows pain. Jesus hung on the cross in physical pain beyond what we suffer. He, too, knew the mental and emotional pain of rejection by his own people.

Pain is not optional for the Christian. But the good news is that in revival, Christians in pain discover renewed hope—even healing. God is always present when his children cry out in pain. When revival comes, bring your pain with you and leave it there. God who is present hears and heals.

---

*As I look back over fifty years of ministry, I recall
innumerable tests, trials and times of crushing pain.
But through it all, the Lord has proven faithful,
loving, and totally true to all his promises.*

David Wilkerson

PRAYER PROMPT: *Father, one of the many reasons I need revival—and perhaps one of the reasons we all need revival—is to experience the healing of our wounds, whether self-inflicted, church inflicted, or inflicted by the sinfulness of this world. In bringing revival, Lord, bring healing!*

AUGUST 20

Revival Is a Celebration

For to me to live is Christ, and to die is gain.
PHILIPPIANS 1:21

Christians are in a constant win-win situation. To continue to live is Christ because Christ imparts his life to us. This brings us great joy while we still live. But we also win over death because death is not loss; it is gain for the believer. Our life here is but a journey whose end is in heaven with our Father and fellow worshippers.

We have known our enemy as the one who is life destroying. But now we know and are indwelt by the one who is live-*giving*, both now and in eternity.

Revival is a celebration of Christ in us and our victory over death.

Christ is the principle of my life, the end of my life, the
joy of my life. If we can say, "for to me, to live is Christ,"
we may comfortably conclude, "and to die is gain!"

THOMAS WATSON

PRAYER PROMPT: *Father, you tend to all my needs as long as I live—and even beyond this life—for to die is but to gain! What an inheritance we have!*

AUGUST 21

God's Plan

*The heart of man plans his way, but
the L*ORD *establishes his steps.*
PROVERBS 16:9

We all make plans, but as the old expression goes, if you want to make God laugh, tell him your plans. *Our* plans can be turned upside down overnight. A lost job, an unexpected medical diagnosis, a failed relationship, financial reverses—these and more can alter our carefully laid-out plans for life.

We are understandably surprised when our plans are disrupted, but God is not in the least bit alarmed. The truth is that for a submitted Christian, God always establishes our steps. He can use revival as a divine reset button in our life. After all, he knows the path that is unknown to us. When our plans are upset, we don't have to know God's revised plan in detail. It's enough that he knows.

> God's plan for each life includes the smallest affairs of that life. The things that come into our experience are not mere chance. "Chance" is not a good word; at least we may not use it to mean something that broke into our life independently of God. Nothing ever comes into our experience by chance, in the sense that it is outside of God's purpose for our life, and beyond God's control.
>
> J. R. MILLER

PRAYER PROMPT: *Lord, my life is not left to chance or random circumstances. Every step I take has been established by you, regardless of my plans. May I then walk ahead day by day, fully confident in your plan.*

AUGUST 22

Expect More!

See, I have set the land before you. Go in and take possession of the land that the LORD swore to your fathers, to Abraham, to Isaac, and to Jacob, to give to them and to their offspring after them.
DEUTERONOMY 1:8

The Israelites were given the promised land. All they had to do was take it. But because there were giants in the land, fear kept God's people from claiming what was already theirs.

In our praying for revival, are we hesitant to ask much from God? Must we rehearse all the promises again to believe, to ask big from the Lord? We can ask too small in prayer, but we cannot ask too big. In fact, God welcomes those who pray big.

Pray big about revival.

Our God will never say, you have drawn too largely; you expect too much. Impossible. It is the joy of his loving heart to answer the very largest expectations of faith.

C. H. MACKINTOSH

PRAYER PROMPT: *Lord, in some ways I tremble to ask big things of you—and yet I know you welcome and favor the large prayers of your people. So, yes, today I pray big about my needs and about revival. Visit me afresh, provoke your people to return to you, and draw lost souls to Christ!*

AUGUST 23

Our Endless Temptations

*Because he himself has suffered when tempted, he
is able to help those who are being tempted.*
HEBREWS 2:18

Are we worried about our various temptations? Do we feel guilt when we are tempted? Are we expecting to be delivered from all temptation by experiencing revival? Such a belief will only lead to disappointment.

Temptation is not sin. Even Jesus was tempted. According to the author of Hebrews, Jesus, having been tempted himself, is able to help us in our hours of temptation.

Revival may strengthen us against certain temptations, but it will not remove all temptations forever. As long as we're in this fallen body, we will be tempted, and often the more mature we become as believers, the more severe the temptations.

> I have explained that you might expect to be tempted to the end of your life, that the nearer you live to God, the more you will be tempted. The presence of temptation in your life is not a proof of deterioration, but the contrary, for the more you know of God on the one hand the more you will know of Satan's temptation, on the other hand.
>
> F. B. MEYER

PRAYER PROMPT: *Lord, the irony of spiritual growth is that we will likely face even greater temptations than in the youthful days of our faith. But, like Jesus, we can resist by declaring the Word of God. Revive my dedication to you in each temptation I face.*

AUGUST 24

The Enemy of Revival Is Self

*A man without self-control is like a city
broken into and left without walls.*
Proverbs 25:28

As joyful as revival is, there may be a letdown when the revival ends. We are not allowed to stay on the mountaintop forever. We must descend into the valleys, bringing the fruit of revival with us.

The biggest letdown may be when we surmise that the entrance of self has played a part in the ebb of revival. As long as Christ is honored, the Father is glorified, and the Holy Spirit is allowed to lead, revival continues.

But seldom does it go on for extended times as eventually the flesh, the self, the carnal nature asserts itself, and man moves to the center of attention.

The glory of extended revival is the continued presence of God and the diminished presence of man.

> Whenever self-effort, self-glory, self-seeking
> or self-promotion enters into the work of
> revival, then God leaves us to ourselves.
>
> Sadhu Sundar Singh

PRAYER PROMPT: *God, when you send revival, help us keep our hands off your work. May self-seeking give way to Christ exalting.*

AUGUST 25

What Is Sin?

*Whoever knows the right thing to do and
fails to do it, for him it is sin.*
JAMES 4:17

What happy lives we could live if there were no sin. But there *is* sin. It impedes our growth as Christians. As for revival, sin hinders revival from coming and works to shut it down when it arrives.

Sin takes many forms. For some Christians certain activities are sinful. While for others, another activity is sinful.

The good news is that God has an answer for sin: repentance, confession, and the appropriation of forgiveness. Satan's goal is for us to wallow in our sin. And even when we are forgiven, he urges us to question our standing with God.

True freedom is keeping short accounts with God. His forgiveness is a never-ending river. It will never run dry. Therefore, we must not let sin reign in our lives.

Always, always, always, take your sin to the cross and leave it there.

Whatever weakens your reason, impairs the tenderness
of your conscience, obscures your sense of God, or takes
off the delight for spiritual things, whatever increases the
authority of your body over your mind, that thing is sin.

SUSANNA WESLEY

PRAYER PROMPT: *Lord, sin hinders or shuts down revival. Teach us all to be sensitive to the moments our flesh is drawn to it, give us the power to deny it, and help us keep sin far away from revival.*

AUGUST 26

When God Says No

> *[Jesus] withdrew from them about a stone's throw, and knelt down and prayed, saying, "Father, if you are willing, remove this cup from me. Nevertheless, not my will, but yours, be done." And there appeared to him an angel from heaven, strengthening him.*
> LUKE 22:41–43

Jesus prayed for the cup of crucifixion to pass from him if God the Father was willing. But we know God's will was for Jesus to drink from that bitter cup. Likewise, we often pray for specific needs and get a no from God. Disappointment or questioning God can follow. But if we could see from God's perspective, we'd understand that God's will works out in our behalf *ultimately*. For every no God gives us, there's a reason—perhaps a reason we'll never know this side of heaven. The same is true for every yes God gives us. In revival, we learn that God is trustworthy in all circumstances. He doesn't ignore our prayers; he, in fact, works out his will in ways that are better than what we had asked for. Faith sees this and is grateful.

> We put our cares into God's hands in prayer, and they do not seem to become less. We think there has been no answer to our supplications. But all the while an unseen hand has been quietly shaping, adjusting, and disentangling for us the complex affairs of our life which made us anxious. We are not conscious of it but our prayers have been receiving continual answer in peace and blessing.
>
> J. R. MILLER

PRAYER PROMPT: *Father, I cast all my cares to you. Sometimes they hinder me from revival living and praying for revival. May your unseen hand shape my life through both victories and trials.*

AUGUST 27

Revival Contentment

*Godliness with contentment is great gain, for we
brought nothing into the world, and we cannot
take anything out of the world. But if we have food
and clothing, with these we will be content.*
1 Timothy 6:6–8

If revival descends on us during a season of discontentedness, that will soon change as the presence of God becomes so real to us that discontent becomes impossible.

God's presence brings God's will, and his will is contentment for every believer because contentment is a sign of resting in the Lord. One of the takeaways from revival is just that: a simple but sure rest in the providence of God. What God wills we accept with joy. What God does not will, we reject.

The goal is always the contentment of rest.

Christian contentment is that sweet, inward, quiet, gracious
frame of spirit, which freely submits to and delights in
God's wise and fatherly disposal in every condition.

Jeremiah Burroughs

PRAYER PROMPT: *Lord, visit me with your presence and help me find total contentment in you. No matter what situation you have in store for me, I believe you will supply anything I need.*

AUGUST 28

Compromise Is Defeat

> *Shadrach, Meshach, and Abednego answered and said to the king, "O Nebuchadnezzar, we have no need to answer you in this matter. If this be so, our God whom we serve is able to deliver us from the burning fiery furnace, and he will deliver us out of your hand, O king. But if not, be it known to you, O king, that we will not serve your gods or worship the golden image that you have set up."*
> DANIEL 3:16–18

Men and women of God must be like Shadrach, Meshach, and Abednego in their unwillingness to compromise their faith. Offers to compromise come from the world, the enemy, and even from well-meaning friends. Compromise is tempting; otherwise it would be easy to say no. These tempting offers can come in fancy wrapping with a bright bow on top. Most of our offers to compromise come in our daily lives, but even in revival, we may be faced with compromise. We may be convicted of some activity God wants us to forgo. It may be a relationship that must end or forgiveness that must be offered. If we would see our lives changed through revival, we must commit all. No compromise.

> The gospel of Christ admits of no compromise. It demands our all. If it required less, it would be unworthy of its great author and finisher. I rejoice that it requires all. This is its glory.
>
> JARED WATERBURY

PRAYER PROMPT: *God, your gospel is complete and so good, there's never a reason for compromising my faith. What is there of value that I would find worthy of compromising for? Nothing!*

AUGUST 29

The *Other* Revival

"Lead us not into temptation, but deliver us from evil."
MATTHEW 6:13

Just as there are revivals among God's people, there also exist—especially in our day—revivals of evil. In certain epochs of our world's story, evil appeared subtly. But in our cultural moment, evil is obvious to those with eyes to see. The turning of many to the occult, Internet pornography, and entertainment with demonic themes is tragic. Visiting or participating in them will only lead the unsuspecting person away from Christ.

But revival among God's people brings a person closer to Christ.

As we pray *for* revival, we also must pray *against* the forces of evil in our communities. When Jesus taught his disciples to pray, the prayer was short, but it included the important phrase that God would "lead us not into temptation, but deliver us from evil." More than ever, that, along with prayer for revival, should be our plea.

> Our . . . duty is to pray night and day that God
> may intervene, and drive back the flood of evil
> which seems bursting on our country.
>
> J. C. RYLE

PRAYER PROMPT: *God, I pray against any revival of evil. Surround your people with a hedge of protection. Keep us safe from the designs of the enemy. Bring true revival of faith and healing to replace the revival of violence, occultism, and sexual immorality.*

AUGUST 30

The Faithfulness of God

He will cover you with his pinions, and under his wings you will find refuge; his faithfulness is a shield and buckler.
Psalm 91:4

God proves he cares for us by his continued faithfulness. Among his many attributes is his loyalty to his people. God cannot, in fact, ever act unfaithfully. Thus, we can put our full trust in him. In praying for revival, we can know our prayers will be answered. We know that God answers prayers that are according to his will. And is it his will to bring revival? Yes, of course! God desires revival more than we do. But he knows revival will only come to a desperate people. Revival will mean nothing to a self-satisfied people. He comes for the insatiable. God's faithfulness toward the desperate prayers of his children is why we can trust him in all things, including attending to our prayers.

> It has ever been one of the brightest traits in Jehovah's character, that he has proved himself faithful notwithstanding the faithlessness of his people. This rock has never been shaken, this foundation cannot be removed, this truth cannot be invalidated, that our God is a faithful God. In every age of the world, in all the trying circumstances in which the church has been placed, and in every individual believer's experience God has been found faithful.
>
> James Smith

PRAYER PROMPT: *Lord, you are faithful. Despite my own occasional faithlessness, you remain true. With you, there is no variance in your commitment to me. As I have prayed for needed revival, you will surely respond in faithfulness.*

AUGUST 31

The Joys of Private Prayer

"When you pray, go into your room and shut the door and pray to your Father who is in secret. And your Father who sees in secret will reward you."
MATTHEW 6:6

In most revivals there is much corporate prayer—and rightly so. We know where two or three are gathered, Christ is there also. But corporate prayer must not replace private prayer where nobody sees or hears but God. We must be careful to make time to pray alone. For many, this is accomplished by having a set prayer time every day and a specific private place to pray and worship.

To neglect private prayer is to delay the blessings of revival. What keeps you from regular, private prayer? Whatever it is, be done with it.

It is impossible to live the life of a disciple without definite times of secret prayer. You will find that the place to enter in is in your business, as you walk along the streets, in the ordinary ways of life, when no one dreams you are praying, and the reward comes openly, a revival here, a blessing there.

OSWALD CHAMBERS

PRAYER PROMPT: *Lord, hear my prayer as I call out to you in the private place, just you and me. Speak to me as I quiet myself and listen for your voice.*

SEPTEMBER 1

To Be Forgiven of Much Is to Love Much

"I tell you, her sins, which are many, are forgiven—for she loved much. But he who is forgiven little, loves little."
Luke 7:47

During revival, many Christians feel a deep conviction of sin. Some cry out for mercy and receive it. Revival can reveal the depths of our sin that we had not realized before the revival.

Confession and repentance bring a wonderful awareness of God's overwhelming graciousness. But rest assured, God's mercy—though free to us—cost God his only Son.

We do well to be thankful to God, but with every conviction of sin, may we be reminded that our sins were not casually forgiven. A price was paid—a price none of us can ever repay.

> The deeper one's sense of sin is, the livelier is his gratitude for pardon and saving mercy. . . . In like manner the deeper one's sense of sin, the profounder will be his humility; and humility is the King's highway to holiness and happiness and heaven.
>
> William S. Plumer

PRAYER PROMPT: *Father, may I never forget or take for granted your love for me as shown in Christ. May I be one who loves much because I have been forgiven much.*

SEPTEMBER 2

Revival Is Not Entertainment

Let there be no filthiness nor foolish talk nor crude joking, which are out of place, but instead let there be thanksgiving.
EPHESIANS 5:4

If some come to revival expecting to be entertained, they will either be disappointed or convicted. What happens in revival has no relationship to performance. There are no entertainers during revival. There is only One for whom we applaud, and that is our Lord and Master.

Neither is there foolish talk, sensuality, or mockery during revival. There is abundant joy, but never is it manifested as anything unholy. Revival is easily disrupted or ended when the spirit of worldly entertainment creeps in. Revival isn't a time for consuming futile amusements; it's a time to be consumed by the living God.

We should come to church not anticipating entertainment—but expecting the high and holy manifestation of God's presence.

A. W. TOZER

PRAYER PROMPT: *Lord, there is joy in revival—great joy—but I pray for a revival free of Christian celebrities and entertainment antics.*

SEPTEMBER 3

Spiritual Gifts—Which Are Yours?

*Each has his own gift from God, one of
one kind and one of another.*
1 CORINTHIANS 7:7

We ask for too little in prayer. God's storehouse is always full. His supply of revival life never wanes. Why then do we ask for small things—often mere comforts—when much more and much better await our prayers?

Have we sought God for our spiritual gifts? They, too, await our asking for and by faith receiving. Consider what the exercise of your gifts might mean for the body of Christ. If you know your gifts, use them. If you don't know your gifts, ask. The body of Christ functions best when each one employs his or her own spiritual gift, and revival is all the sweeter when gifts are being used in full measure.

Bowing daily before a God of infinite power and love, in whose hands are unsearchable riches [most Christians] never ask for anything but fleeting earthly comforts and worldly trinkets! They ask only for things for their bodies, or to beautify their homes making no requests for the heavenly and spiritual gifts that God has for their souls! We should learn to ask for the best things in all God's treasure house!

J. R. MILLER

PRAYER PROMPT: *Dear Lord, thank you for my spiritual gifts. Use them, I pray, to your best advantage. Reveal to me any gifts I may be unaware of.*

SEPTEMBER 4

A Summons to More Prayer

> *[Jesus] told them a parable to the effect that they*
> *ought always to pray and not lose heart.*
> Luke 18:1

When we pray, we must expect results. But we must also remember that revival comes on God's timetable, not ours. We can never become discouraged when revival tarries. It will come in due time. In the meantime, we must continue in prayer, asking God to strengthen us and give us patience. Under no circumstances are we to give in and become slothful in prayer. The longer revival delays, the more determined our prayers should be.

> Oh brother, pray; in spite of Satan, pray; spend hours
> in prayer; rather neglect friends than not pray; rather
> fast, and lose breakfast, dinner, tea, and supper—and
> sleep too—than not pray. And we must not talk about
> prayer, we must pray in right earnest. The Lord is
> near. He comes softly while the virgins slumber.
>
> Andrew Bonar

PRAYER PROMPT: *Lord, I admit that we long for revival. Nevertheless, no matter how delayed revival is in our eyes, we know it's right on time according to your schedule. Till then, we continue to pray expectantly.*

SEPTEMBER 5

Revival Is God Filling His Vessels

*You prepare a table before me in the presence of my
enemies; you anoint my head with oil; my cup overflows.*
PSALM 23:5

We all experience some degree of spiritual exhaustion at one time or another. Even Jesus took his disciples aside to rest. Revival likewise recharges us. We experience a fresh touch from God that fills our hungry hearts. But we don't have to wait for revival to be filled. God supplies fresh power in response to our need and our asking.

Don't delay in asking and receiving a touch from God. The banquet table is prepared.

If you are starving and can find nothing to satisfy your
hunger, then come. Come and you will be filled.
JEANNE GUYON

PRAYER PROMPT: *Lord, when you bring revival, you bring a banquet! I come, Lord. Fill me afresh!*

SEPTEMBER 6

Revival and the Will of God

The Lord is not slow to fulfill his promise as some count slowness, but is patient toward you, not wishing that any should perish, but that all should reach repentance.
2 Peter 3:9

We often think of the results of revival in our own life. But revival is like a rock thrown into a lake—the ripples continue well beyond where the rock plunges into the water. Local revival can spread to wider boundaries.

During the Welsh revival of 1904, the movement of God spread quickly from village to village. The prayers for revival of just a few intercessors can cause the ripple effect to spread even to parts unknown.

The will of God is the blessings of revival to reach many, not a few.

Prayer is not conquering God's reluctance,
but taking hold of God's willingness.
Phillips Brooks

PRAYER PROMPT: *Lord, when you send revival, send it with ripples that reach beyond human boundaries. Make waves, Lord!*

SEPTEMBER 7

Guarding Our Time

Man is like a breath; his days are like a passing shadow.
PSALM 144:4

Time waits for no one. We all have twenty-four hours in a day. How we spend it is up to us. Do we use it by "killing time"? Or do we invest it in revival living? Do we allow ourselves to become spiritually lazy, or do we press on with renewed Holy Spirit energy, taking rest periods only when we're tired?

Living for God's glory means guarding our time, spending it carefully as if it were money. We are all moving toward eternity. May we do so with wisdom regarding our hours, weeks, and years.

O God, impress upon me the value of time and give
regulation to all my thoughts and to all my actions. O God,
help me to live for your glory. As the years roll over me,
may I withdraw my affections from time, and feel that in
moving through the world, I am moving toward eternity!

THOMAS CHALMERS

PRAYER PROMPT: *Lord, you are apart from time, but I am not. Help me as I make time my ally, not my foe. Teach me how to be a good steward of my days on earth, even as I reach out toward eternity.*

SEPTEMBER 8

Preparing for the Wedding

Let us rejoice and exult and give him the glory, for the marriage of the Lamb has come, and his Bride has made herself ready.
REVELATION 19:7

No matter how long we've been a Christian, we're all still in the process of preparation for the day when the church is joined to Christ as the bride to her Bridegroom.

Revival gives us as near a foretaste of that day as God will allow. The resplendent joy, the overwhelming sense of gratitude, the feasting at the wedding banquet—all are awaiting us on that day. But until then, we have revival to whet our appetite.

> Life here on earth is creating an environment where God is preparing a bride for his Son. Suppose that any of the past transgressions of the Lamb's wife could be brought against her on that marriage day, any one instance of unfaithfulness to her promised betrothal, would it not be sufficient to prevent the marriage, mar the wedding supper, and drive the bride away for very shame? No, there is no truth in God's word more certain than the complete forgiveness of sins, and the presentation of the Church to Christ at the great day faultless before the presence of his glory, with exceeding joy.
>
> J. C. PHILPOT

PRAYER PROMPT: *Dear Lord, what a wedding day that shall be! May we all consider your revival to be a time of preparation. Let us rejoice and exult now, giving you the glory!*

SEPTEMBER 9

A Second Wind

*They who wait for the Lord shall renew their strength;
they shall mount up with wings like eagles; they shall
run and not be weary; they shall walk and not faint.*
Isaiah 40:31

One beautiful blessing of revival is the "reviving" of tired Christians who long for a second wind. They have run their race well, and now they long for the strength to continue, but they despair for their lack of spiritual energy.

When God comes in revival power, that power is available to all who will receive it—and freely so. God sees the weary seasoned believers with weak knees and delights in renewing their strength.

Are you spiritually exhausted? God sees you. He will give you the strength you need for the tasks ahead. You shall indeed walk and not faint.

> While even the young and the strong who depend
> on their own strength or resolution will utterly fall,
> if you depend on God you will renew your strength.
> Upward, higher and higher, you shall mount in faith
> and hope. Onward in the heavenly race you shall run
> with patience and perseverance. You shall neither faint
> nor grow weary until you reach the City of the Living
> God. Oh, that you would pray, and pray perpetually.
>
> George Everard

PRAYER PROMPT: *Father, you are the God of second wind and second chances. Renew my waning strength. I long to walk again and not faint. Daily I wait upon you, Lord, for your empowerment.*

SEPTEMBER 10

A New Song

He put a new song in my mouth, a song of praise to our God.
PSALM 40:3

The mercies of God are new every morning and are ours for the taking. With each new day and each new mercy, we find a new song—a new praise to our God—in our mouth.

Revival, like each new morning, brings with it fresh mercies and new songs of praise.

Note that the psalmist tells us God is the one who puts the new song in our mouth; we need only open our mouths and release the song.

The fresh mercies of revival call for new songs of praise. What mercies has God extended to you this week? This month? This year? Sing out your new song.

Fresh mercies, especially such as we never
before received, call for new songs.
MATTHEW HENRY

PRAYER PROMPT: *Father, as I open my mouth to declare your new mercies, put a song on my lips—a song of praise to you.*

SEPTEMBER 11

Being Jesus to Others

> *"Then the King will say to those on his right, 'Come, you who are blessed by my Father, inherit the kingdom prepared for you from the foundation of the world. For I was hungry and you gave me food, I was thirsty and you gave me drink, I was a stranger and you welcomed me, I was naked and you clothed me, I was sick and you visited me, I was in prison and you came to me.' Then the righteous will answer him, saying, 'Lord, when did we see you hungry and feed you, or thirsty and give you drink? And when did we see you a stranger and welcome you, or naked and clothe you? And when did we see you sick or in prison and visit you?' And the King will answer them, 'Truly, I say to you, as you did it to one of the least of these my brothers, you did it to me.'"*
> MATTHEW 25:34–40

Revival changes our hearts. Though we may have lived for our own interests, now we see Jesus in the homeless and the hopeless. We see him in the hungry, in the sick, and in the prisoner. In seeing, we are moved to action. For what we have seen in revival, we now take to those outside the church walls. In so doing this to Jesus's "brothers," we are doing it to Jesus himself.

> A good many are kept out of the service of Christ, deprived of the luxury of working for God, because they are trying to do some great thing. Let us be willing to do little things. And let us remember that nothing is small in which God is the source.
> D. L. MOODY

PRAYER PROMPT: *God, you require so little of us—things we ought to be doing anyway. And yet you require so much of us—a fully surrendered life. Let me be useful in small things, however I can be used.*

SEPTEMBER 12

Turning the World Upside Down

When they could not find them, they dragged Jason and some of the brothers before the city authorities, shouting, "These men who have turned the world upside down have come here also."
ACTS 17:6

Jason had taken in Paul and Silas, but a mob raided Jason's house and took Jason before the authorities, complaining that the men he harbored had "turned the world upside down."

Does today's church create similar complaints? In revival, there can be a fresh turning of the world upside down. Surely our lives will be turned upside down and, hopefully, our churches as well.

Of course, we know that in turning the world upside down, we're really setting the world right side up again. Be prepared, for surely in revival *your* world will be upended.

> The chief danger of the Church today is that it is trying to get on the same side as the world, instead of turning the world upside down. Our Master expects us to accomplish results, even if they bring opposition and conflict. Anything is better than compromise, apathy, and paralysis. God give to us an intense cry for the old-time power of the Gospel and the Holy Ghost!
>
> A. B. SIMPSON

PRAYER PROMPT: *Lord, what can I do to see my world turned upside down? Yes, pray for revival! If ever an event can turn us upside down, it's revival brought by your hand.*

SEPTEMBER 13

Revival Opens Our Eyes

*Open my eyes, that I may behold
wondrous things out of your law.*
PSALM 119:18

When God uses revival to open our eyes, what do we see? We become aware of God's majesty evidenced in his presence. We become aware of our smallness, our weakness, and our poverty in light of his riches. We see needs like never before. Our heart is at once both troubled by the pain of others and comforted in our own pain. Opened eyes result in an opened heart.

When our eyes are opened to the wondrous things from God's law, we remember the words of Jesus: "You shall love the Lord your God with all your heart and with all your soul and with all your mind. This is the great and first commandment. And a second is like it: You shall love your neighbor as yourself. On these two commandments depend all the Law and the Prophets" (Matt. 22:37–40).

You are never used of God to bring blessing until God has
opened your eyes and made you see things as they are.

ALAN REDPATH

PRAYER PROMPT: *Father, open my eyes to see wondrous things out of your law. May revival remove my blinders.*

SEPTEMBER 14

Revival and Church Leadership

Brothers, if anyone is caught in any transgression, you who are spiritual should restore him in a spirit of gentleness. Keep watch on yourself, lest you too be tempted.
GALATIANS 6:1

Our present era may be one of the saddest in church history. Scandals seem to abound. Pastors are involved in sexual immorality, financial mismanagement, and some are even embracing false teaching. Revival can be a new beginning for all who repent of their sins, but it is only a beginning. The fruit of revival in a failed church leader will be seen soon enough. So will a failure to live out the fresh chance revival offers to those caught up in sin. David fell into a sexually immoral sin by his own choice; yet he repented of his sin and God used him.

At this crucial time, we need to pray for God to raise up new righteous leaders in the church and restore repentant church leaders to usefulness. May revival bring about godly leadership in God's churches.

The religious revival we ought to long for, pray for, and work for is a revival that shall affect the morals and ethics of the Church as well as its worship and religious sentiment; and ennoble the whole life of those who bear the Christian name.

ROBERT DALE

PRAYER PROMPT: *Father, I pray for church leaders everywhere. Draw them close to you, keep them from temptation, protect them from burnout. Bring supporters like Aaron who can hold up the weary hands of leaders like Moses among us.*

SEPTEMBER 15

The Fervency of Revival

Do not be slothful in zeal, be fervent in spirit, serve the Lord.
ROMANS 12:11

Why is prayer an oft-repeated theme on these pages? Is it not because of our neediness in light of God's abundant provision? Are we not instructed by God to present our needs to him with the promise that he will answer? But how then do we pray?

With fervency! Not only fervency in prayer but also fervency in living. The Christian life need never be dull as long as God is active in our lives.

Don't become complacent with repeated urges to pray, for prayer is our gateway to the Father. It pierces the walls of heaven. Fervent prayer brings revival.

> It is only fervency in prayer, which will make
> a man prevalent with God. Fervent prayer hits
> the mark, and pierces the walls of Heaven!
> FREDERICK MARSH

PRAYER PROMPT: *Lord, give me a heart for fervent prayer and a zeal for living. May my fervency be known in my service to you. Multiply my effectiveness for you, Father.*

SEPTEMBER 16

"I'll Believe It When I See It"

Now Thomas, one of the twelve, called the Twin, was not with them when Jesus came. So the other disciples told him, "We have seen the Lord." But he said to them, "Unless I see in his hands the mark of the nails, and place my finger into the mark of the nails, and place my hand into his side, I will never believe." Eight days later, his disciples were inside again, and Thomas was with them. Although the doors were locked, Jesus came and stood among them and said, "Peace be with you." Then he said to Thomas, "Put your finger here, and see my hands; and put out your hand, and place it in my side. Do not disbelieve, but believe." Thomas answered him, "My Lord and my God!" Jesus said to him, "Have you believed because you have seen me? Blessed are those who have not seen and yet have believed."
John 20:24–29

When it comes to revival, many are doubters like Thomas. If revival comes, they will believe even though they may not have had eyes to see it coming. The Lord Jesus, who was gracious to Thomas, is gracious still and will show himself to even the most skeptical, if they will finally acknowledge what they have denied. Then, like Thomas, they will surely declare, "My Lord and my God."

If we are satisfied with our state . . . if, like the members of the church at Laodicea, we suppose that we are rich, and . . . have need of nothing . . . can you doubt the need of a revival? Are not you the strongest proofs of this necessity?
John Angell James

PRAYER PROMPT: *Lord, let us not doubt like Thomas but instead be fervent, expectant believers like John, Mary, Mary Magdalene, or like the brave Stephen who showed only grace toward his executioners.*

SEPTEMBER 17

Not I, but Christ

I have been crucified with Christ. It is no longer I who live, but Christ who lives in me. And the life I now live in the flesh I live by faith in the Son of God, who loved me and gave himself for me.
GALATIANS 2:20

The need for revival often becomes apparent when we see that dry religion has replaced a vital relationship with the living Christ. We must cast aside the dry bones of religion and return to true fellowship with our living God. From God's point of view, his relationship with us is always alive. If there's a broken connection, it's on our end, not his.

Revival is a reviving of that intimate relationship.

———

True Christianity is not merely the believing a certain set of theological propositions. It is to live in daily personal communication with an actual living person, Jesus the Son of God!

J. C. RYLE

———

PRAYER PROMPT: *Father, I praise you that Christ lives in me, and I no longer call my life my own. I live now by my faith in your Son, who loved me and gave himself for me. I lay aside the dry bones of religion and take up the new life of Christ.*

SEPTEMBER 18

Hearing God in the Silence

Behold, the LORD passed by, and a great and strong wind tore the mountains and broke in pieces the rocks before the LORD, but the LORD was not in the wind. And after the wind an earthquake, but the LORD was not in the earthquake. And after the earthquake a fire, but the LORD was not in the fire. And after the fire the sound of a low whisper.
1 KINGS 19:11–12

Elijah may have been expecting God to speak through the great and strong wind or perhaps in an earthquake or fire. But no, God spoke with a low whisper. God still does that. Sometimes we expect revival to be noisy (and sometimes it may be), but also sometimes revival can be found in the low whisper of God.

Be careful how you look for God in revival. Look not to the noise but to God's low whisper.

When God speaks he speaks so loudly that all the voices of the world seem dumb. And yet when God speaks he speaks so softly that no one hears the whisper but yourself.

HENRY DRUMMOND

PRAYER PROMPT: *Father, it's easy to hear you when you speak loudly, but less so when you whisper. And yet when you whisper, it's like you're revealing a secret or reminding me of your love. I will listen closely, Lord, for your gentle whisper.*

SEPTEMBER 19

The Treasure Hidden in the Field

"The kingdom of heaven is like treasure hidden in a field, which a man found and covered up. Then in his joy he goes and sells all that he has and buys that field."
Matthew 13:44

The fully surrendered Christian quickly discovers the treasure hidden in the field we call the kingdom of heaven. He or she also finds that selling all to have this treasure is worth the cost.

Not all, however, seek the treasure in the field. It takes full surrender. It takes selling *all*.

Revival offers us fresh perspective on how valuable the kingdom of heaven truly is. Surrendering all for it then becomes easy.

> Christ's riches are unsearchable, and the gospel
> is the field this treasure is hidden in.
> Thomas Goodwin

PRAYER PROMPT: *O Lord! You have hidden treasure in the field for me. Through the power of the gospel, you have given me eyes to see just how valuable your kingdom is. Thank you, Father, for such riches, reserved for the surrendered soul.*

SEPTEMBER 20

An Oxymoron: Revival Is Free, but There's a Cost

"Whoever does not take his cross and follow me is not worthy of me. Whoever finds his life will lose it, and whoever loses his life for my sake will find it."
MATTHEW 10:38–40

In God's economy, the lost life is the found life. We may find in revival a small measure of that found life. We find that this God who makes his presence known is worth losing what this earthly life offers.

In revival, we may well be faced with making a decision about our future. This decision may be costly, but it is worth the experience of his presence and power. In the short run, it feels painful. In the long run, when we experience the tidal wave of his peace and empowerment and nearness, it feels like the nothing but gain.

> If you look up into his face and say, "Yes, Lord, whatever it costs," at that moment he'll flood your life with his presence and power.
>
> ALAN REDPATH

PRAYER PROMPT: *Lord, this is my prayer for revival: "Whatever it costs!"*

SEPTEMBER 21

Dwelling on the Other Side of the Grave

We were buried therefore with him by baptism into death, in order that, just as Christ was raised from the dead by the glory of the Father, we too might walk in newness of life.
ROMANS 6:4

Many Christians understand that baptism is a picture of having died, going down into the grave and rising to resurrection life. But we often only live out the first half of that truth: we die, but we don't rise again to live out the second part of that biblical truth.

Revival is like that. If we don't come away from revival to live a life of resurrection power, we've missed a key part of revival. The truth of revival is near to the truth of Romans 6.

It behooves every Christian to set aside the old buried life and live out of the new revived resurrection life. We must live on the other side of the grave—the resurrection side.

> O! whence comes this new life! surely it could never be struck out of vows, resolutions, and Christless endeavors, nor hammered out of the united force of the whole powers of the soul, called forth together as in a solemn day. But they have been planted together with Christ, therefore they rise up with him, in the likeness of his resurrection. . . . They now bring forth fruit unto God.
>
> THOMAS BOSTON

PRAYER PROMPT: *Lord, thank you for resurrection life! I praise you that not only did I die with Christ; I also rose with him. And this is your provision in a victorious life.*

SEPTEMBER 22

"I Want You"

We love because he first loved us.
1 JOHN 4:19

Revival is a vivid reminder of the intense love God has for each of us. The presence of God is the presence of a loving father, a shepherd who has left the ninety-nine in search of the one missing sheep. We each have been that wandering sheep.

If we could fully open our eyes to the extent of God's love, it would revolutionize our lives. In revival and out of it, the repeated message of heaven is God's declaration, "I love you."

Pray for revival eyes to see God's love today and ears to hear his words—"I want you."

The most blessed words God speaks to a person; what a miracle of love it is that God should love us when there was nothing lovely in us. We were rather fit to be loathed than loved! We had something in us to provoke God's fury, but nothing to excite his love. What love, passing understanding, was it that Christ should die for sinners!

THOMAS WATSON

PRAYER PROMPT: *God, it is the miracle of the ages that you should first love us, rather than us first loving you. Thank you for the love I know on this side of heaven as I eagerly await an even greater comprehension of your love in eternity.*

SEPTEMBER 23

Revival Is Inviting God into Your Present Need

Casting all your anxieties on him, because he cares for you.
1 PETER 5:7

God's care for us is seen in his invitation to cast all our anxieties on him. He can carry them all and not feel the burden that weighs so heavily on us. But how do we *do* this casting of our anxieties on him? As with so much in the Christian life, it's by faith. Faith is the muscle we use to lift our burden and cast it on the Lord. When faith comes in, anxiety exits.

Revival reminds us who God is, how strong and available he is. And so a revived heart invites God to lift our anxieties.

> The beginning of anxiety is the end of faith, and the beginning of true faith is the end of anxiety.
>
> GEORGE MUELLER

PRAYER PROMPT: *As always, Lord, today I cast all my anxieties on you because you care for me.*

SEPTEMBER 24

Spiritual Resources Trump Natural Resources

Just as day was breaking, Jesus stood on the shore; yet the disciples did not know that it was Jesus. Jesus said to them, "Children, do you have any fish?" They answered him, "No." He said to them, "Cast the net on the right side of the boat, and you will find some." So they cast it, and now they were not able to haul it in, because of the quantity of fish.
JOHN 21:4–6

What were the disciples thinking? Jesus wasn't with them, so they opted to return to their fishing boats—only to come up empty. Disappointment on top of disappointment. But then, Jesus came along and instructed them to cast their nets on the right side where, sure enough, their nets were overwhelmed by fish.

It's common for us to toil along according to our own natural wisdom and fail, only to have Jesus come along and give us instructions that trump our natural inclinations. Revival is like that. We have labored long and brought forth little for the Lord. But then in his time, God sends the revival we've been praying for ,and what we had hoped for is now ours—but not by our own power. Trust in God and his resources today, not your own calculations.

It is just Christ-like to turn our total defeat into unprecedented success, through the giving of his Word and the believing of it.

JAMES SMITH

PRAYER PROMPT: *Father, you see how often I exhaust my own resources to accomplish what only you can do. Today, I cast my net on the side of your choosing.*

SEPTEMBER 25

Laying Aside Every Weight

Therefore, since we are surrounded by so great a cloud of witnesses, let us also lay aside every weight, and sin which clings so closely, and let us run with endurance the race that is set before us.
HEBREWS 12:1

Sin is a heavy weight in our lives. It clings to us, slowing us down in the race before us. It robs us of revival.

Some sins have been with us for a long time; others are more recent sad additions. But the author of Hebrews encourages us by reminding us that we're surrounded by a cloud of sympathetic witnesses, thus enabling us to lay aside the weighty sins and run the race with endurance.

We can do this. We can rely on the power of God to keep us.

God expects nothing from Alan Redpath but failure. I, as a man, am no different today from the day before I was converted. Five minutes after I've finished preaching I would be capable of committing any sin imaginable but for the grace of God. Alan Redpath is no different as a man from what he was as a youngster. And the sins that beset him then beset him now, were it not for a constant, continual dependence upon the blood of Jesus, and the grace of God, and the power of the Holy Spirit to keep me.

ALAN REDPATH

PRAYER PROMPT: *Lord, my continual dependence is on the blood of Christ, your grace, and the power of the Holy Spirit. These three are my life jackets in the storm that is this life.*

SEPTEMBER 26

Perpetual Revival

And the disciples were filled with joy and with the Holy Spirit.
Acts 13:52

What is God's desire for our filling with the Holy Spirit? As much as we're filled with joy and the Holy Spirit during revival, this doesn't mean that our day-to-day life shouldn't also be joyful and Spirit filled. Corporate revival shouldn't end with a return to what we experienced before revival. Indeed, isn't it God's will for us always to be joyful—even during adversity? Aren't we always to be filled with the Holy Spirit, even before or after experiencing revival?

When the disciples waited in the upper room for the Holy Spirit to come, that was the last time they had to wait. Once the Holy Spirit is given, we can be filled with the Holy Spirit's peace and joy, no matter the circumstances.

What is needed for life is the perpetual filling of the Spirit which is the normal condition of those who are living in the way of God, and the specific fillings to overflowing which may always be counted on when special service demands.

G. Campbell Morgan

PRAYER PROMPT: *Father, I pray for the perpetual filling of your Spirit so that I may live the revival life. I pray for the constant joy of the Spirit, even in the face of hard times and life's occasional adversities.*

SEPTEMBER 27

Continue in Prayer

*Continue steadfastly in prayer, being
watchful in it with thanksgiving.*
COLOSSIANS 4:2

Why do we pray? Why do we continue to pray when the heavens seem like brass? We pray because we must, because we know our God, because we've seen God answer so many times in the past.

The worst thing we can do is stop praying. That's akin to confirming Satan's lie that God isn't listening or that he purposely withholds his blessings. A revival-praying Christian knows to pray and not give up. Ever!

Steadfast praying, being watchful for God's answer, and giving thanks will eventually see the fruit of our prayers.

> We long for revivals; we speak of revivals; we work
> for revivals; and we even pray a little for them. But
> we do not enter upon that labor in prayer which
> is the essential preparation for every revival.
>
> OLE HALLESBY

PRAYER PROMPT: *Father, I will continue to pray for revival and not give up. I believe every Christian is called to long for revival and thus pray for it as the fulfillment of your will. Teach us, Lord, to labor in prayer!*

SEPTEMBER 28

Revival and Spiritual Warfare

*The weapons of our warfare are not of the flesh
but have divine power to destroy strongholds.*
2 Corinthians 10:4

Through natural eyes we may see the enemy at work in our lives or in the lives of those close to us. But when we enter the arena to engage the enemy, our natural abilities fail. We simply cannot in the power of our flesh subdue the powers that attack us. We *must* turn to our spiritual weapons. Not only are they more powerful than worldly weapons in dealing with the forces of darkness, but they are also weapons that cannot be broken or conquered.

In revival, there will be an attempt by the enemy to shut down the work of God. But if spiritually mature believers take up their weapons, they will exercise divine power to fortify the strongholds that protect revival and strike down the forces that seek to tear them down. In every spiritual battle, don't go out on the battlefield with weapons of the flesh. Take up your mighty spiritual weapons and prevail!

Only those who are spiritual perceive the reality of
the spiritual foe and hence engage in battle. Such
warfare is not fought with arms of the flesh. Because
the conflict is spiritual so must the weapons.

Watchman Nee

PRAYER PROMPT: *Father, you have given me both armor for the war I face, but also the weaponry. I rely on your divine power as I destroy the strongholds in my life.*

SEPTEMBER 29

Living for Eternity

"Truly, truly, I say to you, whoever hears my word and believes him who sent me has eternal life. He does not come into judgment, but has passed from death to life."
JOHN 5:24

We who believe have passed from death to life. It's not a future event; we have already made that passage. Heaven is real and awaits us, but we need not wait to have the joy that all Christians are privy to.

While we once lived for this life only, unsuspecting there was something better, now we have believed and have entered into life everlasting. Therefore, we must set our eyes on the reality that what we hope for in heaven is ours now.

In revival, our ears must be open to hear and our eyes open to the riches prepared for us.

Oh, live for eternity! This poor world is passing away;
the reality is to come, and a glorious reality it is. How
important it is to walk so as to please God in all things!

MARY WINSLOW

PRAYER PROMPT: *Father, I am blessed to know that I now have everlasting life. It's not just for when I die. I praise you for the wonderful benefits of believing in your Son.*

SEPTEMBER 30

The Hymns of Revival

About midnight Paul and Silas were praying and singing hymns to God, and the prisoners were listening to them, and suddenly there was a great earthquake, so that the foundations of the prison were shaken. And immediately all the doors were opened, and everyone's bonds were unfastened.
Acts 16:25–26

When they had sung a hymn, they went out to the Mount of Olives.
Matthew 26:30

If we ever question the power of hymns, we only need to think of Paul and Silas and the mighty earthquake that unfastened the prisoners' chains. Or we might think of that glorious first Communion supper that concluded with Jesus and his disciples singing a hymn. Rest assured, during revival there will be singing, likely both hymns and choruses. Whenever we're in the presence of singing to the Lord, sing with power. See your own chains fall off. See yourself at that first Lord's Supper. Hymns invite the angelic audience.

Revive us again, fill each heart with thy love.
May each soul be rekindled with fire from above.
Hallelujah! Thine the glory, hallelujah! Amen!
Hallelujah! Thine the glory, revive us again.

W. P. Mackay

PRAYER PROMPT: *Lord, unto you I sing praises and hymns that touch my soul. Father, may you inhabit my praises.*

OCTOBER 1

Revival across Desert Sands

*A voice cries: "In the wilderness prepare the way of the
LORD; make straight in the desert a highway for our God."*
ISAIAH 40:3

When this world seems like a waterless desert, it's time for revival to open a highway to God in the wilderness.

Christians always have a choice: Are we content with the desert sands? Do we even know we're *in* a wilderness? Are we lulled into lethargy by our daily routines, or do we believe God for a revival highway out of the desert?

When we pray, we are laying the pavement for God's highway. Christians in previous generations paved the road with their prayers; we can too. The heroes in heaven are the ones who prayed while on earth. Aim for a satisfied end to your labors and answers to your prayers.

> To look back upon the progress of the divine kingdom upon earth is to review revival periods which have come like refreshing showers upon dry and thirsty ground, making the desert to blossom as the rose, and bringing new eras of spiritual life and activity just when the Church had fallen under the influence of the apathy of the times.
>
> E. M. BOUNDS

PRAYER PROMPT: *Father, we're in a desert now. We long for a highway of revival that leads us to lusher ground. May our prayers lay the pavement for your revival freeway.*

OCTOBER 2

Who, *Me*?

O LORD, you have searched me and known me! You know when I sit down and when I rise up; you discern my thoughts from afar. You search out my path and my lying down and are acquainted with all my ways. Even before a word is on my tongue, behold, O LORD, you know it altogether. You hem me in, behind and before, and lay your hand upon me. Such knowledge is too wonderful for me; it is high; I cannot attain it.
PSALM 139:1–6

God is acquainted with our every action and our words before they're spoken; even our thoughts are known by him. He knows our every need, including our need for revival. He watches tenderly over us, hearing our pleas for revival. All we have or can have comes from his generous hand. The knowledge of God is high, and, along with the psalmist, we cannot attain it. But we can trust him in all things.

> God's all-seeing eye and all-pervading presence are indisputable. His thorough knowledge of all the events in which we are intermixed. . . . His distinct perception of every thought, of every word and deed, of every step taken, of every wish conceived, are acknowledged truths. Never do we come in or go out, never do we rise or sit down, but his eye marks us. Our lips never open, no utterance ever sounds, but his all-hearing ear discerns the significance. . . . We are always surrounded by his power, and never can escape his hand.
>
> HENRY LAW

PRAYER PROMPT: *Lord, I worship you for your awesomeness. You know my every thought; you anticipate my every action. You know my prayers before I utter them. Thank you, Father, for the careful attention you pay to my life.*

OCTOBER 3

In His Presence

Seek the LORD and his strength; seek his presence continually!
PSALM 105:4

Power for living comes from being in the presence of the Lord. There are no shortcuts. In revival, we experience God's presence so completely that we simply want to bask in his love. Words fail us. Prayer has been offered, and now we have nothing to add. God needs no additional information. Now as we rest in his presence, not only are we satisfied, but so is God. He enjoys being in our presence as much as we enjoy being in his presence. Perfect communion. *This* is revival.

There come times when I have nothing more to tell God. If I were to continue to pray in words, I would have to repeat what I have already said. At such times it is wonderful to say to God, "May I be in Thy presence, Lord? I have nothing more to say to Thee, but I do love to be in Thy presence."

OLE HALLESBY

PRAYER PROMPT: *God, I love it when words fail me in prayer because my heart is so full. May I now simply be in your presence? You are enough.*

OCTOBER 4

Revivals Happen Best on Dead-End Streets

When you pass through the waters, I will be with you; and through the rivers, they shall not overwhelm you; when you walk through fire you shall not be burned, and the flame shall not consume you.
Isaiah 43:2

We appreciate revivals the most when they happen when we are at our lowest. When the church of God is weak and ineffective, that's when revival is needed most. That's true both in corporate revival and personal revival.

Many Christians have been brought low by life's circumstances or their own bad choices. But when believers see no hope for their present trouble and cry out to God, he hears and passes through the fire and the flood with us. Such sweet revival will never be forgotten.

If you are on a dead-end street, you're ready for revival.

Fiery trials make golden Christians! Sanctified afflictions are spiritual promotions.

William Nicholson

PRAYER PROMPT: *Lord, you know my needs as well as your church's needs. Come in power and carry us through. Supply our needs. Fill our souls.*

OCTOBER 5

An End to Anemic Prayer

Being in agony [Jesus] prayed more earnestly; and his sweat became like great drops of blood falling down to the ground. And when he rose from prayer, he came to the disciples and found them sleeping for sorrow, and he said to them, "Why are you sleeping? Rise and pray that you may not enter into temptation."
Luke 22:44–46

Jesus prayed often, but only in the garden of Gethsemane are we told he was in agony and thus prayed "more earnestly." So in earnest was he that he sweated, as it were, great drops of blood. How is it when we pray for revival? Are we praying in earnest? Or are our prayers anemic? Are our prayers diluted by our drowsiness? Will the Lord return to find us asleep?

Anemic prayers for revival don't secure God's blessing. Nothing less than a wrestling with God for a move of his Holy Spirit will bring revival. God hears the prayers that call for his hand to move. He's watching for intercessors who pray awake, who pray "more earnestly" even in agony, who do not surrender to sleep.

You must pray with all your might. That does not mean saying your prayers, or sitting gazing about in church or chapel with eyes wide open while someone else says them for you. It means fervent, effectual, untiring wrestling with God. This kind of prayer be sure the devil and the world and your own indolent, unbelieving nature will oppose. They will pour water on this flame.

William Booth

PRAYER PROMPT: *Father, when my prayers are weak or half-hearted, know that I desire change. Empower me through the Holy Spirit to pray more earnestly. Bring an end to my anemic prayers.*

OCTOBER 6
Though None Go with Me

*"My sheep hear my voice, and I know
them, and they follow me."*
JOHN 10:27

We are all sheep in need of a shepherd. We hear the voice of Jesus and follow him into green pastures. Revival is a time of intimate fellowship with our Good Shepherd, who leads us toward his will for us. Though the path isn't always smooth, the presence of the Shepherd reassures us.

If you hear the voice of the Shepherd call your name, be quick to listen. You will be given an assignment—one suited to your gifts, with an eternal reward to be bestowed.

Christ's sheep follow Him, they walk in the narrow
path He has marked out, they do not refuse because it
is sometimes steep and narrow but wherever the line
of duty lies they go forward without doubting.

J. C. RYLE

PRAYER PROMPT: *Good Shepherd, I follow you to the lush grass where you would have me graze. I have wandered in the past, but you found me and carried me home. I will never leave your presence again.*

OCTOBER 7

God Is Looking for Vigilant Hearts

*Keep your heart with all vigilance, for
from it flow the springs of life.*
PROVERBS 4:23

Our physical hearts keep us alive. When the heart stops, so do we. In the spiritual life, our inner heart determines whether we live or die spiritually. The springs of life flow from a vigilant heart, but we're often unaware of the threats to our spiritual heart. We may then neglect the required vigilance to keep our heart protected and aflame for the Lord.

For many, revival is a time of resetting the heart, a time to become more aware of the treasure within each of us. Know this: our enemy wants to rob us of that treasure. He wants us to set our hearts on anything but God. Our vigilance and the Lord's protection are the only safeguards against his tactics.

———

> Keep your heart as you would keep a treasure. A man
> who has a great treasure of money and jewels, will keep it
> with lock and bolt so that it is not stolen. Christian, you
> carry a precious treasure with you, even all that you are
> worth—a heart! The devil and the world would rob you
> of this jewel. Oh, keep your heart as you would keep your
> life. If you are robbed of this treasure, you are ruined.
>
> THOMAS WATSON

———

PRAYER PROMPT: *Father, I'm well aware of the treasure within me. Make my heart a vigilant one against the enemy's attempts to rob me of my treasure or set my heart on lesser things. I pray for an even greater measure of heavenly treasure in my life—a revival with newfound riches.*

OCTOBER 8

Heirs of the Kingdom

*Has not God chosen those who are poor in the
world to be rich in faith and heirs of the kingdom,
which he has promised to those who love him?*
JAMES 2:5

What an inheritance awaits every Christian! If we only had eyes to see our destiny. But through the eyes of faith, we *can* see; we *can* know that what God has planned for us exceeds our expectations. We who are poor now will be rich in heavenly wealth. We who are sick shall be well. Our homes shall be eternal and maintenance free. Revival is a time of rejoicing both for what we have now in Christ and for what we will inherit from our heavenly Father.

My poor brother, my poor sister!
Look up! Look forward!
Your cottage will soon be exchanged for a mansion!
Your sickness will soon be exchanged for health!
Your poverty will soon be exchanged for wealth!
Your sin will soon be exchanged for perfect holiness!
Your earth will soon be exchanged for Heaven!
You will not always be poor! You will not be poor for long.
Jesus will soon come—and then you will reign with Him!
For you, an inheritance is reserved in Heaven!
For you, a mansion is being prepared!
For you, glory, honor, immortality,
even eternal life, are in reserve!

JAMES SMITH

PRAYER PROMPT: *Lord, you prepare an inheritance for me that cannot be taken or shaken. It is mine by virtue of Christ. I now enjoy a pretaste of that which is to come. Praise you, Father!*

OCTOBER 9

The Mystery of Revival

Oh, the depth of the riches and wisdom and knowledge of God! How unsearchable are his judgments and how inscrutable his ways!
ROMANS 11:33

Revival is truly unexplainable. It is a sovereign move of God and yet comes in response to our prayers. It can be as short as a few days or last for years. It can have a leader but never a usurper. It can be loud, or it can be quiet. It can attract the unsaved, or it can repel unbelievers.

In short, the ways of God in revival are often a mystery. If there's no mystery, we might wonder if it's really God's revival.

If you can explain what is happening in a church, apart from the sovereign act of God, it is not revival.
MARTYN LLOYD-JONES

PRAYER PROMPT: *O Lord, your ways are the ways of mystery yet fully perfect as designed by you. I don't need to understand; I just need to enjoy revival as it comes from you.*

OCTOBER 10

Revival Is a Community Affair

As we have opportunity, let us do good to everyone, and especially to those who are of the household of faith.
GALATIANS 6:10

Though revival is among God's people, it also results in good for the local or national community. Good works flow from revival. Orphans and widows are cared for. Addicts are given new life. Churches are revitalized. Families are strengthened. The weak and the sick are cared for. Even crime rates can go down.

These results happen because revival brings home the reality that God is a Giver of good things, and we, his people, become great givers, having received new life through revival.

Every community can benefit from revival. What are the needs where you live that can benefit from revival?

A man of a right spirit is not a man of narrow and private views, but is greatly interested and concerned for the good of the community to which he belongs, and particularly of the city or village in which he resides, and for the true welfare of the society of which he is a member.

JONATHAN EDWARDS

PRAYER PROMPT: *God, I pray for my community. I pray for revival that will touch the hearts you're now preparing to receive new life as a wave of evangelism accompanies your outpouring. You know the needs of my community. Supply healing in all the broken parts.*

"He has paid for my sins and given me His own righteousness. Praise be to God!"

OCTOBER 11
Revival and the Glory of God

From him and through him and to him are all things. To him be glory forever. Amen.
ROMANS 11:36

Though revival is a time for joy, it's also a time for mourning over our sin. It's a time to glimpse the holiness of God and realize how far we are from that holiness. It's a time of gratitude for the imputed righteousness of Christ every believer receives at salvation. We are holy because the holy one died to ensure that our sins—our lack of holiness—were forever dealt with. Because of all that revival is for us, we bow down and give God the glory. We can do nothing else.

He has paid for our sins and given us his own righteousness! Praise be to God!

A necessary pre-cursor of any great spiritual awakening is a spirit of deep humiliation growing out of a consciousness of sin, and fresh revelation of the holiness and power and glory of God.

JOHN R. MOTT

PRAYER PROMPT: *God, when I think of my past, sin-filled life, I join with John Newton in proclaiming your grace as amazing. Thank you for giving me the righteousness of Christ! May the Holy Spirit reveal any hidden sin in my heart.*

All my sins are forgiven; because of that revival, I bow down and give God the glory.

My God is the eternal OPTIMIST!

OCTOBER 12

The Optimism of Revival

> May the God of hope fill you with all joy and
> peace in believing, so that by the power of the
> Holy Spirit you may abound in hope.
> ROMANS 15:13

This world is full of troubles. It's easy to become depressed about crime, wars, and man's inhumanity. On a personal level, our individual problems may cause us to feel hopeless. But revival is about hope and optimism. It would be difficult for one to go through revival and remain defeated by troubling circumstances. No, when we leave revival, we bring the joy we experienced with us. We watch the news knowing that our redemption is drawing nearer day by day despite the predicted wars and rumors of war. We know, too, that all our personal problems have a heavenly solution. And if we accept by faith the fact that God will cause all these things to work together for our good, we can have the weight of worry lifted from our heart.

> Beloved reader, if you are the possessor of this hope; if
> your soul rejoices in its purifying, elevating, heart-soothing
> influence; render all praise, thanksgiving, and obedience
> to him who, as the God of hope, has planted this blessed
> hope within your soul as a sun that will never set.
>
> OCTAVIUS WINSLOW

PRAYER PROMPT: Father, you are the eternal optimist because you know all things, and you work all your plans to culminate in a glorious eternity where there can be no pessimism. Lord, may I not see my cup as half full or half empty but, instead, overflowing.

This world is full of problems. But revival is about hope and optimism
All my personal problems have HEAVENLY solutions!!!

OCTOBER 13

Facing the Future

I know the plans I have for you, declares the LORD, plans for welfare and not for evil, to give you a future and a hope.
JEREMIAH 29:11

Sometimes we worry too much about the future. Will we face sickness, financial loss, broken relationships? Will this world's events plunge us into despair? What does God say to these concerns? He offers a promise of a future with hope. He has plans for each of us, tailor-made for our benefit and for his use.

Revival is a time to affirm our trust in God for a divinely inspired future. To worry in the light of revival is to miss out on God's clear intent for us. Do not worry! God has a plan for you.

The future is as bright as the promises of God.
ADONIRAM JUDSON

PRAYER PROMPT: *Lord, I entrust my future to you. Bring forth your plan for my life. Give me a future and a hope of your choosing.*

OCTOBER 14

Doctrines

As for you, teach what accords with sound doctrine.
Titus 2:1

Is doctrine important? Paul, writing to Titus, thought so. But not just doctrine, it must be *sound*. In other words, *truth*. For many Christians the word *doctrine* sounds too heady, too academic. But rightly taught and understood, the Bible presents many doctrines that are important for the believer to grasp. There are basic doctrines of the faith which all believers hold as primary. There are other secondary doctrines that Christians have the space to disagree on. To use a secondary doctrine as a sword to wound others who have a different interpretation of certain Scripture passages to misuse doctrine. Worse is to know all sorts of doctrine and practice none of it in everyday life.

During revival, can you praise God next to your born-again brother or sister who, while adhering to the common basic doctrines of the faith, may have a different view of how the end times will unfold or whether a specific level of tithing is a must for Christians today? These and other issues will be resolved in eternity. But until then, let's not hinder revival over honest differences of opinion. Instead, let's understand doctrine as live-giving truth, and let's ultimately remember that an unlived doctrine is a dead doctrine.

> There is scarcely anything so dull and meaningless
> as Bible doctrine taught for its own sake. Truth
> divorced from life is not truth in its biblical sense,
> but something else and something less.
>
> A. W. Tozer

PRAYER PROMPT: *Father, the life-giving doctrines essential to the gospel are dear to me. I pray for a collaborative heart toward my brothers and sisters, who disagree with me on certain secondary doctrines, and a heart more interested in living my beliefs than arguing about them.*

OCTOBER 15

An Undivided Body of Christ

*I appeal to you, brothers, by the name of our Lord
Jesus Christ, that all of you agree, and that there
be no divisions among you, but that you be united
in the same mind and the same judgment.*
1 CORINTHIANS 1:10

Is there any place in the Bible calling for a divided church? No, there isn't. Quite the contrary. Jesus prayed for us to be united. Paul preached against division, and even King David declared, "Behold, how good and pleasant it is when brothers dwell in unity!" (Ps. 133:1).

Make no mistake, the unbelieving world is watching. When they see Christians divided, they don't see Christ. It's true that we're divided from the world, but we are not divided from God or from one another. Revival has a tendency to root out division and unite believers or to move on when division persists.

Divisions in the church always
breed atheism in the world.
THOMAS MANTON

PRAYER PROMPT: *O Lord, how it must grieve you when your church is divided. Bring healing, compassion, and repentance from our tendency to divide from the brothers and sisters we declare as wrong simply because they disagree with us about futile things.*

OCTOBER 16

Godliness

While bodily training is of some value, godliness is of value in every way, as it holds promise for the present life and also for the life to come.
1 TIMOTHY 4:8

We don't often hear the word *godliness* these days, but Paul thought that godliness "is of value in every way." Why then are we not more eagerly seeking true godliness in our own lives? After all, Paul also said that godliness holds promises for both this life and the life to come. One sure effect of revival is a coming face-to-face with true godliness as the presence of God envelops us. We also, by contrast, will come to terms with our own ungodliness.

If for no other reason, revival must come to cure the church of its tendency not to reflect the God it claims to worship.

The revival which is most urgently needed is a revival of practical godliness. Sunday preaching is not enough; we need more sermons all through the week.

THEODORE CUYLER

PRAYER PROMPT: *Father, I'm often beset with temptations that are truly ungodly. Forgive me, Lord, and help me turn my rudder to move me toward a godly lifestyle. In revival, may your church be cleansed of ungodliness and transformed to look more like you to a watching world.*

OCTOBER 17

Revival Is Not a Measure of Spirituality—Love Is

Love is patient and kind; love does not envy or boast; it is not arrogant or rude. It does not insist on its own way; it is not irritable or resentful; it does not rejoice at wrongdoing, but rejoices with the truth. Love bears all things, believes all things, hopes all things, endures all things. Love never ends.
1 CORINTHIANS 13:4–8

If there is a test for one's Christianity, it is surely the ability to love. Jesus tells us unbelievers will know we're Christians by our love. In 1 Corinthians 13, Paul recounts exactly what love is, including bearing all things.

Many well-taught Christians may measure their faith by their knowledge of the Word. But if there is no love attached to their faith, Paul tells us their knowledge benefits nothing. If we would be revived, we must also become filled with love—the kind of love that is a verb.

> Our love to God is measured by our everyday fellowship with others and the love it displays.
> ANDREW MURRAY

PRAYER PROMPT: *Father, if revival has only one effect on me, may it be an increase in my ability to love you and care for others.*

Handwritten note: The test of your Christ-ianity is surely your ability to LOVE. → Love God, othe ppl., thyself!

OCTOBER 18

On the Other Side of Revival

John answered them all, saying, "I baptize you with water, but he who is mightier than I is coming, the strap of whose sandals I am not worthy to untie. He will baptize you with the Holy Spirit and fire."
Luke 3:16

When we're in the revival crowd, we experience revival. But when we leave, do we carry the revival fire with us in order to set others aflame with revival? Or will our revival fire turn to ashes once removed from the revival bonfire? We must not waste revival when it comes. We must fan the flame with continued prayers, much thanksgiving, and fervent evangelism. Our flame must not go out!

Look well to the fire of your souls, for
the tendency of fire is to go out.
William Booth

PRAYER PROMPT: *Father, may I not only burn with revival enthusiasm during the coming glorious days, but may I continue to be aflame with heavenly passion until my dying day.*

OCTOBER 19

The Fruit of Revival is PRAYER,

> *By this my Father is glorified, that you bear much fruit and so prove to be my disciples.*
> JOHN 15:8

As we pray for revival, we pray with certainty. But even if revival tarries, we will have benefited from the time on our knees. Prayer is its own reward. The fruit of revival, of many things, is more prayer, more calling out to God, more seeking of God. Praying for revival is a win-win proposition. Prayer for revival is never wasted.

> All revival begins, and continues, in the prayer meeting. Some have also called prayer the great fruit of revival. In times of revival, thousands may be found on their knees for hours, lifting up their heartfelt cries, with thanksgiving, to heaven.
> HENRY BLACKABY

PRAYER PROMPT: *Father, in praying for revival, I'm doubly blessed. First, I get to request the promise of revival; second, there is the fruit that is prayer itself. Prayer feeds my spirit daily and deepens my dependence on you.*

Revival continues in PRAYER
PRESENCE
PRAYER + are the fruits of revival,
+ PROMISE

OCTOBER 20

Spiritual Brain Fog

> *Now may the God of peace himself sanctify you completely,*
> *and may your whole spirit and soul and body be kept*
> *blameless at the coming of our Lord Jesus Christ.*
> 1 Thessalonians 5:23

We live in an age when denominations that once stood for righteousness have ceased preaching the sermons that engender a desire for righteousness. Various doctrines are discussed and argued over in front of a world needing answers. In such a situation it is imperative that we rid ourselves of the spiritual brain fog and declare the unfiltered gospel with clarity. Revival has a way of bringing spiritual sunshine to dissolve our spiritual brain fog. As we pray, we must be clear in our petitions. What do we want from revival? Why do we want it? What keeps revival at bay?

If we would be clear thinkers and lucid pray-ers, we must clear ourselves of all spiritual brain fog.

Nothing can overturn the mind which abides in faith.

Stephen Tyng

PRAYER PROMPT: *Father, God of peace, I pray you will sanctify me entirely: body, soul, and spirit. May all spiritual brain fog be replaced by clarity of mind as I focus my prayers on revival.*

OCTOBER 21

The Needed Revival

"Will not God give justice to his elect, who cry to him day and night? Will he delay long over them? I tell you, he will give justice to them speedily. Nevertheless, when the Son of Man comes, will he find faith on earth?"
Luke 18:7–8

Spiritual apathy among God's people is a great enemy of revival. When Christ returns, will he indeed find faith on earth? Will we continue in our slumber, or will we awaken to the possibilities of revival? Will the fruit of revival be reveling in God's presence, repentance for sin, compassion for the lost, evangelistic zeal, and a healing of the wounds of the hurting? Will he find a church eager to enter eternity as a bride has readied herself for the wedding? What is needed is a pervasive revival that touches a worldwide population. Do we have the kind of faith for revival on that scale? How big is our God? Indeed, he is big enough to deliver us from apathy into white-hot passion for himself and for good works done in his name!

The revival we need is a deliverance from that spiritual apathy and laxity which now characterizes the average Christian, a return to self-denial and closer walking with God, a quickening of our graces, and the becoming more fruitful in the bringing forth of good works.

Arthur Pink

PRAYER PROMPT: *Lord, we need revival not just for revival's sake or for our own benefits. We need revival for the fruit it brings with it—the good works wrought by those touched by revival.*

OCTOBER 22

Beware of Mockers and Scoffers

*Blessed is the man who walks not in the counsel of the wicked,
nor stands in the way of sinners, nor sits in the seat of scoffers.*
Psalm 1:1

Mockers and scoffers at our faith will always be part of the Christian's lot. If we're not mocked, we might question why not. Lukewarm Christians are safe, but Christians on fire for God are open targets for accusers. Revival is no exception. If we take revival seriously, surely bystanders will try to undermine our experience. Preparing for revival includes preparing for earthly humiliation and possibly the loss of friends.

We must always remember the promise of God that there is a blessing to those mocked for his name.

> To be laughed at is no great hardship to me. I can delight
> in scoffs and jeers. Caricatures, lampoons, and slanders are
> my glory. But that you should turn from your own mercy,
> that is my sorrow. Spit on me, but, oh, repent! Laugh
> at me, but, oh, believe in my Master! Make my body as
> the dirt of the streets, but damn not your own souls!
>
> Charles Spurgeon

PRAYER PROMPT: *Lord, I pray for the mockers of revival. They truly are ignorant of what they're missing—most of all a relationship with you. Bring them in, Father. Let them see all they're missing.*

OCTOBER 23

Pray in the Spirit

The Spirit helps us in our weakness. For we do not know what to pray for as we ought, but the Spirit himself intercedes for us with groanings too deep for words. And he who searches hearts knows what is the mind of the Spirit, because the Spirit intercedes for the saints according to the will of God.
ROMANS 8:26–27

Great prayer warriors will recount the many times they found no more words to pray and relied on the unuttered groans of the Spirit to intercede through them. As we pray for revival, we will experience such times, and we should welcome the loss of words. After all, our prayers for revival issue from our heart of desperation.

When we leave the prayer closet, we should feel relieved by our groaning prayers. Our prayer life should satisfy both us and God.

> The Holy Spirit needs us to accomplish his intercessory ministry, and we certainly need him to accomplish ours. What a privilege to be invited to join in this heavenly partnership. He wants to be free to think through our minds, feel through our hearts, speak through our lips, and even weep through our eyes and groan through our spirits. When a believer is thus at the disposal of the Holy Spirit, praying in the Spirit will be a reality.
>
> ARTHUR WALLIS

PRAYER PROMPT: *Father, when my prayers no longer find words, hear the groaning of your Spirit, laboring over the many needs I see. At such times, pray through me, Holy Spirit.*

OCTOBER 24

A Glimpse of God's Unseen Hand

Behold, I have engraved you on the palms of my hands.
Isaiah 49:16

When all seems hopeless, when it seems the heavens are brass, and the prospect for revival is dim, that's when we must lean on God all the harder. We become bold yet reverent in our prayers. We push back against the forces that attempt to halt revival. Above all, we put our trust in the one who has engraved us on the palm of his hands.

It is in those times of hopeless chaos when the sovereign hand of God is most likely to be seen.

Thomas Chalmers

PRAYER PROMPT: *Father, we do not always see or perceive your hand at work, and yet your hand is always about your business, never idle. This same hand of yours has my name engraved on it. Your hand is my protector and the impetus for my own hand to be about the work you have assigned me.*

OCTOBER 25

God's Unrelenting Love for Sinners

> *The scribes of the Pharisees, when they saw that he was eating with sinners and tax collectors, said to his disciples, "Why does he eat with tax collectors and sinners?" And when Jesus heard it, he said to them, "Those who are well have no need of a physician, but those who are sick. I came not to call the righteous, but sinners."*
> MARK 2:16–17

Decisions are made in revival. Backsliders return to Christ, rededications are made, and sinners are drawn to the Savior. Revival, then, serves as a hospital for the spiritually sick. When criticized by the Pharisees for eating with sinners, Jesus explained that he was reaching out not to those who are well but to those who are sick with sin. It's not for us to show God's anger at sinners but to display his unrelenting love for sinners and offer them the new life in Christ we enjoy. Our prayers for revival must include a plentiful harvest of new believers.

> God is light—perfect holiness. God is love—pure benevolence. His holiness and his benevolence both prompt him to rejoice when sinners escape from sin. Sin is that abominable thing which he hates. . . . It plunges sinners into the lowest depths of guilt and wretchedness. It pollutes them with a stain, which all the waters of the ocean cannot wash away, which all the fires of Hell cannot remove; from which nothing can cleanse them, but the blood of Christ.
>
> EDWARD PAYSON

PRAYER PROMPT: *Lord, when you bring revival, let it be as a huge net, saving many from sin, suffering, death, the enemy, and hell.*

OCTOBER 26

Wholly His

*"All that the Father gives me will come to me, and
whoever comes to me I will never cast out."*
JOHN 6:37

If we learn anything from revival, it's that we are wholly his. We do not belong to ourselves, nor are we attached to this world. Our kingdom is now *his* kingdom. We are heirs of a great inheritance. We are never alone in this world; we have an ever-present Father. How is this possible? By the simple but costly purchase of us by the blood of Christ. We are his entirely, wholly, irrevocably, eternally.

I am his by purchase and I am his by conquest; I am
his by donation and I am his by election; I am his by
covenant and I am his by marriage; I am wholly his; I am
peculiarly his; I am universally his; I am eternally his.

THOMAS BROOKS

PRAYER PROMPT: *Lord, we all need a sense of belonging. And for the believer in Christ, we have the confidence of being possessed by you. We are wholly yours!*

OCTOBER 27

Changing the Way We Think

Finally, brothers, whatever is true, whatever is honorable, whatever is just, whatever is pure, whatever is lovely, whatever is commendable, if there is any excellence, if there is anything worthy of praise, think about these things.
PHILIPPIANS 4:8

Many Christians fall into a mental rut that is often filled with negative, powerless, or futile thoughts. When God visits us with his reviving presence, it changes the way we think, viewing things in a new, right-side-up way compared to the world's upside-down way of thinking. We read about this new way in Paul's letter to the Philippians. Pure thoughts, just thoughts, lovely thoughts are the everyday call of the Christian but also the fruit of revival. The world loves to dwell on that which is false, dishonoring, unjust, chaotic, and laughable. Are we willing to allow revival to turn all these upside-down thoughts right side up again? Are we willing to let revival change the way we think?

Remember that among the thousands of thoughts that pass through your mind in a day, there is not one hidden from God! He understands your thoughts afar off, and in his sight the thought of foolishness is sin. Therefore be watchful. Do not dwell on anything that may pollute the mind. Cast away murmuring thoughts, angry thoughts, impure thoughts and pray that God would preserve you from them.

GEORGE EVERARD

PRAYER PROMPT: *Father, I pray for victory over my thought life. I choose to think only on the things that are worthy of a Christian.*

OCTOBER 28

Exalting Christ, Our Lord

God has highly exalted him and bestowed on him the name that is above every name, so that at the name of Jesus every knee should bow, in heaven and on earth and under the earth, and every tongue confess that Jesus Christ is Lord, to the glory of God the Father.
PHILIPPIANS 2:9–11

Revival is about exalting Jesus Christ, not about wanting an emotional high. If we seek revival for an outbreak of emotional goose bumps, we're going to end up disappointed. Goose bumps are momentary; they don't change lives.

There is a seriousness about revival that precludes preoccupation with self. The irony is that as we worship the Lord in revival, we experience a spiritual lift that stirs our hearts. But the emotions must always follow, not lead in revival.

> It is Christ who is to be exalted, not our feelings.
> We will know Him by obedience, not by emotions.
> Our love will be shown by obedience, not by how
> good we feel about God at a given moment.
> ELISABETH ELLIOT

PRAYER PROMPT: *Father, if nothing else should occur during revival, let there be an exalting of Christ. For when Christ is exalted, everything else falls into place as it should.*

OCTOBER 29

What Do We Want from Revival?

*Oh that you would rend the heavens and come down,
that the mountains might quake at your presence.*
Isaiah 64:1

What do we want from revival? Do we not want a return to the power that birthed the church and has seen it expand for two thousand years? Do we not want the God of consuming fire to burn away the dross in our lives? Do we not want to feel God's heartbeat for the wounded and the lost?

If we want little from revival, then it's little we shall have. We must want and seek much, much more from God's reviving work.

> [The Christian church] is at a low ebb, and greatly needs a revival. . . . Among those who profess to be followers of Christ, how little is there of real piety, and of vital godliness! Whether among pastors or their flocks, we behold but little of that primitive simplicity, or of that entireness of devotion to God, which characterized the apostolic age. . . . We want to see the lighting down of his arm among us; and such displays of his power and glory as he gave when he shook the room where his people were assembled, and filled them all with the Holy Spirit. . . . In a word, we are looking for times of refreshing from the presence of the Lord: and for these we should be earnestly pleading with God in prayer; saying, with the prophet, "Oh that you would rend the heavens and come down, that the mountains might [quake] at your presence."
> Charles Simeon

PRAYER PROMPT: *Lord, I ask for a return to the power that birthed the church and has revived her down through the centuries when it was at a low ebb. Rend the heavens and come down!*

OCTOBER 30

Lament in Revival

*Why, O Lord, do you stand far away? Why
do you hide yourself in times of trouble?*
Psalm 10:1

Just as worship and praise both precede and continue through revival, so too does lament. We all have much to lament—if not on our own behalf, surely, we can lament the weakness of the church today. We can lament over broken families, warring nations, and the advance of evil in our world.

God honors our lamentations. He hears them and accepts them just as he does with our praises and our petitions. Don't hesitate to lament in your prayer times. Every lament you raise up carries weight with God.

> The God of the Bible, is the God of the broken-hearted. The world cares little for broken hearts. Indeed, men often break hearts by their cruelty, their falseness, their injustice, their coldness and then move on as heedlessly as if they had trodden only on a worm! But God cares. The broken-heartedness of His people attracts Him. The lament of grief on earth, draws him down from Heaven!
>
> J. R. Miller

PRAYER PROMPT: *Lord God, you hear my lamentations as a father hears the groans of his child. Know that my lamenting is for your people. Oh, that my lamentations would stir your heart and bring a fresh wind of your presence!*

OCTOBER 31

We Are God's Messengers to the Next Generation

These words that I command you today shall be on your heart. You shall teach them diligently to your children, and shall talk of them when you sit in your house, and when you walk by the way, and when you lie down, and when you rise.
DEUTERONOMY 6:6–7

God instructed his people to teach his commands to their children. The blessings of God followed his commandments; thus, to obey was to be blessed. Hebrew children were taught from a young age to know their history and their God.

Today, we who are Christians must likewise instruct our young in the ways of the Lord. We must teach them to obey God's Word and to love and serve him. If we fail to pass down the Lord's teaching to this generation of children, succeeding generations will be worse off. Praying children are more likely to avoid the sin-inducing traps of the enemy.

During times of family prayer, we must teach our children to pray for revival in their generation.

The prayers of God's saints strengthen the unborn generation against the desolating waves of sin and evil.

E. M. BOUNDS

PRAYER PROMPT: *Lord, how easy it is to pray for the next generation and the children just coming up. The world is theirs to intercede for, to raise up their generation's prayer warriors, pastors, and evangelists. Guard, O God, our children! Fill them with a holy hunger to know and serve you.*

NOVEMBER 1

Praying Specifically

*Whatever you ask in prayer, believe that you
have received it, and it will be yours.*
Mark 11:24

When praying for revival, pray specifically. Pray for your church, your town, your nation. Pray for your unsaved friends and relatives. But be aware that asking is the first third of successful praying. The second third is believing—often despite temptations to doubt. The third part is receiving. All three parts are important, or Jesus wouldn't have mentioned all three.

Many Christians do well with asking, but believing and receiving are more challenging. But why pray at all if we don't expect God to answer? Expectancy in prayer is key. If you pray for revival, start praising now for its soon arrival. God honors bold, specific, and expectant prayer.

Expect God to do as you have asked. Unless there is
this expectancy, faith is not fully in exercise. It is this
expecting from him which honors and pleases God, and
which always draws down from him answers of peace.

Arthur Pink

PRAYER PROMPT: *Lord, you are my Father and you hear my prayers. Today, I pray specifically for my loved ones and others who need prayer. I pray, too, for revival to come to my church fellowship and to my town.*

NOVEMBER 2

Revival and Healing

Is anyone among you sick? Let him call for the elders of the church, and let them pray over him, anointing him with oil in the name of the Lord. And the prayer of faith will save the one who is sick, and the Lord will raise him up. And if he has committed sins, he will be forgiven.
JAMES 5:14–15

Among our prayers for revival, we cannot forget to pray for those who are sick. Testimonies abound telling of both mental and physical healing during revival. As revival comes to us, let us present the sick for prayer and believe God for his will in healing.

Though sickness is part of this broken world, praying for healing can bring the supernatural touch to bear on sickness. God knows we can serve him better when we are healthy. We ask him in faith, and we trust him with whatever result accords with his will.

We are a spiritual people living in a natural world. Sickness and its consequences abound in the world. What joy, then, for the believer to learn from the Word of God the way of healing for the sick! The Bible teaches us that it is the will of God to see his children in good health. The Apostle James has no hesitation in saying that the prayer of faith shall save the sick, and the Lord shall raise him up. May the Lord teach us to hearken and to receive with simplicity what his Word tells us!

ANDREW MURRAY

PRAYER PROMPT: *Lord, your Word instructs us to pray in faith for a return to good health. I pray that with revival will come testimonies of great healing, both physical and spiritual.*

NOVEMBER 3

The Arrows of God

Count it all joy, my brothers, when you meet trials of various kinds, for you know that the testing of your faith produces steadfastness. And let steadfastness have its full effect, that you may be perfect and complete, lacking in nothing.
JAMES 1:2–4

What must happen first in order to see a miracle? It's that we're facing a seemingly impossible situation.

And so trials are invitations for God to intervene in our troubles. A severe need is an arrow in our life pointing us to God. If we follow the arrow, it will lead us to God. He will be there—and with him, the answer to the impossible situation we face.

———

The arrow of prayer, feathered with a divine promise, springing from the bow of faith, and winged by the power of the Spirit, will overcome every obstacle, pierce every cloud, and fasten itself upon the throne of the Eternal God!

OCTAVIUS WINSLOW

———

PRAYER PROMPT: *Father, I know my trials test my faith and eventually produce steadfastness. But as I go through trials, may my prayers be as arrows headed for the target of steadfastness.*

NOVEMBER 4

Revival Is Fellowship with Jesus Christ

*God is faithful, by whom you were called into the
fellowship of his Son, Jesus Christ our Lord.*
1 CORINTHIANS 1:9

What is the Christian life but fellowship with our Creator and the Lover of our soul? Not only that, but this fellowship is one into which we were called by God himself. Never let us think we were born again by our own choosing. We were *called*. Isn't this a breathtaking truth?

We may enjoy good relationships with our earthly friends, but none can compare to our fellowship with God. For many, revival is a fresh awakening to the reality of our true fellowship with God. Such a revelation changes us.

> Human fellowship can go to great lengths, but not all
> the way. Fellowship with God can go to all lengths.
> OSWALD CHAMBERS

PRAYER PROMPT: *Lord, what a joy to enter into fellowship with you. You are not only my father but also my helper, friend, and advocate. No one on earth can match friendship with you.*

NOVEMBER 5

God's Word as the Template for Our Thoughts and Our Lives

The word of God is living and active, sharper than any two-edged sword, piercing to the division of soul and of spirit, of joints and of marrow, and discerning the thoughts and intentions of the heart.
HEBREWS 4:12

God's Word is our sword. It is alive and active, discerning our thoughts and our heart's intentions. It is a template for all we do, our plumb line of truth. We are instructed in life's principles as laid out by God in the Bible. During revival, Jesus, the living Word is exalted, but the written word, too, is honored and adhered to. Anything that happens counter to the Word is not part of God's plan for revival. If the revival is not true to the Word, it's not God's revival.

———

[The Word of God] is sharper than any two-edged sword, for it will enter where no other sword can, and make a more critical dissection: it pierces to the dividing asunder of the soul and the spirit, the soul and its habitual prevailing temper; it makes a soul that has been a long time of a proud spirit to be humble, of a perverse spirit to be meek and obedient. Those sinful habits that have become as it were natural to the soul, and rooted deeply in it, and become in a manner one with it, are separated and cut off by this sword.

MATTHEW HENRY

———

PRAYER PROMPT: *Thank you, God, for your Word! It is the template for all my thoughts and actions. Deepen my understanding of this vital weapon in the warfare I face daily. May revival be a time of embracing your Word in an even more powerful way.*

NOVEMBER 6

Revival Is the Means, Not the End

*Be patient. Establish your hearts, for the
coming of the Lord is at hand.*
JAMES 5:8

While revival is a wonderful visitation from God, it is merely the means and not the end of God's plan. Someday, this earth's history will culminate, and God will establish new heavens and a new earth, at which time the need for intermittent visits from God will be no more, for we will forever—and in full measure—bask in his presence.

Our present revivals are mere foretastes of glory—and weak ones at that. It's vital that we not keep our eyes on revival itself but see it as we glimpse into our greater end.

Have patience, then, for the coming of the Lord.

> The patience that God requires is a disposition to bear all that he has appointed for us, without complaining; yes, with resignation and hope; to wait God's time for the mercies we need or for answers to the prayers we put up. . . . Are you impatient? Then confess it, and mourn over it before God! Impatience will make you miserable, and lead you to dishonor God. Watch against it!
>
> JAMES SMITH

PRAYER PROMPT: *God, patience is hard but necessary. Give me, then, the patience to wait for answers to my prayers and, ultimately, for your final coming. May I have the disposition to accept all you have appointed for me here and now as I patiently wait for the day of your return. Visit me afresh, giving me the staying power I need until your final visitation.*

NOVEMBER 7
Establish the Peace of God in Your Life

*May the Lord of peace himself give you peace at all
times in every way. The Lord be with you all.*
2 THESSALONIANS 3:16

True revival brings peace, not chaos. If confusion and disruption interrupt what God is doing, revival will not last. For the Holy Spirit doesn't bring disorder in revival; he brings peace. Even when revival isn't quiet, it's still peaceable.

If we find no peace during revival, we must first look inside: Is something amiss we need to deal with? Or is the lack of peace because the revival has become an exercise in self-seeking?

The Holy Spirit carries a spirit of peace. If we would have the peace of God, it will be because we are surrendered to the Prince of peace.

> Self-seeking is the gate by which a soul departs
> from peace; and total abandonment to the
> will of God, that by which it returns.
>
> JEANNE GUYON

PRAYER PROMPT: *Holy Spirit, thank you for your peace during revival. Though our loud praises may ring out, they are full of peace. Protect us from a heart that seeks self, thereby protecting our peace.*

NOVEMBER 8

"Do Whatever He Tells You"

On the third day there was a wedding at Cana in Galilee, and the mother of Jesus was there. Jesus also was invited to the wedding with his disciples. When the wine ran out, the mother of Jesus said to him, "They have no wine." And Jesus said to her, "Woman, what does this have to do with me? My hour has not yet come." His mother said to the servants, "Do whatever he tells you."
JOHN 2:1–5

When revival happens, we may wonder if we have any part to play. We deem ourselves as having nothing to contribute. But we must remember the wedding at Cana. The wine was gone, leaving only water to offer the guests. But Mary, the mother of Jesus, told the servants to do whatever Jesus told them. The result was the best wine at the wedding. We can also think of the boy whose only small role was to contribute two fishes that would feed more than five thousand. No contribution is too small if we all just do whatever Jesus tells us.

Consider David Brainerd, missionary to Native Americans. He did what he could in his twenty-nine years of life, and it was enough to fulfill God's will for him.

When Jesus is present, no offering is too small.

> Lord, let me make a difference for you that is utterly disproportionate to who I am.
> DAVID BRAINERD

PRAYER PROMPT: *Heavenly Father, I have only a little to contribute. Please multiply it as I do whatever you tell me. Make my part in revival utterly disproportionate to who I am.*

NOVEMBER 9

Unashamed

*I am not ashamed of the gospel, for it is the power
of God for salvation to everyone who believes,
to the Jew first and also to the Greek.*
ROMANS 1:16

If we would experience revival, we must forsake any shame for the gospel. The early Christians were brave followers of Christ, unashamed of their Master and bold in preaching the good news.

Revival has a way of branding our hearts with the love of Christ that any remnants of shame are melted away. Know this: God will not send revival where it will be shamed or unwelcome.

Search your heart. Is the gospel a cause of embarrassment to you? Are you reluctant to share Christ for fear of rejection? Do you associate with the Christian faith privately but refuse to do so publicly? Are you willing to become unashamed?

If we would have the presence and the power of Christ
among us, we must have his cross too; for if we are ashamed
or afraid of his cross, he will not come to us in power.

JOHN ANGELL JAMES

PRAYER PROMPT: *Father, how could I ever have shame for the gospel or for revival? Both are a privilege to experience. Thank you for not being ashamed to call me your child.*

NOVEMBER 10

Deeper Intimacy through Discipline

For the moment all discipline seems painful rather than pleasant, but later it yields the peaceful fruit of righteousness to those who have been trained by it.
Hebrews 12:11

How disciplined are we in prayer? In life?

The prayer that brings revival is pointed and unrelenting. It will not be denied. But as we pray, we must not let distractions or wandering thoughts steal our attention. We must hold fast to our cry for revival.

Likewise, we must not allow laziness and procrastination to derail us from doing God's will. While discipline may be painful, we can know that it will produce the fruit of righteousness.

The battle of prayer is against two things in the earthlies: wandering thoughts and lack of intimacy with God's character as revealed in his word. Neither can be cured at once, but they can be cured by discipline.
Oswald Chambers

PRAYER PROMPT: *Lord, as I seek you for revival, strengthen me against all wandering thoughts. Bring alive the intimacy we share in prayer. Give me ideas to create a more disciplined prayer life.*

NOVEMBER 11

The Measure of Our Lives

> *"Well done, good and faithful servant. You have been faithful over a little; I will set you over much. Enter into the joy of your master."*
> MATTHEW 25:23

Who among us doesn't yearn to hear the Lord say, "Well done, good and faithful servant"? At our conversion, those words should have become our life's goal. And truly, the final measure of our lives will be what the Holy Spirit was able to accomplish through us as we pursued God's plan.

But we err if we think our role must be larger than life. God's assignments come both big and small, and both are necessary. If we're faithful at our church, if we love others (in deed, not just in words), and if we love and pray for revival, we will have accomplished much.

> It is not great things that God requires of us, unless our mission is to do great things. He only asks that we be faithful in the duties that come to our hand in our commonplace days. That means: 1. that we do all our work as well as we can; 2. that we serve well in all of our varied relationships of life; 3. that we stand heroically in our lot, resisting temptation and continuing true and loyal to God; 4. that we fulfill our mission in all ways according to the grace given unto us, using every gift and talent for the glory of God and the good of others.
>
> J. R. MILLER

PRAYER PROMPT: *God, I pray you'll keep me focused on the life you have designed for me. I set aside my own desires, my own will, that your will might be done.*

NOVEMBER 12

The Lord's Table

*The cup of blessing that we bless, is it not a participation
in the blood of Christ? The bread that we break, is
it not a participation in the body of Christ?*
1 Corinthians 10:16

In the Lord's Supper, we are called to remember Christ's sacrifice for our sins. There is great significance in taking the bread and the cup. The bread speaks of his broken body; the cup speaks of his atoning blood. A celebration of the Lord's Supper during revival may heighten our appreciation for the work of Christ. But let us always draw near when offered the bread and the cup, "for as often as you eat this bread and drink the cup, you proclaim the Lord's death until he comes" (1 Cor. 11:26).

> Draw near in the holy sacrament of the supper. God is again coming to us in that ordinance; an ordinance appointed for the most special nearness out of Heaven. . . . Here we may sacramentally touch his precious body and blood, and feed upon it. Oh! Let us be sure to meet him there; he will not break the appointment. Let us draw near, draw by the veil with the hand of faith: whatever be between him and us, let us closely unite with God in his Son, and come even to his seat, come forward, for we will be welcome.
>
> Thomas Boston

PRAYER PROMPT: *Lord, draw near to me during the celebration of Communion. Keep me mindful of the broken body and the spilled blood of Christ. Revive me as I partake of the bread and the cup.*

NOVEMBER 13

The Power of Fasting

"Is not this the fast that I choose: to loose the bonds of wickedness, to undo the straps of the yoke, to let the oppressed go free, and to break every yoke?"
ISAIAH 58:6

Prayer for revival is effective, but fasting adds weight to our intercessions. Sadly, many Christians rarely combine their prayers with fasting, despite the scriptural admonition to do so.

When fighting a war, an army uses its most effective weapons to their best advantage. Fasting, along with prayer, is a weapon we must employ in our war against the enemy. Some Christians have found that the best fasts are from evening to evening. If our health allows for fasting with prayer, then we must include this ancient practice in our spiritual battle for revival.

> In giving us the privilege of fasting as well as praying, God has added a powerful weapon to our spiritual armory. In her folly and ignorance, the church has largely looked upon it as obsolete. She has thrown it down in some dark corner to rust, and there it has lain forgotten for centuries. An hour of impending crisis for the church and the world demands its recovery!
>
> ARTHUR WALLIS

PRAYER PROMPT: *Lord, as your people pray for revival, may we also see a return to the important part fasting plays in intercession. Lead us, Lord, in this ancient practice.*

NOVEMBER 14

Servanthood and Revival

*If anyone serves me, he must follow me; and where
I am, there will my servant be also. If anyone
serves me, the Father will honor him.*
JOHN 12:26

One of the Christian principles contrary to the world is that becoming great in God's kingdom means becoming a servant. The way up is down. The way to be exalted is to be humbled.

When Jesus washed the feet of his disciples, he was serving them—men who one would expect to be washing his feet.

How do we show our willingness to serve others? Some Christians literally follow Jesus's example by conducting foot-washing ceremonies. Others remember Jesus's admonition to serve him by caring for the sick, visiting those in prison, and remembering the poor. There are ample opportunities to serve Jesus by serving others, even during revival. We just need to look for the opportunities to serve. A revived Christian is always a serving Christian.

One of the principal rules of religion is, to lose no occasion
of serving God. And, since he is invisible to our eyes, we
are to serve him in our neighbor; which he receives as if
done to himself in person, standing visibly before us.

JOHN WESLEY

PRAYER PROMPT: *Father, help me see your image in the people I meet. Let me look at others through the revival eyes of love.*

NOVEMBER 15

Standing on the Shoulders of Those Who Have Blazed the Trail

Faith is the assurance of things hoped for, the conviction of things not seen. For by it the people of old received their commendation.
HEBREWS 11:1–2

When we think of the "people of old," we're remembering the pioneers of the faith and of revival. They prayed for revival, just as we are doing today, and they enjoyed the fruit of their prayers as their revivals literally changed the world. Pioneers such as Jonathan Edwards, George Whitefield, John Wesley, Evan Roberts, Jessie Penn-Lewis, Dwight Moody, Charles Finney, and many others too numerous to list here. They were not Christian celebrities but servants of the Lord doing what they knew from God to do. Credit also goes to the nameless thousands who did no more than pray until they saw the rain of revival begin to fall. These men and women stood fast in prayer and would not relent, and neither must we. Whether our names are written down or not, may God add our presence to the future pages of revival history.

Revival comes from heaven when heroic
souls enter the conflict determined to win
or die or if need be, to win and die!

CHARLES FINNEY

PRAYER PROMPT: *Lord, send revival in answer to my prayers. I remember the brave prayer warriors of Christian history. May that fervent spirit dwell also in me!*

NOVEMBER 16

No Room for Human Glory

I am the LORD; that is my name; my glory I give
to no other, nor my praise to carved idols.
ISAIAH 42:8

Revival is such a level playing field. Just as there are no celebrities in revival, so too is there no room for pride. If we are ever offered kudos for any of our efforts—prayer or otherwise—we must refer the praise to God. For no man, not even the most ardent prayer warrior, can take credit for revival. Though prayers bring revival, revival does not bring glory to those who pray. During revival or outside of it, in all seasons we must learn to immediately deflect any praise to God.

From the November 16, 1889, entry
in Andrew Bonar's journal:

I see very plainly that the Lord has been teaching me, and that I needed the teaching that I was not necessary as an instrument when revival work was spreading in the city. I fear I had secret conceit of my importance, and the importance of old friends. But the Lord works by independent instruments in this place and that; in this person and in that.

PRAYER PROMPT: *God, you alone can bring revival, and you alone are to be praised during revival. All glory pointed to a person must be reflected onto you.*

NOVEMBER 17

Coming to Grips with Our Sin

*Whoever conceals his transgressions will not prosper, but
he who confesses and forsakes them will obtain mercy.*
Proverbs 28:13

Revival is a time to come clean with God. Are we concealing sin from whom no sin can be concealed? Why are we waiting to deal with our sin? The promise is that in confessing and forsaking our sin, we obtain mercy. But if we continue to conceal our sin, we will not prosper.

There is joy in confession, repenting, and obtaining God's mercy. Pain only comes from continuing in sin, short-circuiting our spiritual life. It may seem odd, but the deeper we go in the Christian life, the more aware we become of our sin; and the quicker we deal with it, the deeper we can go.

> The nearer a man gets to God,
> the greater he sees his sin.
> Martyn Lloyd-Jones

PRAYER PROMPT: *Lord, I harbor no known sin in my life. If there is sin, reveal it to me so I can deal with it fully by appropriating the forgiveness that is in Christ.*

NOVEMBER 18

On Earth as It Is in Heaven

*"Your kingdom come, your will be done,
on earth as it is in heaven."*
MATTHEW 6:10

We are all called to pray for revival individually. But the church at large is also called to pray. How is it with your church? Is revival praying practiced? Is it encouraged? One person can pray and be heard by God, but imagine the impact of thousands praying in their churches!

Our prayer for revival is that God's will be done on earth as it is in heaven. Surely revival is God's will, so we must pray and not faint. So much depends on our prayers!

> When the churches are aroused to their duty, men
> of the world will be swept into the Kingdom.
> A whole church on its knees is irresistible.
>
> EVAN ROBERTS

PRAYER PROMPT: *Lord, I believe our prayers for revival please your ears. I believe you hear and answer our prayers in accordance with your will. Please, God, send out a call to your churches to be on their knees for revival.*

NOVEMBER 19

Watching and Waiting with Silent Expectancy

*For God alone, O my soul, wait in
silence, for my hope is from him.*
PSALM 62:5

God honors our prayers for revival both spoken and unspoken. We need not raise our voice in order to be heard. Silent prayer is our friend. Many Christians assume silent prayer as less effective because their thoughts can wander or they might become sleepy. The best antidote for that, whether in vocal or silent prayer, is to walk or stand as you pray.

Some intercessors have prayed for revival in their city by taking prayer walks in different parts of town. On each block, they pray for revival and blessing, and they stand against the work of the enemy in that neighborhood.

Pray aloud or pray silently but pray!

> A season of silence is the best preparation
> for speech with God.
> SAMUEL CHADWICK

PRAYER PROMPT: *Father, you hear my prayers before I even speak them. You know exactly how and when to answer my spoken and unspoken requests. You know my prayers for my neighborhood and for widespread revival in my city.*

NOVEMBER 20
Lord, Help My Unbelief!

*Jesus said to him, "'If you can'! All things are possible for
one who believes." Immediately the father of the child
cried out and said, "I believe; help my unbelief!"*
Mark 9:23–24

In today's time, when we see many who have once professed Christ turning away, it's easy to disbelieve God can bring about a revival that will invigorate the church. But belief is key to revival.

Even if we must cry out, "Lord, I believe; help my unbelief!" we still must pray with whatever faith we have. We must also remember that revival is most successful when God's people are desperate. We might even say in keeping with the father who confessed his unbelief that desperation trumps disbelief.

Pray on in belief. And when you sense any unbelief, simply cry out to God in desperation to end it. He will always honor a desperate cry.

Believe that God means just what He says.
Cast away unbelief for evermore.

Jonathan Goforth

PRAYER PROMPT: *Father, I do believe, but whatever remains of disbelief, I pray you will help my unbelief. I pray that the fruit of revival will be the end of all unbelief in my heart.*

NOVEMBER 21

The Inner Life

That according to the riches of his glory he may grant you to be strengthened with power through his Spirit in your inner being.
EPHESIANS 3:16

We often think of revival as an outward experience. We see and hear the things of revival. But we mustn't forget that revival's primary purpose has more to do with our inner life than our outer life. Our hearts are changed through revival, affecting our outer life, not vice versa.

One proven way into our inner life is meditating on God and his Word. When we feast on the Bible, we are increasing our inner strength with the ability to pass through the trials of life. In turn, those on the outside see this transformation and want to learn more about it.

Always let revival have its way with your inner life first.

We may profitably meditate, with God's blessing, although we are spiritually weak. The weaker we are, the more meditation we need to strengthen our inner man. Meditation on God's Word has given me the help and strength to pass peacefully through deep trials.

GEORGE MUELLER

PRAYER PROMPT: *Lord, allow your Spirit to strengthen my inner being. Empower me through your Word. Revive my inner life as I lay down the fleshly attempts of godliness through my outer life. Work* in *me before you do anything* through *me.*

NOVEMBER 22

Abiding Fruit

"You did not choose me, but I chose you and appointed you that you should go and bear fruit and that your fruit should abide, so that whatever you ask the Father in my name, he may give it to you."
JOHN 15:16

A true revival will produce abiding fruit—fruit that remains long after the revival has ended. Changed lives go on to change other lives.

A revival in name only will, at best, produce poor fruit that doesn't last. It may produce goose bumps and an adrenalin rush but no significant life changes. Those roused by emotional excitement will not continue to walk in Christian maturity. The supposed revival began and ended at the church doors.

Learn to discern real revival from mere religious excitement. Look for the abiding fruit of *changed lives.*

Do not mistake religious excitement for true revival. Often during a time of special emphasis people can get all excited. It is the continuing work that I am interested in, not how many came forward during a meeting. A year later how many are still going on with the Lord? That is where the true measure of a revival is discovered. It is not in the excitement of the meeting itself, but in the lasting fruit.

CHUCK SMITH

PRAYER PROMPT: *Lord, revival does excite me, but allow that passion to provoke real, daily change in my life. Do not let this experience begin and end as a momentary adrenalin rush or an emotional high.*

NOVEMBER 23

No Shrinking Back

You have need of endurance, so that when you have done the will of God you may receive what is promised. For, "Yet a little while, and the coming one will come and will not delay; but my righteous one shall live by faith, and if he shrinks back, my soul has no pleasure in him." But we are not of those who shrink back and are destroyed, but of those who have faith and preserve their souls.
HEBREWS 10:36–39

We pray for revival and nothing changes. No revival appears on the horizon. So, what do we do? We pray with endurance. We are in this for the long haul. We pray for and expect revival. *We will not give up.*

We may also find our other prayers seemingly unanswered. Our children are prodigals. Our relationships are shaky. Our job is tedious. Our health is poor. Do we then shrink back in our prayers? Or do we persist in trusting God's promises? Prayers that are slow to be answered reveal our mettle. Will we give in, or will we believe God regardless of apparent roadblocks?

We should not grow weary in a Christian course. We should not tire in our race. . . . Let us not shrink back from Christ's colors. . . . We must not only hold forth our profession of faith but hold fast our profession. The crown is not given to him who fights but to him who overcomes.

THOMAS WATSON

PRAYER PROMPT: *Refresh me, Lord, as I continue praying for revival in the land. I choose today to be steadfast and unmovable in persistent prayer until the answer comes.*

NOVEMBER 24
The Hidden Life of the Christian

You have died, and your life is hidden with Christ in God.
Colossians 3:3

The hidden life is the life of Christ dwelling in the believer. It is not seen, but its actions are seen in the Christlike deeds of serving others. The hidden life is not for self-satisfaction. It is seeking to find the lost, to bind up the brokenhearted, to bring forgiveness to sinners. Revival is an experience in which the hidden life of Christ within is expressed through worship and characterized by joy. The Christian life is a deepening awareness of the power of a hidden life.

> There is nothing so deep, nothing so hidden, as the life of God in the soul. It seems to be enshrined in the lowest depths of a man's heart. It does not float upon the surface, like a cork upon the water, but sinks deep, very deep, into the very bottom of the soul. Therefore hidden from the eyes of a profane world; hidden from the professing world; and what is more, sometimes hidden from the subject of it himself. A child of God often cannot see his own faith, nor can he discern the life that is bubbling and streaming up in his own bosom. It is not a lake, spread abroad in the meridian sunshine, to attract every eye; nor is it a brook that flows babbling on over the clear pebbles; but it is a well . . . hidden from view. Be careful to live the hidden life.
>
> J. C. Philpot

PRAYER PROMPT: *Father, though my life is hidden in you, I pray for visible results as I live out Chistlikeness in my day-to-day living. On the days I am tempted to fall back into apathy, revive the hidden life within and set me aright!*

NOVEMBER 25
A Clear Conscience

*I always take pains to have a clear conscience
toward both God and man.*
Acts 24:16

If you enter your prayer closet with a questionable conscience, you must make sure you leave the closet with a cleared one. A clear conscience gives us boldness in our prayers.

The best course is to stay away from sin altogether. We must know our triggers to sin and avoid them ruthlessly. Learning to resist the magnetic pull of sin by reckoning ourselves dead to sin as Paul teaches us in Romans 6 and relying on the power of the Holy Spirit are keys to an overcoming life. And an overcoming life empowered with a clear conscience has power when praying for revival.

> Be firm as a rock against every enticement to pleasure or profit, at the cost of a good conscience. Be able to say "No," to mean it, and to stick to it, though the wary tempter has a tongue as smooth as oil and as musical as a siren's note. Avoid the very first step in evil. Don't break the fence with the idea that you can soon make up the breach. Don't go a little way in the wrong direction imagining that you can easily make up what is lost.
>
> George Everard

PRAYER PROMPT: *God, you have offered a simple but profound solution to my sin. Because Christ paid the price, I can confess, repent, and be forgiven of my sin. Knowing the sin has already been paid for, I come to you now and unburden my conscience. You know exactly which thoughts and deeds are weighing me down with guilt. Take them now, so that I might move on to freely and lightly pray for revival.*

NOVEMBER 26

No Return to Egypt

*"I am the LORD your God, who brought you out of
the land of Egypt, out of the house of slavery."*
EXODUS 20:2

In the Old Testament, "the land of Egypt" is analogous to the world. Before we were Christians, we all belonged to "Egypt." We were in bondage, often unaware of our lost state. But then God came and rescued us. He freed us and called us to a better land, a better way. But along the way, we, like the journeying Israelites, tend to forget the true value of our deliverance. We might even claim to miss our Egyptian pleasures. We may grumble about our trek across the desert. We lose sight of the promised land, a land that is already ours.

Revival changes all that. When God is in our midst, we never harken back to a bitter past. We hunger for God's manna—for the Bread of Life who is Christ—not the old garlic and leeks of Egypt. In revival, God reminds us that he has delivered us from the world, the flesh, and the devil, and he is journeying with us all the way to our promised land.

> Soar back through all your own experiences. Think
> of how the Lord has led you in the wilderness and
> has fed and clothed you every day. How God has
> borne with your ill manners, and put up with all your
> murmurings and all your longings after the sensual
> pleasures of Egypt! Think of how the Lord's grace
> has been sufficient for you in all your troubles.
>
> CHARLES SPURGEON

PRAYER PROMPT: *Father, you have brought me so far from my days in Egypt and my wandering the wilderness. I pray you will constantly renew my memory of where I've come from and where I'm headed. Revive my thanks for your deliverance, and renew my hope for the land of promise.*

NOVEMBER 27

What if There Is No Revival?

You do not have, because you do not ask.
JAMES 4:2

Imagine this world continuing to spin without hope for revival. What we now see in the world are just the birth pangs preceding Christ's return. Without a serious repentance, the birth pangs will increase. And though we yearn for Christ's return, we also long to see more people saved, spared from the judgments coming to this planet. Imagine, also, the revival that is coming. Think of the salvations, the restorations, and the joy of revival. We cannot let the opportunity pass! The object of our prayers—and revival—is blessing, not the curse that comes with no revival. If we do not have revival, are we truly asking? James says we do not have because we do not ask. So ask! Pray on! Don't let the image of a world with no revival become reality.

> Many of God's people throughout the world are praying for a quickening of the spiritual life of the Church in revival power, but wherever there is a mighty working of God, you may settle it that there will be a mighty working of the powers of darkness in opposition to it. . . . Too often, in the past God's people have been so ignorant of Satan's devices that he has succeeded in stopping revival before they were aware of what he was doing. The armor of God is designed that we may stand against the wiles of the devil and in order to do this, we must be alert and able to recognize them.
>
> JESSIE PENN-LEWIS

PRAYER PROMPT: *Lord, I pray not just for revival but for a thwarting of the schemes of the enemy to prevent revival.*

NOVEMBER 28

Standing Strong

We who are strong have an obligation to bear with the failings of the weak, and not to please ourselves.
ROMANS 15:1

God is looking for men and women whom he can invest with his strength. Such are people who know they're weak and are thus willing to trade their weakness for God's strength. And what does God do with these divinely empowered Christians? He uses them in the lives of others. His strength working through weakness searches out and ministers to the hurt and broken. Revival is a time for the weak to become strong in faith and for the strong in faith to offer their strength to the weaker brothers and sisters who need a helping hand.

It will not do for us to take merely the things that belong to the gentle side, and think of these as the whole of Christian character. Christ was infinitely gentle. The warmth of his heart made a tropical summer all about him. But behind the gentleness, was also infinite strength. We must be like him, not only in gentle warmth but also in truth and strength and righteousness. We must be to others, not only tenderness but also strength to lean upon, and stability in which they may find refuge.

J. R. MILLER

PRAYER PROMPT: *Lord, I ask for your supernatural strength—not just for myself but so I might help the ones you have for me to serve. Father, broaden my shoulders. Help me stand strong.*

NOVEMBER 29

Renewing Our Mind

*Set your minds on things that are above,
not on things that are on earth.*
COLOSSIANS 3:2

Revival can be a crash course in renewing our mind. We become aware of heaven's realities and earth's liabilities. Being given a glimpse of heavenly joy, our previously disordered life now yearns for more of God's intervention in our life. Our sin is seen both as horrendous and thoroughly atoned for by the blood of Christ. And what sin has undone in our lives is now renewed by God's boundless grace. None of us escape the need for a renewed mind. Jesus had to rebuke his disciples many times for their constant earthly, untransformed mind. Peter even had to suffer a stark rebuke in which Jesus told him he regarded the things of man, not God (Matt. 16:23). Later, of course, the disciples underwent a transformation of grace, much as we must do.

Grace is as large in renewing us as sin was in defacing.
STEPHEN CHARNOCK

PRAYER PROMPT: *Lord, my mind needs renewal—even revival. Incline my heart to your Word. May your grace be to me as deep and healing as sin was in debasing me.*

NOVEMBER 30

God's Word and Revival

"The words that I have spoken to you are spirit and life."
JOHN 6:63

In all seasons but especially during revival, we honor God's Word, which brings us life. We do not read the Bible as we read any other book. We're aware of the life-giving words on the pages of the Word. Revival is a time to read the Scriptures in our private time but also to hear the Word preached. It's a time to take the Word in, to internalize the Word. In so doing we're taking in an eternal message to all who will believe. Then, having taken in the Word of life, we must live the Word. We must *do* what we believe.

> The Word is not a mere dead letter that will soon vanish away: it lives in the mind of God: it lives in the decrees of Heaven: it lives and will live forever: nor will millions of ages cause it to be forgotten, or in the least enervate its force. All besides this shall wax old, and decay: but this shall endure, without the alteration of one jot or tittle of it, to all generations.
>
> CHARLES SIMEON

PRAYER PROMPT: *Lord, your Word is eternal, and in its pages I find the way to eternal life through faith in Christ. Instruct me through your Word to become the mature and useful Christian you mean me to be. As a prayer warrior, I ask you to keep revival fire paramount in my intercession.*

DECEMBER 1

Be Watchful!

Be sober-minded; be watchful. Your adversary the devil prowls around like a roaring lion, seeking someone to devour.
1 Peter 5:8

Revival awakens us to the spiritual realities of the kingdom of God. But we will also become more awake to the tactics of the enemy to rob us of all that revival gives us. Therefore, we must always be awake and watchful lest we lose the blessing of revival and fall back into our old pre-revival ways, perhaps even returning to our old sinful patterns.

Satan's battle plans are always working against us. This roaring lion is always on the loose, always prowling, seeking to devour us. If we are sober minded and watchful, we will notice his schemes, fight back in the power of the Lord, and have victory over him.

> Satan continually lies in ambush, and watches to draw us to sin. The devil stands girded for battle. He is always fishing for our souls. He is either laying snares, or shooting darts. Therefore we had need watch him, that we be not decoyed into sin. Most sin is committed for lack of watchfulness.
>
> Thomas Watson

PRAYER PROMPT: *Lord, sharpen my discernment so that I'm not caught unaware of my adversary who comes prowling like a roaring lion. I shall have no fear of him, nor shall I allow him to undermine my prayers for your revival.*

DECEMBER 2

The Ancient Paths

Thus says the LORD: "Stand by the roads, and look, and ask for the ancient paths, where the good way is; and walk in it, and find rest for your souls. But they said, 'We will not walk in it.'"
JEREMIAH 6:16

Scoffers will say revival is too old-fashioned. They picture large tents, sawdust aisles, and mourning benches. Those who dismiss moves of God as old-fashioned are forgetting how successful revivals have been in history. What worked in earlier years will still work in the twenty-first century, though perhaps adapted to the times. God still moves today, though not always in tents, sawdust, and mourning benches. If anything, we should pray for a return to the ancient paths God has established. Let us never say of revival, "We will not walk in it."

> On these [ancient] truths [the early Christians] lived, and for them they were ready to die. Armed with these truths, without gold to bribe or the sword to compel assent, they turned the world upside down . . . and in two or three centuries altered the whole face of Society. Can we mend these "old paths"? Does human nature require any different medicine? I believe the bones of the oldest human skeleton that ever was unearthed are just like the bones of men in these days, and I believe the moral nature and hearts of men, after the lapse of ages, are just the same. We had better ask for the "old paths."
>
> J. C. RYLE

PRAYER PROMPT: *Father, you are still the same as you were since before the first day of creation. You are the "ancient of days." You lead us on the old tried-and-true paths if we will only follow. Lord, we will live by the ancient truths that offer far more wisdom than the new paths.*

DECEMBER 3

Your Revival

Let the favor of the Lord our God be upon us, and establish the work of our hands upon us; yes, establish the work of our hands!
PSALM 90:17

During a revival season (or outside of it), what work has God called you to? Have you presented yourself to God unreservedly? Do you view your hands as vessels for his hands to work in the world? If so, there is work for you—and for only you—to do. It may be as an intercessor, a missionary, or a marketplace worker who supports God's work with your paycheck.

May the favor of the Lord be upon us, and may the work of our hands be established by God, who has called us. When your work is finished, God will call you home. You cannot leave this life with your assignment incomplete.

Are we not all immortal till our work is done?
ROBERT MURRAY M'CHEYNE

PRAYER PROMPT: *Lord, keep me alive and healthy only until my work here is finished; then call me home. If there is a special assignment you have for me during a forthcoming revival season, make it clear to me, and I will walk in it!*

DECEMBER 4

To What People Are You Called?

I am speaking the truth in Christ . . . that I have great sorrow and unceasing anguish in my heart. For I could wish that I myself were accursed and cut off from Christ for the sake of my brothers, my kinsmen according to the flesh.
ROMANS 9:1A–3

Has God put a certain populace on your heart? Down through the centuries, godly men and women have gone into the fields to harvest souls for whom they carried a burden. For Paul, it was his fellow Jews. Hudson Taylor answered the call to China. God beckoned David Livingstone to Africa.

If you have a call to a special people, *go*. If not, pray and support those who do go.

> When I was about twelve or thirteen years of age, I was walking home with my father [William Booth, founder of the Salvation Army] when he led me for the first time in my life into a drinking saloon. I have never forgotten the effect that scene produced upon me. The place was crowded with men, many of them bearing on their faces the marks of brutishness and vice, and with women also, disheveled and drunken, in some cases with tiny children in their arms. There, in that brilliantly lighted place, noxious with the fumes of drink and tobacco, and reeking with filth, my father, holding me by the hand, met my inquiring gaze and said, "Willie, these are our people; these are the people I want you to live for and bring to Christ." The impression never left me.
>
> BRAMWELL BOOTH

PRAYER PROMPT: *Lord, bring revival to "my" people, If I cannot go to them, I will pray for and financially support those who can go.*

DECEMBER 5

The Sudden Onset of Revival

Suddenly there came from heaven a sound like a mighty rushing wind, and it filled the entire house where they were sitting.
Acts 2:2

When the early disciples were gathered together in prayer, the Holy Spirit filled the entire house "suddenly."

It seems ironic that we pray at length for revival that doesn't come. So on we continue to pray. But then, like with those early disciples, the outpouring comes suddenly.

Though as long as revival comes, we really don't care if it's sudden, just as long as it comes. Nevertheless, let us be on our toes, waiting for the coming of the Holy Spirit's outpouring in revival. Suddenness may indeed be God's strategy for revival.

> Since revival may be likened to a strategic attack,
> it is plain that—as in the realm of human conflict,
> so in the spiritual—the effect of every attack
> is heightened by the surprise factor. In revival
> God works suddenly and unexpectedly.
>
> Arthur Wallis

PRAYER PROMPT: *Lord, whether sudden or not, we are waiting for the outpouring of your Holy Spirit. Soon, Lord, soon!*

DECEMBER 6

The Gift of Revival

*Every good gift and every perfect gift is from above,
coming down from the Father of lights, with whom
there is no variation or shadow due to change.*
JAMES 1:17

Let us never forget that when we ask God for revival, we're asking him for a gift. We cannot produce revival or earn it; revival must be given freely by God. And when the gift of revival comes, we must remember not to idolize the gift but instead to keep our eyes on the Giver.

Let us also remember that revival is not a gift God gives begrudgingly (none of his gifts are). They are given lavishly and for the purpose of revealing his love to his people.

When revival comes, enjoy the gift as freely as God has given it.

Be careful that you do not become so enamored of
God's good gifts—that you fail to worship the giver.

A. W. TOZER

PRAYER PROMPT: *God, your greatest gift is salvation, but surely revival is near the top of the list of your many additional gifts. For all your gifts—but especially revival—we worship you, the Giver.*

DECEMBER 7

For the Sins of the Whole World

*He is the propitiation for our sins, and not for ours
only but also for the sins of the whole world.*
1 JOHN 2:2

Among other benefits of revival is that it is in some respects a celebration of who God is and his gracious forgiving of not only our sins but also the sins of the whole earth if they would call on him as Lord.

This is our message to the nations: because of Christ's sacrifice on the cross, God forgives our sins, gives us his righteousness, and offers us everlasting life, from the least to the greatest. May every revival prayer contain gratitude to God for his willingness to blot out our transgressions and to forget all our sins, no matter our nationality.

And because he does so, we too can let go of the burden of past sins and remember them no more. Is this not a reason to celebrate?

> The task of the Church after Jesus'
> resurrection and ascension was to proclaim
> the forgiveness of sins to all nations.
>
> CHARLES STANLEY

PRAYER PROMPT: *Father, may revival spread the good news of the gospel here and around the globe.*

DECEMBER 8

Revival Reminds Us of Home

We know that if the tent that is our earthly home is destroyed, we have a building from God, a house not made with hands, eternal in the heavens.
2 Corinthians 5:1

Though we often fail to ponder death, it's worth remembering that earthly death is the doorway to our eternal home. Heaven is where we will see God. It's where we will dwell securely, free from all fear. Much will be given us in heaven, but nothing good will be lost. In God's eternal presence, all our earthly sorrows will be turned to joy, and all our tears will be turned to laughter.

Because revival gives us a fresh experience of God's presence, it also offers a glimpse of heaven; for revival, like heaven, brings us a sense of what "home" is really like. So, can our thoughts of heaven, the glorious other side of death, be too frequent? I think not.

Heaven is now our true, abiding home. . . . While on earth we are strangers and pilgrims, far from our final rest. And while such is our condition here, should we not often think of our heavenly home? Should not Heaven attract us more and more as we journey through life?

David Harsha

PRAYER PROMPT: *Lord, every day brings me closer to coming home to heaven. I pray for a sense of what heaven is like through revival. I long to be home at last.*

DECEMBER 9

God on Display

*The LORD your God is in your midst, a mighty one who will
save; he will rejoice over you with gladness; he will quiet
you by his love; he will exult over you with loud singing.*
ZEPHANIAH 3:17

If we are ever to hear God exulting over us with loud singing, it will likely be in revival. A revival of his people pleases God. He rejoices in us with gladness, quiets us with his love. Best of all, he is in our midst. Since he exults over us, how then can we not also exult over God with the delightful singing of revival?

When God gazes on his redeemed people—the purchase
of Jesus' blood, his own chosen ones—it seemed as if
the great heart of the Infinite could restrain itself no
longer but, wonder of wonders and miracle of miracles,
God, the Eternal One, sings out of the joy of his soul!

CHARLES SPURGEON

PRAYER PROMPT: *God, in revival I will listen for your voice singing over your people. It may even be that you will be singing with delight through the voices of your people!*

DECEMBER 10

The Fruit of the Spirit Is the Fruit of Revival

*Walk in a manner worthy of the Lord, fully
pleasing to him: bearing fruit in every good work
and increasing in the knowledge of God.*
COLOSSIANS 1:10

The goal of all faithful Christians is to live a life pleasing to the Lord, walking in a manner worthy of the Lord. We want our every good work to be fruitful. The insight we receive from revival gives us new strength to live that God-pleasing life. We come away with a renewed vision of what our life can be. We determine to look ahead, not behind. While we once bore no fruit, now we bring forth the fruit of the Holy Spirit. We learn to walk upright spiritually, in a manner pleasing to the Lord, reducing our stumbles. The worst thing for a revived Christian to do is to look back with regret at that which cannot be changed. The best course is to look ahead at what God wants to do through us.

> What makes Heaven so happy? Just this: all there keep
> the eye and heart intently fixed upon this one thing—
> pleasing God. What would make us permanently
> and solidly happy on earth? Only this: to aim always
> and in everything to please God. Ah! if we did this,
> we would have few cares, few fears, and no falls!
>
> JAMES SMITH

PRAYER PROMPT: *Lord, my greatest desire is to live a life pleasing to you. Help me as I walk in a manner worthy of you.*

DECEMBER 11

A Natural Love

*Little children, let us not love in word or
talk but in deed and in truth.*
1 John 3:18

God's love is the theme of revival. He would have us both receive and give out love. Our faith is in vain if we love only in our words but not in our deeds.

The mark of true revival is the naturalness of the love we have. As the Holy Spirit reproduces the life of Christ within us, he is reproducing the love of Christ. No one has given, or ever will give, more than Christ; and he still gives today, often through the hands of his revived children. Hands motivated by love, not duty.

We need not feign love. We need not serve out of a sense of duty. We need only to receive and give. Repeat daily.

Just as there's no feigning true revival, so too is
there no feigning the true Christian life. In revival
God visits us with his presence. In the Christian
life, he comes not to visit, but to stay.

The true standard of greatness is service. It is not what
our life is in gifts, in culture, in strength; but what we
do with our life, which is the real test of character.

J. R. Miller

PRAYER PROMPT: *Lord, of all the outcomes from revival, may I be of more service to your people, motivated by a fresh perception of your love. May your love for me have tangible results.*

DECEMBER 12

Looking to Jesus

Looking to Jesus, the founder and perfecter of our faith, who for the joy that was set before him endured the cross, despising the shame, and is seated at the right hand of the throne of God.
HEBREWS 12:2

In revival we encounter the founder and perfecter of our faith. We understand that it was for future joy that he endured the cross. We too have a future joy, but like Christ, we must endure our daily crosses, though none compare to what he endured.

During our hardest days, we must look to Jesus. We must turn our eyes away from this present world and focus our vision on the joys of the Christian life, both here and in heaven.

It's good to expect joy after suffering. If we don't look for joy, we will have wasted our suffering.

I would fix all my thoughts and desires on Christ's glory! The more I see of the glory of Christ—the more the painted beauties of this world will wither in my eyes and I will be more and more crucified to this world. It will become to me like something dead and putrid, impossible for me to enjoy!

JOHN OWEN

PRAYER PROMPT: *Father, during every coming trial, help me look to Jesus and to the joy that follows suffering. To the extent that I suffer, so may my joy be also. Where your people struggle to handle suffering the right ways, may you revive us all to approach suffering the way Christ did.*

DECEMBER 13

Live for God Today

*Do not boast about tomorrow, for you do
not know what a day may bring.*
PROVERBS 27:1

Most of our troubles center around future uncertainty. Even though we look back at God's past faithfulness, we hesitate about what might happen tomorrow. But God knows about our tomorrows and has prepared us, if only we will believe. Every tomorrow that arrives has the stamp of God's care on it. Even if tomorrow brings grief or regret, God supplies the needed strength to weather the storm.

Our revival prayers must thank God for today and surrender tomorrow to his perfect will.

> God is down in front. He is in the tomorrows.
> It is tomorrow that fills men with dread. God
> is there already. All the tomorrows of our life
> have to pass him before they can get to us.
>
> F. B. MEYER

PRAYER PROMPT: *God, you know that my hope for my tomorrow is for revival, both to me personally and to my family, my friends, my city, and my country. Please help me look positively about each tomorrow, expecting the best. Give me grace for today and no worries about tomorrow.*

DECEMBER 14

Revival: Small or Large, It Doesn't Matter

Do not overlook this one fact, beloved, that with the Lord one day is as a thousand years, and a thousand years as one day.
2 PETER 3:8

True revival pray-ers know not to give up praying *ever*. And odd as it seems, a true pray-er will not feel defeated as months and perhaps years go by with no sign of revival. Every revival God sends, he sends in due time. Revival praying means pressing on in intercession across the ages.

A true revival pray-er will also not be disappointed if the revival prayed for is less than what was expected. It's natural to want large-scale revival, but when smaller regional revival occurs—often unreported to the church at large—God has a way of taking small beginnings and doing great things. A single new ministry birthed in a small revival may grow to have a huge impact worldwide. Just as we must refrain from dictating the time of revival to God, so must we refrain from dictating the size of revival. We may even pray specifically for small revivals to break out in various pockets of the world.

> For ten or eleven years I have prayed for revival. I could sit up all night to read or talk about revivals.
>
> EVAN ROBERTS, INFLUENTIAL IN THE
> GREAT WELSH REVIVAL OF 1904–1905

PRAYER PROMPT: *Lord, I do not dictate the size of revival. You do mighty things through even small revivals. Send the blessing of revival in any size and I will be rejoicing.*

DECEMBER 15

Revival and Restoration

If the foundations are destroyed, what can the righteous do?
PSALM 11:3

When praying for revival, we must also pray for the reformations that undergird revival. Revival without change in the hearts of God's people, without renewed churches, will only have a fleeting effect.

In praying for reformation, we're enlarging our request for revival. We're asking God for *more* than a quick visit of his presence that refreshes our spirits. We want the coming revival to have the full effect that God intends. We want substantial, ongoing change to the body of Christ, as needed. A return to holiness, to righteousness, to Spirit-filled living, to churches on fire for God. Revival, yes. But lasting reformation, too!

> Often men have acted as though one has to choose between reformation and revival. Some call for reformation, others for revival, and they tend to look at each other with suspicion. But reformation and revival do not stand in contrast to one another; in fact, both words are related to the concept of restoration. Reformation speaks of a restoration to pure doctrine, revival of a restoration in the Christian's life. Reformation speaks of a return to the teachings of Scripture, revival of a life brought into proper relationship to the Holy Spirit. The great moments in church history have come when these two restorations have occurred simultaneously.
>
> There cannot be true revival unless there has been reformation, and reformation is incomplete without revival.
>
> FRANCIS SCHAEFFER

PRAYER PROMPT: *Father, as I pray for revival, I pray for the deep changes that reform and restore. Repentance, holiness, the breaking of sin's torturous chains—all this and more, I pray.*

DECEMBER 16
Emptying Ourselves

If anyone cleanses himself from what is dishonorable, he will be a vessel for honorable use, set apart as holy, useful to the master of the house, ready for every good work. So flee youthful passions and pursue righteousness, faith, love, and peace, along with those who call on the Lord from a pure heart.
2 TIMOTHY 2:21–22

It's impossible to be full of self and full of Christ. If we are full of self, there is no room for Christ. And if we empty ourselves, we will be filled with Christ.

In revival, we become acutely aware of the One who seeks to fill us, and we gladly submit to the emptying of self.

If we're afraid of losing something important when we empty ourselves, we are not focusing on the gain we have in Christ. We must never fear the emptying of self. For to be filled with Christ, we're ironically made completely the selves we were always meant to be.

> Self-emptiness prepares us for spiritual fullness.
> RICHARD SIBBES

PRAYER PROMPT: *Father, it is right that I empty myself to make room for your fullness. I focus not on the rubbish I lose but on the treasures I gain.*

DECEMBER 17

Revival: Hunger for God Realized

*Jesus said to them, "I am the bread of life; whoever comes to me
shall not hunger, and whoever believes in me shall never thirst."*
JOHN 6:35

God comes to the hungry and thirsty and fills them with himself. Hunger is the prerequisite—though we cannot recreate divine hunger or thirst—that must come from God. He creates the void he intends to fill. This hunger is the impetus for us to pray for revival. For in revival, we are fed the Bread of Life as we come to him and believe in him.

Yes, Jesus is the bread that satisfies and the water that quenches our thirst. We must therefore consider our hunger for God as a gift from God.

> God will fill the hungry because he
> himself has stirred up the hunger.
> THOMAS WATSON

PRAYER PROMPT: *Father, of all the things you do in the hearts of men and women, I love that you birth a hunger for yourself in us that can only be satisfied by you. This is the hunger that drives us to our knees for revival. Fill us, then, Lord. Satisfy our hunger and thirst!*

DECEMBER 18

Revival and Nominal Christians

Having the appearance of godliness, but denying its power.
2 Timothy 3:5

What revival joy to see throngs of nominal Christians find that what they've only believed casually or culturally is real and will change their lives. Perhaps some of us have been there: brought up in the church but never allowing the reality of the gospel to seize our heart. Many cold hearts have been warmed by a divine awakening. It was so with John Wesley, a nominal Christian until his own revival experience caused him to say upon reading Luther's preface to the epistle to the Romans, "I felt my heart strangely warmed. I felt I did trust in Christ, Christ alone, for salvation; and an assurance was given me that He had taken away my sins, even mine, and saved me from the law of sin and death."

> Never have there been so many millions of nominal Christians as there are today, and never has there been such a small percentage of real believers. Never has Christendom been so crowded with those who have a form of godliness, but who are strangers to its transforming power. We seriously doubt whether there has ever been a time in the history of this Christian era when there were such multitudes of deceived souls within the churches, who truly believe that all is well with their souls, when in fact the wrath of God abides on them!
>
> Arthur Pink

PRAYER PROMPT: *Father, open the eyes of those whose faith is merely mental assent to Christianity but has not yet reached their heart. May revival bring new life to them, even to their own surprise.*

DECEMBER 19

The Power of Revival in Our Personal Ministry

I do not account my life of any value nor as precious to myself, if only I may finish my course and the ministry that I received from the Lord Jesus, to testify to the gospel of the grace of God.
ACTS 20:24

What a day it will be when we all rest from our labors and simply relish being in the presence of the Lord. Yes, we all want to, like Paul, finish our course well. But then, also like Paul, we must not count our life here as precious but be willing to lose it for the sake of the Lord.

For many believers, the work God has called them to seems hard, but they press on. And so must we, whatever our work. What a joy it is to undertake an impossible work for the Lord, for we can only achieve the impossible through him.

May we all pray that in revival we're faced with a call from God that seems impossible through natural eyes.

> There are three stages in the work of God: Impossible; Difficult; Done.
> HUDSON TAYLOR

PRAYER PROMPT: *Father, use revival to fan the flames of personal ministry. Refresh the laborers in your vineyard. May their prayers accomplish what is impossible in the natural.*

DECEMBER 20

Leaving Our Nets

[Jesus] said to them, "Follow me, and I
will make you fishers of men."
MATTHEW 4:19

More than two thousand years later, Jesus is still calling for men and women to follow him. Some of us must leave our "nets" to do so. But the loss is really a gain. After walking with Jesus for three years, witnessing the grandest event of all time on Calvary, and then receiving the Holy Spirit and the commission to preach the gospel, these fishermen did indeed become fishers of men until their dying day.

Do we, too, follow Jesus in his Great Commission? If so, we will have no regrets. May revival recharge our batteries to serve him well for the remainder of our lives.

These fishermen left their all to follow him. And this is what we also must do, in heart at least, and in act also, if fidelity to him require it: nor on any other terms than these will he acknowledge us as his disciples. And is he not worthy of being served thus? Did his disciples ever find cause for regret that they had forsaken all for him? No! Nor shall we.

CHARLES SIMEON

PRAYER PROMPT: *Lord, I leave my nets behind to pursue your calling. Give me the power and the vision of my predecessors in ministry. Hear my prayers for success in my labors.*

DECEMBER 21

Endless Prayer for Revival

Pray without ceasing.
1 Thessalonians 5:17

Men and women of God who are faithful in prayer for revival will not give up. They pray until the answer is manifest. They see the rain clouds of revival on the horizon and are encouraged that the downpour will soon be upon them. On the other hand, there are those who say they want revival and toss up a bullet prayer now and then, assuming those kinds of prayers are sufficient.

In the Gospels, Jesus frequently taught that we should pray and not give up. The apostle Paul encouraged the Thessalonian believers to pray without ceasing. He wasn't referring to bullet prayers; he meant for them to pray on until the revival rains began to fall—and even then, to keep praying for them to continue.

So must we, day after day, seek God for life-changing revival. Never give up!

If the spiritual life be healthy, under the full power of the Holy Spirit, praying without ceasing will be natural.

Andrew Murray

PRAYER PROMPT: *Lord, as I pray, I find it so natural to lay my concerns and petitions before you. With the Holy Spirit guiding my prayers, ceaseless prayer is possible.*

DECEMBER 22
No Task Is Too Little

Whoever gives one of these little ones even a cup of cold water because he is a disciple, truly, I say to you, he will by no means lose his reward.
MATTHEW 10:42

Our natural tendency is to think of large and more important ways to serve the Lord, forgetting that there are no small jobs in God's kingdom. According to Jesus, giving a cup of cold water to a child is worthy of reward.

The truth is that few Christians are called to be seen in service. Most of us serve where God plants us, often in seemingly small, invisible places. Many Christians have suffered regret by trying to be what they are not and trying to do what they have not been called to do.

Happy are those who have found their place of service, whether large or small. It may be during revival that, for each of us, our place of service may be revealed.

> There are many of us that are willing to do great things for the Lord, but few of us are willing to do little things.
>
> D. L. MOODY

PRAYER PROMPT: *Lord, I'm willing to do what I think are little things in your service, knowing that if the deeds of all of us who are called to small things were added together, it would surely be an unimaginably big thing. I'm happy, Father, wherever you plant me.*

DECEMBER 23

On Being Single-Hearted for the Lord

*The light of the body is the eye: if therefore thine eye
be single, thy whole body shall be full of light.*
Matthew 6:22 (kjv)

There is much in today's world to catch the eye of even the most devout Christian. There are pleasures and temptations available today that believers in the past never had to face. To be effective in such a world, we must have an unclouded eye and a single heart for the Lord's work. This requires us to quickly refuse to linger on the world's eye candy, to quiet the tempting whispers of our enemy, and to forever set aside ambitions to be great in this present life.

Revival gives us a glimpse of the joys of the kingdom in which we live and serve. The most important prayer some believers must pray is, "Lord, give me a single heart for your kingdom!"

> Blessed are the single-hearted, for they shall enjoy much peace. . . . If you refuse to be hurried and pressed, if you stay your soul on God, nothing can keep you from that clearness of spirit which is life and peace. In that stillness you know what His will is.
>
> Amy Carmichael

PRAYER PROMPT: *Dear Lord, my heart sings for you. My eyes are unclouded by the world's attraction. I am entirely yours.*

DECEMBER 24

Revival and Personal Sacrifice

*Through him then let us continually offer up
a sacrifice of praise to God, that is, the fruit
of lips that acknowledge his name.*
HEBREWS 13:15

If good works are done because we feel duty bound to perform them, something is wrong. Serving God in any capacity is a privilege, not a chore. Most Christians who have served well have gone through deep waters. Many faced hunger, sickness, danger, rejection, and more; but in all this, they never thought of it as a sacrifice. Fulfilling one's calling satisfies the soul in ways reluctant sacrifice can never match.

Consider your work for the Lord. Is it a sacrifice or a privilege? The answer will reveal how fruitful your work will be.

> People talk of the sacrifice I have made in spending so much of my life in Africa. Is that a sacrifice which brings its own blest reward in healthful activity, the consciousness of doing good, peace of mind, and a bright hope of a glorious destiny hereafter? Away with the word sacrifice. Say rather it is a privilege. Anxiety, sickness, suffering, or danger, now and then, with a foregoing of the common conveniences and charities of this life, may make us pause, and cause the spirit to waver, and the soul to sink; but let this only be for a moment. All these are nothing when compared with the glory which shall be revealed in and for us. I never made a sacrifice.
>
> DAVID LIVINGSTONE

PRAYER PROMPT: *Father, I delight to serve you. Any sacrifice I make is worth the privilege to be your child. What you ask of me, I will do. No regrets.*

DECEMBER 25

The Inner Shrine

*"My soul magnifies the Lord, and my
spirit rejoices in God my Savior."*
Luke 1:46–47

For many of us, our tendency is to be consumed with outer service to the Lord but less so with our inner life. Mary was a young woman chosen by God to bear the Savior. Her reply was to magnify the Lord in her soul and for her spirit to rejoice in God her Savior. What is our response to the Christmas message? For the world, there is much outer activity and much preparation. But do we rejoice in our spirit and soul? Is Christmas only an outer event? Or was it perhaps the beginning of the biggest revival until the Lord's future return? It was a time when the presence of God came to live among us, suffer for us, and rise from the dead for us.

The reality of Christmas and a revival based on the coming of Christ must bring to each of us an inward change. If we rise from revival and proceed to busy ourselves once again with outward duties to the neglect of inward worship, we have missed the recommissioning aspect of revival and the meaning of Christmas. Our outward duties should not be neglected, but they are secondary to matters of the Spirit. If we are led by the Spirit, we will do the outward. For the strong inner life eventually expresses itself in good works and rejoicing.

> There must be the inward worship within the
> shrine if there is to be outward service.
>
> Alexander Maclaren

PRAYER PROMPT: *Dear Lord, it's so easy to become preoccupied with outer matters during this time of year, often to the neglect of my inner being. As I celebrate Christmas, may my response be Mary's response. May my soul magnify you, O Lord.*

DECEMBER 26

Love Your Enemies

"I say to you who hear, Love your enemies, do good to those who hate you, bless those who curse you, pray for those who abuse you."
Luke 6:27–28

One of the hardest commands Jesus left with us was to love our enemies. It seems like an impossible task when our enemies have caused us harm and are still arrayed against us. Nevertheless, the Word of God is clear: in loving our enemies, we must do three things—do good, bless them, and pray for them.

This *sounds* doable. And given the actions of God toward us, who were his enemies before we were saved, it seems reasonable. But after an attack from those who hate us and have wronged us, the ire within starts to rise. Nothing can soothe our anger except the Spirit of the Lord who enables us to quiet our anger and love our enemy despite all feelings to the contrary. In loving our enemy, we actively demonstrate the kind of love we have received.

In revival we sense the love of God who has reached out to save his enemies. When we consider that we were once his enemy and his love sought us out, how can we then refuse to love *our* enemies?

Let your kindness be as limitless and as unconstrained by personal feelings as God's; for it is a necessary qualification to our being the children of God, that we should love our enemies.

William Bacon Stevens

PRAYER PROMPT: *Father, you are a great example of loving enemies, for you loved each believer when we were your enemy. Help me, by faith, to love, to do good, and to pray for my enemies.*

DECEMBER 27

When God's Plan Takes an Unexpected Turn

*I am sure of this, that he who began a good work in you
will bring it to completion at the day of Jesus Christ.*
PHILIPPIANS 1:6

Some Christians enter revival during a difficult time. There have been disappointments, pain, rejection, frustration, and profound depression—some of which has been self-inflicted. Revival is often an "urgent care" clinic for the hurting or the spiritually bankrupt who will allow the Holy Spirit to minister to them through worship, prayers, preaching, and confessions of sin.

Consider that revival is God's chosen way to help the hurting. It's no secret that revival changes lives. Depression is replaced by joy, painful wounds are bound up, and disappointment is exchanged for faith. Dryness has given way to renewed joy. All of this has been arranged by God for us. Come to the Lord and bring your wounds with you. Receive power from the Holy Spirit.

O arise, and pray, and agonize for the outpouring of the
Spirit upon your soul; give up your lifeless religion, your
form without the power, your prayer without communion,
your confessions without brokenness, your zeal without
love. And O, what numerous and precious promises cluster
in God's word, all inviting you to seek this blessing!
OCTAVIUS WINSLOW

PRAYER PROMPT: *God, I come to revival with any known or unknown wounds. Bind up my wounds, remove any pain, and bring joy in place of sadness.*

DECEMBER 28
Gaze upon Jesus and Live

*So Moses made a bronze serpent and set it on
a pole. And if a serpent bit anyone, he would
look at the bronze serpent and live.*
NUMBERS 21:9

When the Israelites complained while wandering through the wilderness, God sent poisonous serpents whose bite was fatal. But when they repented, God directed Moses to raise up a bronze serpent so that all who looked upon it would live. Later, Jesus would likewise be lifted up so that all who looked upon him in belief would survive the stinging death of sin (John 3:14–15).

In revival, we're reminded to cast our eyes on Jesus lifted up—either by one glance to be saved for the first time (if we were not a Christian previously) or to stare and be reminded of his previous saving grace (if we were). As others have wisely noted, the glance at Jesus saves; the gaze sanctifies.

Today, the death sting of the serpent is stilled for all who will gaze at Christ lifted on the cross and believe.

> The Gospel brazen serpent may be seen from the
> most obscure corner, and a crucified Jesus may be
> savingly looked to, even from the ends of the earth.
> WILLIAM NICHOLSON

PRAYER PROMPT: *Father, I look to Christ, raised up for me just as the brazen serpent was raised so that all who looked up were saved. May my look not be merely a glance but a gaze.*

DECEMBER 29

Revival, the Healing Agent for Spiritual Disease

*A joyful heart is good medicine, but a
crushed spirit dries up the bones.*
PROVERBS 17:22

A physical disease can put us down for a while, or it can even kill us. Just so, spiritual disease can severely hinder our relationship with the Lord. But just as many diseases now have cures, God also offers a cure for all spiritual disease.

It may sound simplistic to offer joy as medicine for the spirit, but it's difficult to meet a joyful Christian who is spiritually sick. And unlike medicine for the body that requires a prescription and may taste bitter, God's medicine is free and delightful to the taste.

Revival is a place of joy. One could say it's a dispensary of God's joy so that all who ail spiritually can come and find healing.

In the gospel there is a salve for every sore and a
remedy for every malady. There is no spiritual disease,
but there is power in Christ for the cure of it!
MATTHEW HENRY

PRAYER PROMPT: *Lord, in many ways, revival is a hospital where those with spiritual ailments are made whole again. Revive my life, Father. Restore the joy of my salvation.*

DECEMBER 30

Encourage One Another

*Therefore encourage one another and build
one another up, just as you are doing.*
1 Thessalonians 5:11

The Christian family worldwide is a family of encouragers. We bear one another's burdens, pray for one another, and share both joys and griefs. In revival we are touched by joy, and it then behooves us to take that joy outside the walls of revival to infect others.

We would be surprised at how many people we regularly encounter who are silently carrying a heavy load. Are we sensitive to the needs of the weary and heavy laden? Joy is but one thing we export from revival. We also offer compassion, counsel (when asked), and a helping hand. The fruit we bring from revival can be endless. There is something to meet every need. Joy and encouragement are great evangelistic tools.

> The law of love bids us bear one another's burdens, and there
> is no other way in which we can do this so effectively, as
> by living a life of joy. He who goes among men throughout
> the day with glad heart and cheerful face, speaking some
> encouraging words to everyone he meets, saying something
> uplifting in every ear is a wonderful inspirer of strength,
> courage, and hope, in others. His is a divine ministry
> of good to others. He makes everyone a little braver and
> stronger. Weary plodders pluck up fresh energy after
> meeting him. Fainting ones awake to new courage when his
> hopeful words have fallen upon their ears. The influence
> of such a habitual encourager never can be measured!
>
> J. R. Miller

PRAYER PROMPT: *Father, as I follow Jesus, may I, like him, become a burden-bearer for others. Infuse a fresh empathy within me that causes me to reach out and touch others as Christ did.*

DECEMBER 31

To Lose Is to Gain

What does it profit a man to gain the whole world and forfeit his soul? For what can a man give in return for his soul?
MARK 8:36–37

It seems we're daily assaulted by temptations to be something other than what we are. Self-help books abound telling us to promote ourselves, have pride, build bigger barns, to *find* ourselves. But Jesus tells us this is all wrong. What we gain today may be lost tomorrow—and certainly will be lost at our departure from this life.

We find ourselves only in Christ. He has now become our life; we are no longer our own. What then will we take from this past year into the new year? What awaits us in the next twelve months?

We pray that it will be a year of great revival. We commit ourselves to yet another year of beseeching God to turn our world upside down with a revival that will precede the Lord's return.

> To give oneself up is not a loss, it's a gain. What we lose in surrender is what we want to lose and what we need to lose. What we gain is what we want to gain and what we need to gain. Let your life throughout the coming year be a silent witness to the Gospel. Strive to assist Christ's ministers, in your families and among your friends and acquaintances, by speaking to them of the things pertaining to the kingdom of God, by showing them what great things your heavenly Father has done for you.
>
> J. C. RYLE

PRAYER PROMPT: *Lord, though our year has ended, you need no calendar to determine between one day and the next or one year and the next. So I will continue to pray for revival every day, month, and year until we see the outpouring of your Spirit as promised.*

A Final Note from R. A. Torrey

Hark, I hear a noise! Behold a shaking! I can almost feel the breeze upon my cheek. I can almost see the great living army rising to their feet. Shall we not pray and pray and pray and pray, till the Spirit comes, and God revives His people?

What is needed is a general revival, but if we cannot have a general revival, sweeping over the whole earth, we can have local revivals and state revivals and national revivals. It is not necessary that the whole Church get to praying to begin with. Great revivals always begin first in the hearts of a few men and women whom God arouses by His Spirit to believe in Him as a living God, as a God who answers prayer, and upon whose heart He lays a burden which no rest can be found except in the importunate crying unto God. Oh, may He, by His Spirit, lay such a burden upon our hearts today. I believe He will!

Works Cited and Recommended Resources

Websites

Many of the quotes in *Our Cry for Revival* came from the Grace Gems website (https://www.gracegems.org), a wonderful treasury of writings from Christian leaders who are now with the Lord.

Other valuable sites consulted in the preparation of *Our Cry for Revival* include:

> Christian Quotes (http://Christian-quotes.ochristian.com)
> Sermon Index (SermonIndex.net)

Priscilla Shirer quote on "X" https://twitter.com/PriscillaShirer/status/1111246166237147137.

Thomas Watson: https://www.ccel.org/ccel/watson/commandments.iii.ii.html.

Charles Spurgeon: https://apprenticeshiptojesus.wordpress.com/2007/09/12/charles-spurgeon-quotes/.

Books

Barabas, Steven. *So Great Salvation: The History and Message of the Kewick Convntion.* Eugene, OR: Wipf & Stock, 2005.

Bartleman, Frank. *Azusa Street, An Eyewitness Account.* Newberry, FL: Bridge-Logos, 1980.

Cairns, Earle E. *An Endless Line of Splendor: Revivals and Their Leaders from the Great Awakening to the Present.* Carol Stream, IL: Tyndale House Publishers, 1986.

Grubb, Norman. *Rees Howells Intercessor*. Fort Washington, PA: Christian Literature Crusade, 1987.

Lewis, E. Elvet. *With Christ among the Miners*. Cincinnati, OH: Jennings & Graham, 1907.

Lloyd-Jones, Martyn. *Revival*. Wheaton, IL: Crossway Books, 1987.

Matthews, David. *I Saw the Welsh Revival*. Chicago: Moody Bible Institute, 1957.

Nel, Olea. *South Africa's Forgotten Revival: The Story of the Cape's Great Awakening in 1860*. Maitland, FL: Xulon Press, 2008.

Ravenhill, Leonard. *Revival Praying*. Bremerton, WA: Bethany Fellowship, 1962.

Reid, Reverend William. *Authentic Records of Revival, Now in Progress in the United Kingdom*. Wheaton, IL: Richard Owen Roberts, 1980.

Roberts, Richard Owen, ed. *Glory Filled the Land: A Trilogy on the Welsh Revival*. Austell, GA: International Awakening Press, 1989.

Stewart, James A. *Invasion of Wales by the Spirit through Evan Roberts*. Fort Washington, PA: Christian Literature Crusade, 1975.

Terry, Lindsay. *I Could Sing of Your Love Forever*. Nashville, TN: Thomas Nelson, 2008.

Tracy, Joseph. *The Great Awakening: A History of the Revival of Religion in the Time of Edwards and Whitefield*. Carlisle, PA: Banner of Truth, 1976.

Torrey, R. A. *The Power of Prayer*. Grand Rapids, MI: Zondervan, 1955.

Towns, Elmer, and Douglas Porter. *The Ten Greatest Revivals Ever*. Ann Arbor, MI: Servant Publications, 2000.

Wallis, Arthur. *In the Day of Thy Power: The Scriptural Principles of Revival*. Fort Washington, PA: Christian Literature Crusade, 2012.

Magazines

The Overcomer (various issues consulted from 1914–1955).

Acknowledgments

Much thanks are due for the many supporters of this book, including my prayer team:

>Elaine Wright Colvin
>Lydia Harris
>Julie-Allyson Ieron
>Sarah Kohnle
>Cecil Murphey
>Michael Reynolds
>Sandy Silverthorne

And especially Doug and Marilyn Couch for their longtime prayers and encouragement.

Thanks to my supportive family, especially my wonderful wife, Beverly.

Thanks to my B&H editors, Logan Pyron and Ashley Gorman, managing/production editor, Kim Stanford, along with the entire B&H team. And to Sue Miholer at Picky, Picky Ink, copy editor extraordinaire.

Much appreciation for my agent, Greg Johnson of WordServe Literary.

About the Author

Nick Harrison is the author of more than a dozen books including *Magnificent Prayer, His Victorious Indwelling: Daily Devotions for a Deeper Christian Life*, and *The One-Year Life Recovery Prayer Devotional*. His books have been endorsed by Anne Graham Lotz, Jerry Jenkins, Liz Curtis Higgs, Chip Ingram, and Lee Strobel.

Nick graduated from San Jose State University with a degree in English and a minor in journalism. For fifteen years Nick served as a senior editor at Harvest House Publishers. Nick and his wife, Beverly—an avid quilter—are the parents of three grown daughters and grandparents to two boys and two girls. Nick's website is http://nickharrisonbooks.com.

Nick's Books

> *Promises to Keep: Daily Devotions for Men of Integrity*
>
> *365 WWJD: Daily Answers to What Would Jesus Do?*
>
> *His Victorious Indwelling: Daily Devotions for a Deeper Christian Life*
>
> *Magnificent Prayer: 366 Devotions to Deepen Your Prayer Experience*
>
> *Walking with Wesley: A Ninety-Day Devotional*
>
> *Power in the Promises: Praying God's Word to Change Your Life*
>
> *The One-Year Life Recovery Prayer Devotional: Daily Encouragement from the Bible for Your Journey toward Wholeness and Healing*
>
> *One-Minute Prayers® for Those with Cancer*
>
> *One-Minute Prayers® for Dads*
>
> *One-Minute Prayers® for Husbands*
>
> *One-Minute Prayers® When You Need a Miracle*